WITHDRAWN

WITHDRAWN

THE UNIVERSITY OF CHICAGO
PUBLICATIONS IN ANTHROPOLOGY

ETHNOLOGICAL SERIES

SUYE MURA
A JAPANESE VILLAGE

SUYE MURA
A JAPANESE VILLAGE

By

JOHN F. EMBREE

須
惠
村

THE UNIVERSITY OF CHICAGO PRESS
CHICAGO · ILLINOIS

THE UNIVERSITY OF CHICAGO PRESS, CHICAGO 37

Cambridge University Press, London, N.W. 1, England
The University of Toronto Press, Toronto 5, Canada

*Copyright 1939 by The University of Chicago. All rights reserved
Published October 1939. Sixth Impression 1958. Composed and
printed by* THE UNIVERSITY OF CHICAGO PRESS, *Chicago,
Illinois, U.S.A.*

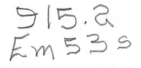

To the memory of Keisuke Aiko—scholar, gentleman,
and good judge of wine—who with tragic fitness was
the first citizen of Suye to die for the machine age.
When returning home one evening in November, 1937,
from Menda Town on his three-wheel motorcycle, he
collided with the Hitoyoshi-Yunomae train. That day
Suye lost her first motor transportation and her most
promising son—and the writer of this book
lost his best friend in Japan.

11096

INTRODUCTION

THERE is an abundance of books on Japan, treating of Japanese life in various aspects. Dr. Embree's book is of a kind that has not hitherto been attempted; it is a description, based on direct observation, of the life of a Japanese village community. Its chief purpose is to provide material for that comparative study of the forms of human society that is known as social anthropology; but it should have an appeal to a wider audience of general readers as giving an additional insight from a new angle into Japanese civilization. For, though we may be inclined to judge the civilization of a nation by its literary or artistic production, by the extent of its commerce, or even by its military achievements, if we wish to understand it, we must remember that its roots are in the ordinary life of the common people. Just how the common men and women live together from day to day in a Japanese village is what Dr. Embree has observed and what he has described in this book.

There is a widespread idea that social anthropology is, or should be, concerned only with the simpler societies which we refer to as primitive, savage, or uncivilized, and that the study of the more advanced societies is to be left to historians, economists, and sociologists. It is true that until about fifteen years ago the field researches of social anthropologists were confined to the preliterate peoples of the world. But in recent years, under the leadership of Professor Fay-Cooper Cole, Professor Redfield, and Professor W. Lloyd Warner, social anthropologists of the

University of Chicago and of Harvard University have carried out important field studies of communities in Sicily, Mexico, Massachusetts, Mississippi, Ireland, and Quebec. In 1935 it was decided to extend this kind of investigation to the literate peoples of eastern Asia, and Dr. Embree's study of a Japanese village is the first of what was planned as a series of connected researches in that region.

What is now known as social anthropology began in the seventeenth and eighteenth centuries with writers who sought to use the accounts of uncivilized peoples given by travelers for the purpose of gaining insight into the nature of social institutions. But it did not become an established study until the second half of the nineteenth century, and it acquired its name only some fifty to sixty years ago. Throughout a great part of the nineteenth century the social anthropologists, with a few exceptions, such as Bastian, did not themselves observe the facts with which their theories were concerned but sought them in the accounts of missionaries and travelers. By the beginning of the present century, however, it had come to be recognized that for the progress of the science it was essential that systematic observations of social life should be made by trained observers having in mind the hypotheses to be tested and the problems to be solved. Field research has thus become just as important to social anthropology as laboratory experiments are to physics and chemistry.

Social anthropology has for its aim to discover valid and significant generalizations about human society and its institutions. The only method by which this aim can ever be attained is by the comparison of a sufficient number of sufficiently diverse types of society. The relatively simpler societies of backward peoples are, for several reasons, of extreme importance to the social anthropologist, but his comparative studies must extend over the whole range of known human societies. Therefore, since the kind of knowledge which he requires about the more advanced societies is not otherwise available, he has to extend his field researches to these.

What is required for social anthropology is a knowledge of how individual men, women, and children live within a given social structure. It is only in the everyday life of individuals and in their behavior in relation to one another that the functioning of social institutions can be directly observed. Hence the kind of research that is most important is the close study for many months of a community which is sufficiently limited in size to permit all the details of its life to be examined.

An assumption, or methodological postulate, that guides those connected researches of which Dr. Embree's is one, is that in social anthropology at the present stage of its development the scientifically most profitable undertaking is the comparative and detailed investigation of forms of social structure. This term—"social structure"—is sometimes used without any clear definition, but is here meant to refer specifically to the network of direct and indirect social relations linking together individual human beings. The method of field anthropology is to investigate the social structure in the concrete observable behavior of individuals, and this necessitates a close study of a community of limited size. The result in the present work is a picture of Japanese social structure in the perspective provided by a single village.

What may be called the basic structure of any society is constituted by personal relations as they are determined by neighborhood, kinship or family ties, and sex and age.

The most important unit in the social structure of rural Japan seems everywhere to be a limited neighborhood group which is exemplified by what Dr. Embree describes under the term *buraku*, which we might translate "hamlet." The internal organization of the hamlet, as it still exists in Suye, with its elected headman, and its households linked together by mutual aid in many economic and social activities and by the social conviviality of parties for the drinking of rice wine, in all probability comes down from very ancient times. The kinship system, which links together households belonging to the same or to different hamlets, has taken on a peculiar form in Japan as the result of the widespread custom of adoption in various forms; this also seems to be an ancient and characteristic feature of Japanese life.

The hamlet is part of a much larger and highly complex structure which is and has for some time been undergoing fairly rapid change. The effects or repercussions of these changes, as they are seen in the hamlet and in the lives of its inhabitants, have been excellently described and analyzed by Dr. Embree and are summarized in his eighth chapter. In abstract structural terms the hamlet is steadily losing its relative independence, and it as a group and its members as individuals are becoming more and more involved in and dependent upon relations with the wider social environment. The immense increase in the facilities for communication, by roads, railways, omnibuses, bicyles; the consolidation of the hamlets into the organized and centrally controlled village (*mura*); the national consolidation which is being effected through the army, nation-wide associations, and official Shinto and emperor worship; the replacement of the local dialect by standard Japanese—all these and many other of the changes that

Dr. Embree has recorded are components of a single process.

This process itself, in the particular form that it has in contemporary Japan, is one example of a general kind that has occurred thousands of times in the course of history and is at the present time observable all over the world. It may reasonably be held that it is the constant and most important constituent of social evolution. The relative isolation, autonomy, and independence of small local communities is the distinguishing feature of the simplest and least-developed societies. The concrescence of these into larger and larger social structures by political, economic, religious, or other organizations is the outstanding feature of human history. One of the major problems of social anthropology is the investigation of processes of this kind in order to determine their general character; this can only be done by the comparative study of a considerable number of concrete instances each of which has been carefully observed and analyzed. The scientific value of Dr. Embree's monograph as providing important material for such a comparative study should commend it to those who have any interest in the fundamental problems of a science of society.

I have drawn attention to this aspect of Dr. Embree's work because its importance may easily be overlooked. But there is much else in his book that is both of general scientific value and of interest to those who wish to know something of the civilizations of eastern Asia. It gives, to my mind very effectively, a synoptic picture of life in a rural community of a country which it is very desirable that we should all know something about.

A. R. RADCLIFFE-BROWN

ALL SOULS COLLEGE, OXFORD

PREFACE

THIS book is an attempt to present an integrated social study of a peasant village in rural Japan. While Suye Mura,[1] the village described, cannot be claimed to represent all rural Japan any more than can any other single village, it is at least representative in many respects. Most Japanese villages depend economically on some single product—the commonest economic bases being rice, fish, and silkworms. In addition are the mountain villages, more or less isolated, dependent on lumber, mushrooms, and other mountain products for a livelihood. Suye is primarily a rice-growing village with silkworms as a secondary source of income and so is representative of a large part of rural Japan. The countryside of Japan is dotted with small towns of five to ten thousand population, surrounded by clusters of villages. The town, being full of shops and on a railroad, supplies the country with manufactured goods and some amusements, the chief of which are *geisha* houses. The country in turn supplies food and customers for the town and girls for the *geisha* houses. Suye is typical of most villages in being one of a cluster around two small towns (Menda and Taragi).

The main forms of rural Japanese society are much the same all over Japan—co-operation, exchange labor, and a religious festival calendar closely correlated with the agricultural seasons—but each region, even each county, has its own peculiar details of language and custom. For instance, obscene songs are typical of rural festivities in general, but the particular words and sex symbols vary from

[1] *Suye* rhymes with *soufflé;* the *y* is scarcely enunciated.

region to region. Thus, while the basic patterns of Suye are typical of much of rural Japan, the lesser details are characteristic only of Kuma County.

A peasant community possesses many of the characteristics of a preliterate society, e.g., an intimate local group, strong kinship ties, and periodic gatherings in honor of some deified aspect of the environment. On the other hand, it presents many important differences from the simpler societies; each little peasant group is part of a larger nation which controls its economic life, enforces a code of law from above, and, more recently, requires education in national schools. The economic basis of life is not conditioned entirely by the local requirements but by the nation, through agricultural advisers. The farmer's crop is adjusted to the needs of the state. In religion and ritual there are many outside influences to complicate the simple correlation of rites and social value, festivals and agricultural seasons. While full of local variations, the rituals and festivals are not indigenous to the community nor is the community spiritually self-sufficient. These characteristics make it impossible to regard Suye Mura as comparable to a purely self-contained preliterate society.[2]

The present study is part of a larger research on types of society in eastern Asia being made by the Social Science Division of the University of Chicago under the direction of Professor A. R. Radcliffe-Brown. The recent wars in

[2] The Japanese peasant village is, however, comparable to other folk communities, using the term "folk" in the sense used by Dr. Redfield in *Tepoztlán* or in *Chan Kom*. Speaking of villages in Yucatan, Redfield says: "These villages are small communities of illiterate agriculturalists, carrying on a homogeneous culture transmitted by oral tradition. They differ from the communities of the preliterate tribesman in that they are politically and economically dependent upon the towns and cities of modern literate civilization and that the villagers are well aware of the townsman and city dweller and in part define their position in the world in terms of these. The peasant is a rustic, and he knows it" (Robert Redfield and Alfonso Villa, *Chan Kom: A Maya Village* [Washington, 1934], p. 1).

Asia and the acceptance by Professor Radcliffe-Brown of the chair of anthropology at Oxford have tended to impede the progress of this larger scheme.

In any study such as this the reader has a right to know how and why the particular village was selected and what qualifications the writer has to undertake the study. Both my wife and I had been in Japan for various periods of time before undertaking the investigations on which this report is based. The field work itself lasted a year and a half (August, 1935–December, 1936) and was made possible through a grant from the Social Science Research Committee of the University of Chicago. The period from November, 1935, to November, 1936, was spent in Suye Mura. I had been a fellow in the Department of Anthropology at the same university during the academic year preceding this field study. My knowledge of Japanese is fragmentary, but my wife can speak the language fluently.

On arrival in Japan I visited various persons connected with the Foreign Office, in order to explain the purposes of the research, and obtained from the office tacit permission to pursue my studies. I also called on certain professors of Tokyo Imperial University and Waseda University for advice and information. After this some twenty-one villages were visited in order to locate a desirable one for study and, just as important, to gain perspective for the research in the village finally selected.[3]

While impossible to determine much about a given village in a brief preliminary visit, Suye was chosen for these reasons:

1. It is relatively small and thus practical for two people to undertake.

2. It does not possess any striking features to make it

[3] No social studies of Japanese village life have been published in English and very few in Japanese. See Bibliography for some recent Japanese studies.

stand out from the general run of rural communities in Japan. It is not too close to any large city; it is not a "model" village, that is, one being reconstructed under government supervision into a superefficient farm-production center, as are many villages in Japan; it is a rice village and is neither outstandingly rich nor outstandingly poor.

3. Suye is far from any military zone, and thus our work did not come under undue suspicion by the military. In any field work by foreigners in Japan this is an important consideration.

4. In Kumamoto we had a very good introduction to any village through Professor S. Kimura and Mr. R. Kojima. In Suye in particular the headman, Mr. T. Morinaga, was most cordial to us, and his nephew, Keisuke Aiko, the only college graduate living in the village, proved our warmest and most understanding friend. It is to the late Mr. Aiko that this book has been dedicated.

I should like to take this opportunity to express my deep appreciation to Professors Shiroshi Nasu and Kunio Yanagida, of Tokyo Imperial University, and Professor Tsubin Odauchi, of Waseda University, for giving me much valuable information and advice; to Mr. K. Ohkawa, the assistant of Professor Nasu and now himself a professor, who was very helpful and visited several places with me; and to Professor Eitaro Suzuki, of the Imperial Agricultural College of Gifu, who supplied much valuable information and advice at the outset of the study. From Professor Suzuki I learned most concerning the various village types to be found in Japan. To Professor Shuzo Kimura, of Kyushu Imperial University, I owe a very great debt of gratitude for his patience and perseverance in visiting with me three rural communities in Kyushu and in explaining the purpose of my study to officials who were often in some doubt as to the honesty of my intentions. Mr. Kojima, of the Kumamoto Prefectural Office, was also of great assistance in this latter respect. Furthermore, he proved a most jovial friend and introduced me to many aspects of town and city life I might not otherwise have known. Such knowledge helped greatly in understanding rural life and its very sharp contrast in Japan to the life of town and city. The numerous other village and prefectural officials with whom I came in contact, especially during the preliminary survey trip, were without exception extremely helpful, and I cannot be too thankful for the many hours which they gave, and the trouble they went to, in order to assist me.

One other important factor in the successful accomplishment of the study was the aid of Mr. Toshio Sano, a graduate of Tokyo Language School, who lived with me and acted as my interpreter and translator. For his painstaking translations of lectures and village records and for his patience with my interpreting demands at all hours of the day and night, I am most grateful.

More than to any official or professor, however, I owe thanks to the people of Suye who so cordially received two foreigners in their midst and with whom both my wife and I formed many a warm friendship. International friendship was never at a higher point than during some of Suye's drinking parties of 1935–36.

In the writing of the present descriptive report on life in Suye, I wish to express my gratitude for the advice and counsel of the staff of the Department of Anthropology at the University of Chicago, more especially to Professors Fay-Cooper Cole, Robert Redfield, and A. R. Radcliffe-Brown. To Professor Radcliffe-Brown belongs any credit for the good points in the pages that follow, for he gave me most of my formal training in searching out the rules of a society. But let no blame for errors fall on his head, for with rare restraint, once he sent me to the field, he did not lay down any rules on what to find or how to find it.

A part of my time as research associate for the University of Hawaii was devoted to the completion of the manuscript for publication, and I wish to thank Dr. F. M. Keesing of the Department of Anthropology of that institution for kindly granting me this opportunity.

I should also like to thank Mr. Yukuo Uyehara, of the University of Hawaii, for his transcription of the characters for Suye Mura which appear on the title-page and for his assistance in the translation of the folk songs. I am indebted to my colleague, Dr. Gordon T. Bowles, for his careful reading of the manuscript. Acknowledgments are due to *Fortune Magazine* for permission to reprint the description of Japanese countryside (p. 12) and for the use of the photograph of a woman spinning (facing p. 40). All photographs in the book, including the one first printed in *Fortune*, were taken by Ella Embree and myself.

JOHN F. EMBREE

TABLE OF CONTENTS

LIST OF ILLUSTRATIONS

PHOTOGRAPHS

FIGURES

MAPS

LIST OF TABLES

CHAPTER I

HISTORICAL BACKGROUND

BEFORE launching on a description of contemporary rural life in Japan and the changes it is undergoing, it is necessary to sketch in a little of the recent history of the country, especially of the years immediately preceding that great social and economic revolution commonly known as the Meiji Restoration. A historical background, when available, is an essential part of any diachronic study.

For over two hundred years before the Meiji era the Tokugawa feudal regime was in power. Primarily a military government carried on in times of peace, after its initial battles against previous rulers its main purpose was to preserve a feudal and military form of government rigid and unchanging.

The Emperor, as nominal head of the state, continued to keep court in Kyoto, while the Tokugawa regime set up actual government in Tokyo (then called Yedo). The country was divided into feudal fiefs each with a lord or *daimyō* having absolute right of jurisdiction in his own province, including the right of taxation. The Tokugawa themselves were in reality simply the largest of such *daimyō* with the largest estate and hence the greatest wealth and power, while most of the lesser *daimyō* merely imitated them in their methods of governing the people. To prevent revolution, each *daimyō* had to spend a part of the year in Tokyo and, while at home, was required to leave his wife and children as hostages behind in the capital. The mass of the people were farmers owing taxes to the feudal lords of the respective districts and controlled by military men (*samurai* and *ashigaru*) who owed allegiance to these same lords.

The *shōgun* or feudal head of the state had a government of officers whose functions were often ill defined. One characteristic of this government was that it discouraged initiative. Responsibility was shifted from man to man because the government's high offices were duplicated or their functions discharged not by individuals but by councils. Its operations were also hampered by a system of rotations under which the elders or councilors of government took turns of duty and were therefore likely to muddle and procrastinate. The system extended right down to the small *kumi*, or group of five persons who formed the unit of rural organization. This was done because it was thought necessary to guard against monopoly of power by one person. This aspect of the government is significant because today in rural regions similar features of divided and rotated responsibility are to be found in local non-official affairs. To prevent political troubles, a system of spies was maintained to give reports on conditions in various provinces.

The government was run partly on Confucian[1] principles with many of its laws ethical in nature. Philosophers were called in to solve economic and other problems of government which they dealt with on ethical rather than practical principles, with the object of preserving unchanged the system of classes. The virtues of loyalty to one's superiors and filial piety were always stressed. Farm-

[1] The Confucianism of Japan is that expounded by Chu Hsi (d. 1200) with special emphasis on loyalty and the ideal of a unified empire under a "Son of Heaven" (see Hu Shih, *The Chinese Renaissance* [Chicago, 1934], p. 18).

ers were urged to be industrious, *samurai* to be economical. Even today similar exhortations are given to the peasant. Laws were broad in nature and frequently were not comprehended by the people, with different punishments for different classes. "It is good Confucian doctrine that the common people should do what they are told, without asking why; and certainly no Japanese ruler went out of his way to explain his commands to his humblest subjects."[2]

This attitude, not new in the country with the Tokugawa, has given to the peasants of Japan a remarkable docility, which still exists, to all that emanates from government sources.

Below the nobles and lords there was a rigid series of social classes each with its own occupations, forms of dress, and types of law prescribed by the government. The highest of these were the soldiers, or *samurai*, who came eventually to be almost a purely parasitic class. Below them in rank came farmers and artisans, then merchants, and, lowest of all, the pariah class called *eta*, made up of former slaves, Korean prisoners, and workers in tanning and other industries involving killed animals.

The *daimyō*'s income consisted of the rents collected from farmers in his domain. A lord would ordinarily take about 50 per cent of each farmer's rice crop, a portion of which he distributed to *samurai* and other retainers.

Travel from province to province was discouraged, and passports were required to cross fief lines. Each province wished to remain a self-contained unit and not to lose any of its produce or to admit any possible spies. The Tokyo government deliberately left roads and bridges in poor repair especially those which led to the capital. This was done in part to prevent any sudden attack on the city.

[2] G. B. Sansom, *Japan: A Short Cultural History* (New York, 1931), p. 451.

Feudal lords often set up border barriers to exact a toll from travelers.

Religion was left to itself so long as it refrained from political activity. In order to check its growing power, the great Shinshū sect was split into two sections (known today as East and West Hongwanji). During this period Buddhism continued, as before, to be the dominant religion, overshadowing and at times assimilating the native Shinto. However, after the split of the Shinshū sect, Buddhism fell into a coma, and no outstanding priest or religious reformer appeared during the Tokugawa regime, or since for that matter.[3] The *samurai* as a class cultivated Zen and developed such formalistic aspects of it as the tea ceremony. Christianity, which had gained a foothold in certain sections of Kyushu, was ruthlessly suppressed early in the Tokugawa regime in conjunction with the expulsion of foreigners and the cleansing of the country. The reason for this was that the rulers justly feared political trouble and possible encroachment by foreign powers in the wake of Christian missionaries. Another aspect of this isolation policy was the prohibition on building seaworthy ships, no Japanese being allowed to leave Japan or, once having left, to return on pain of death.[4]

During the Tokugawa regime the merchant class gradually expanded with an increase in internal travel and

[3] Buddhist beliefs in rural regions today are often far removed from any formal Buddhism found in books. The predominant sect, Shinshū, is a special Japanese form of Amida Buddhism, quite unlike the original teachings of Gautama.

[4] This decree came at a time when Japan was just beginning to expand like Elizabethan England, with rovers and settlers in Manila, Java, and Siam. These growing and expanding Japanese outposts all gradually died out after the isolation policy of the Tokugawa went into effect. It is interesting to speculate on the possible colonial empire that might have been Japan's but for the cautious policy of the Tokugawa in 1633 (see Y. Takekoshi, *The Economic Aspects of the History of the Civilization of Japan* [London, 1930], chap. xxxiv).

trade despite all obstacles. Associations of merchants arose at this time and frequently took over roadside toll gates and exacted tolls from rivals, thus creating monopolies. Rice, the usual form of exchange, became too bulky for commercial transactions during the early period of the regime, and money came into general use with the merchant classes. *Samurai* continued to receive their incomes in rice, however, and right up to the revolution considered money vulgar and beneath their notice. As time went on the merchant class became more and more influential. Many took to rice brokerage and speculating and by the consequent sharp fluctuations in the price of rice great hardships were imposed on both farmers and *samurai*, whose incomes depended upon it. The feudal lords, including the Tokugawa, felt these economic jolts also, for in the last analysis they depended on rice in their roles as squires. The early rice brokers were the forerunners of the modern broker to be found in every rural region, a man who is heartily hated by all farmers.

Peasant farmers had a very rough time. Many got into debt as money became necessary to them for many things which previously they had bartered for rice. Owing to intensified cultivation of the fields, they had to buy such things as manure, agricultural implements, horses, and clothing, with silver, which steadily decreased in purchasing power. Feudal landholders began to exact taxes in money instead of rice at a rate favorable to themselves. Peasants frequently abandoned their farms and went to other regions or cities to avoid their burdens, and frequently they left the lords' fields to go to some temple land or to the manor of a court noble where taxes were less onerous. Infanticide and abortion were freely practiced. The government in reaction tried to control rice prices, but

without avail. They forced farmers to stay on their home-
land and frequently deported them from cities to their
native villages. Laws against infanticide were passed, but
economic necessity continued stronger than law or parental
love.

Many agrarian revolts occurred due to extremes of
poverty, frequently the result of increased pressure by im-
poverished *samurai* and feudal lords. These were often
cruelly crushed.

It is worth observing that the poverty of the peasants forced them,
in many instances, to surrender their land by sale or pledge to creditors,
and there were thus brought into existence two new classes, one of persons who owned land which they did not farm, the other of persons who
farmed land which they did not own. This created new hardships for
agriculturalists and a clash of interests between tenant farmers and
landowners (other than feudal lords). The most curious anomalies
arose, as for example when a landowner reproved his tenant for producing too much rice, because taxation increased in proportion to the
yield, while the tenant objected that unless the yield were high there
was no surplus for his own subsistence. Tenant disputes continued
throughout the 18th and 19th centuries and in some parts of Japan
they have recurred in quite recent years.[5]

The government realized the importance of agriculture
to the state and took great pains to improve it, but little
thought was given to the well-being of the farmer as such.
He was considered to be stupid and of value only as a
rice-producer. "Statesmen thought highly of agriculture,
but not of agriculturalists."[6]

In the city during this period the popular theater—
kabuki—developed, as did puppet shows and color prints.
The now universal three-stringed musical instrument
called *samisen* came into its own. Licensed quarters for
prostitution grew and flourished. The merchants, who had
plenty of money, were the main patrons of the theater and

[5] Sansom, *op. cit.*, p. 509.   [6] *Ibid.*, p. 457.

the arts as well as of the "dream world" of bath girls and courtesans. When the national exuberance and love of the frivolous and obscene would become too marked, the government would issue repressive laws, but, in spite of all, the gay city recreations continued to increase in quantity and variety. It is interesting to note that the government again today is worrying itself about the "morals" of its people by closing dance halls and prohibiting all kinds of sentimental songs.

With the government attempting to control economic forces by fiat, and with the merchants enjoying their wealth in cities while *samurai* and peasant alike suffered, it is clear that the most powerful single factor leading to the Meiji revolution was the change from a purely agricultural to a mercantile economy.

The Shogunate at the beginning of its regime prohibited all foreign trade and all foreigners, except for a little colony of Dutch near Nagasaki, in a desire to keep the country as stable as possible. Thus any new ideas from Europe were excluded. At home, however, a little freedom of research was permitted. It was through this little crack that native scholars gradually realized and spread the idea that the Emperor was the true head of the government and that the *shōguns* were mere usurpers of power. Native Shinto ideas were the better able to make themselves felt with the lowered prestige of Buddhism.

The coming of the West to knock forcibly at Japan's closed doors in 1853 added one more strain to a feudal system already weakened by the growth of mercantilism and the increasing conviction of educated men that the feudal lords were usurpers of the Emperor's divine power.

In the years 1867–68 the Tokugawa government resigned, and there was an armed conflict between the

Shogunate party and the Emperor's party in which the Shogunates were defeated. Feudalism was abolished and the monarchy restored. In the succeeding years many changes took place. The more important innovations were:

1868   Buddhism and Shinto declared separate. The same researches that led in part to the overthrow of the *shōgun* also exposed the foreign origin of Buddhism and the manner in which it had usurped the place of Shinto. One form of Shinto was made into a state cult.

1868–69 Roads hitherto barred by territorial lords opened for free traffic.
   Restrictions on interfief trade and communication removed.

1869   Equality of the four classes—*samurai*, farmer, artisan, and merchant—declared. While technically the merchant had been below the *samurai* and farmer, he held greater actual power for many years before this.

1869   First telegraph built; first newspaper printed.

1870   First primary schools in Tokyo. It was several years before these reached the countryside. Compulsory education began in 1872.
   Vaccination encouraged. Smallpox epidemics, previously fairly common, have practically disappeared in Japan since this time.

1871   Postal service established.
   Men's hair allowed to be cut as they pleased and social distinctions in dress abolished. This had a great leveling influence.
   Choice of crops to be grown made free.

1872   Sunday adopted as a legal holiday.
   Choice of trades and professions declared to be free.

1873   Gregorian calendar adopted.
   Conscription law passed: "While the spirit of this law had its source primarily in the ancient imperial policy that in an emergency all men shall become soldiers and when the emergency passes they shall again become farmers, the form it now took was based upon Western models."[7]

1874   Political parties formed.

---

[7] Inazo Nitobe *et al.*, *Western Influences in Modern Japan* (Chicago, 1931), p. 384.

Public speaking commenced by Fukuzawa.[8] This was an important event. Since then the government has adopted lectures as a branch of its public education. The mass of the peasants, who do not read newspapers, are periodically assembled in a village schoolhouse or lecture-hall and given a two- or three-hour talk by some itinerant government official on new forms of agriculture, on patriotism, or on morality.

1877 Saigō Rebellion. Saigō, a lord of Satsuma in southern Kyushu, dissatisfied with the government's pacific attitude toward Korea, lead a revolt against the government. The newly formed conscript army of commoners received its first real test and won when Saigō was defeated at Kumamoto. This was the last counterrevolutionary move on the part of old feudal lords and *samurai*.

In ensuing years railroads were built and gas engines and electricity introduced.

In addition to these foreign introductions, native law was also changed. The chief motive for this, as well as for several other reforms, was that Japan had concluded several unequal treaties with Western nations and wished at the earliest possible moment to revise them. The feeling of inferiority engendered by these treaties and by the superior mechanical culture of the West gave rise to a virulent nationalism which has, if anything, increased with the years.

With all these radical changes several significant features of life remained unchanged, or merely appeared in a new form:

1. A spy system all over the country to report on conditions.
2. The law code, though supposedly fixed, could by means of certain statutes be broadly interpreted to crush any form of activity including speech and writing which might disturb the ruling powers. Furthermore, in addition to the code, Imperial edicts, laws in themselves, were (and are) issued from time to time. These, while issued

[8] The *Autobiography of Fukuzawa Yukichi* gives an excellent insight into the life of this transition period. Beside the radical innovation of lectures, Fukuzawa also founded the first newspaper and the first university (Keio) in Japan.

in the name of the Emperor were (and are) usually composed not by the Emperor himself but by a clique in power.

3. Continuance, after a brief interval, of military men as actual governors of the country.

4. Education calculated to keep people in their place and serve their Emperor (rather than feudal lord) in time of war.

Professor Hu Shih has referred to the "cultural response" of Japan to Western civilization as one of centralized control as against the "diffused assimilation" response of China. He says:

What has happened in Japan during these seventy years of modernization only represents one peculiar type [of cultural response], which we may call the type of "centralized control." Such orderly and efficient progress in a gigantic task of nation-wide reformation is only possible under such exceptional circumstances as have been described above. Its advantages are most apparent, but it is not without very important disadvantages. The Japanese leaders undertook this rapid transformation at so early a time even the most far-sighted of them could only see and understand certain superficial phases of the Western civilization. Many other phases have escaped their attention, and in their anxiety to preserve their national heritage and to strengthen the hold of the dynasty over the people, they have carefully protected a great many elements of the traditional Japan from the penetration of the new civilization. One of the most evident examples is the state patronage and protection of the Shinto religion. The peculiar extra-constitutional powers of the military caste in the government is another example of compromise. The position of women may also be cited. In short, the rapid cultural transformation in Japan has been achieved with too great a speed and at too early a date to allow sufficient time for the new ideas and influences to penetrate into the native institutions and attain a more thorough cultural readjustment. The whole affair has assumed the form of ingrafting an alien culture on the stock of traditional Japan. Much of the traditional medieval culture is artifically protected by a strong shell of militant modernity. Much that is preserved is of great beauty and permanent value; but not a little of it is primitive and pregnant of grave dangers of volcanic eruption.[9]

[9] *Op. cit.*, pp. 23–24.

Since the Meiji revolution, Japan has become one of the great nations, with ships sailing the seven seas; meanwhile the rural communities have maintained a remarkable stability through all these changes in the capital and other cities of the country. The following pages are devoted to the society as it is found today in one of these rural communities, Suye Mura, and the changes occurring in its local social system.

CHAPTER II

VILLAGE ORGANIZATION

TO REACH Suye Mura from Tokyo, one boards an express train at 3:00 P.M. for Shimonoseki. The view from the train window is predominantly rural—groups of farmers, men and women, transplanting rice if it is spring, family groups gathering it if the month is October. As the train passes through the prefectures of Hiroshima and Yamaguchi, the farmhouses change in shape, the methods of stacking rice vary, and even the type of straw hat the farmer wears changes from region to region.

The fact that Japan is a small, heavily populated nation is reflected in the short distances between settlements, the old well-worn paths, and the scarcity of wasteland.

There are other signs for those who look to see them.

There are the roads always narrow and mostly at the wood's edge or the river's.

There is the straw piled on brushwood bridges off the loam and the trees only growing at the god's house, never in the fields.

There are the whole plains empty of roofs, squared into flats of water, no inch for walking but the dike backs, not so much as a green weed at the foot of the telegraph poles or a corner patch gone wild.

There are the fields empty of crows after harvest: thin picking for black wings after cloth ones.

There are the men under moonlight in the mountain villages breaking the winter snowdrifts on the paddies to save days of spring.

There are the forest floors swept clean and the sweepings bundled in careful, valuable piles.

There are the houses without dogs, the farms without grass-eating cattle. . . . .

Japan is the country where the stones show human fingerprints: where the pressure of men on the earth has worn through to the iron rock.

There is nothing in Japan but the volcanoes and the volcanic wastes that men have not handled. There is no getting away from men anywhere: from the sight of men in the open houses or from the shape of their work in the made fields or from the smell of their dung in the paddy water.[1]

From Tokyo to Shimonoseki is sixteen hours by train. Crossing the straits to Moji and thence again by rail to Yatsushiro is another eight hours. On this trip the train passes through the industrial region of Fukuoka, near which is Yahata, the great munitions center, where no foreigner sets foot. South of Fukuoka is Kumamoto City, primarily important as a rice center, the prefecture of which it is the capital producing some of the best rice in Japan. Kumamoto was also the capital of the old feudal lord and famous anti-Christian Kato Kiyomasa.

Yatsushiro is a small city two hours south of Kumamoto. Here one changes trains and waits an hour for the Hitoyoshi train. During this hour most passengers sit huddled over their bulky hand baggage, and the mothers among them sit patiently as they suckle their babies. A few more adventurous travelers walk out in the town to spend the time drinking *sake* or beer in a little restaurant which, catering to transients, has poor service and anything but pretty waitresses. The rather miserable wait in Yatsushiro is more than compensated for by the gorgeous scenery on the two-hour trip to Hitoyoshi. The railroad runs along the edge of the Kuma River, which has cut a deep gorge in this region. The rapids of this river are famous all over Japan, and tourists often come to Hitoyoshi from Tokyo for the sole purpose of riding down them in summer. Now

[1] From "Of Many Men on Little Land," *Fortune Magazine*, September, 1936.

and then the train passes a little settlement perched precariously between the rough side of the canyon and the rushing torrent. The men of these villages eke out a livelihood at lumbering. About 5:00 P.M. Hitoyoshi, the capital of Kuma County, is reached. This is a town of about ten thousand people, fifty-four miles south of Kumamoto and eight hundred and sixty miles distant from Tokyo by rail. Here are a few rather pathetic hot springs and some small hotels.

A traveler to Suye Mura has now the choice of a bus direct to the village or a train to Menda or Taragi, neighboring towns. The train is cheaper but involves a walk of half an hour or so from the station to the village.

The train runs up the middle of Hitoyoshi basin while the bus runs along the northern edge, passing through numerous villages which lie half in the plain, half in the mountains. After forty-five minutes and a distance of twelve miles, one comes to the end of the bus line and finds one's self in the little *buraku* of Kakui in the agricultural *mura* of Suye.[2]

Here there is neither hotel nor restaurant. Whoever leaves the bus must live here or have a friend's house to welcome him. It being six o'clock by now, the weary traveler is glad of a drink of *shōchū*, a supper of pickle and rice, and the relaxation of a hot Japanese bath.

The island of Kyushu on which is located Suye Mura has figured in Japanese history from earliest times. Jimmu Tennō, the putative first historical ruler of the Japanese people, began his activities here before moving north to conquer the main island. Most of Japan's long and varied relations with Korea were carried on via the west coast of

---

[2] For definitions of *buraku* and *mura* see p. 22.

Kyushu, and in later years it was at various ports of Kyushu, especially Nagasaki, that the first foreign trade with Europeans began, the results of which still cling to the native customs and dialect of the island. During the Meiji Restoration it was Saigō Takamori of southern Kyushu who fought the last battle against the new order of things.

On the one hand, Kyushu is and always has been regarded as outlying and barbarous by the residents of the nation's capitals at Kyoto and Tokyo; and, on the other, it is always recognized as the origin of the imperial line and as having contributed some of the best and strongest men to the nation.

The prefecture of Kumamoto (which is about half the size of Connecticut) is located in the middle of this important island. Kuma County, in the southeast corner of the prefecture, is a flood plain encircled by maturely dissected mountains and drained by the waters of the Kuma River. The vivid effect of being surrounded by mountains is reflected in the story still told by the small children and old women of Kuma: After the sun goes down in the west, it goes, during the night, secretly round behind the mountains to the east where it climbs up again in the morning. From the eastern end of the basin Mount Ichifusa, the sacred mountain of the region, rises to a height of six thousand feet. The Kuma River originates here and, after flowing through Kuma County, runs north through Yatsushiro, finally emptying into the Sea of Yatsushiro off the western coast of Kyushu (see Map I).

Formerly a separate daimyoate under the rule of the lords of Sagara for three hundred years, Kuma has long been off the main line of change in Japan. It is a hundred and twenty-five miles south of Hakata, the chief port of

MAP I

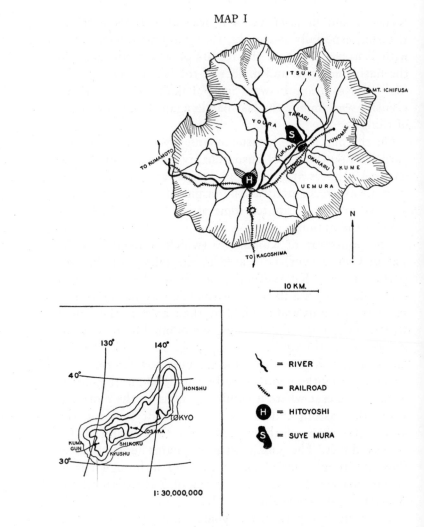

Kuma County

olden days for intercourse with the Asiatic mainland, and is too far off the beaten track to have felt much direct influence of foreign trade and early Christianity, as did the more favorably located regions to the north and south of it.

Sagara was one of the lesser lords, having a fief yielding about 18,000 *koku* of rice. Kato of Higo immediately to the north had, for instance, 520,000 *koku*. Despite Kato's wealth, he never succeeded in conquering Sagara, who seems to have ruled a buffer state between the powerful lords of Higo to the north and Satsuma to the south.

Hitoyoshi, the capital of old Kuma, is located on the Kuma River, and, before the advent of the railroad fifteen years ago, its chief means of transportation of rice to the nation's great cities was via this river north to Yatsushiro and thence to Kumamoto and other centers north and east. The railroad, first built for military expediency rather than for practical profit, affected Kuma profoundly, bringing it much closer to the nation's capitals, so that today, superficially at least, Kuma County is much like any other rural district. Kuma retains, however, many a turn of speech and social form characteristic of an older era and is in some ways ten to fifteen years behind rural districts near Tokyo and Kyoto. In methods of farming and schooling, on the other hand, it is much like the rest of the nation due to a national system of agricultural guidance and education.

The climate of Kuma is cold from December to March, the first frosts coming in early November or late October, the last ones in April. During the fall nights heavy mists settle in the valley, chilling the morning air and turning cobwebs to silver. By ten or eleven the sun breaks through, dries off the silver, and warms up the air. There is seldom more than two or three inches of snow on the ground at a time, and what there is usually comes in January or February. The temperature rarely falls below 20° F. Plum blossoms come out on leafless trees in February, cherry, peach, and camellia in early April, azalea in May, and pear in June. Lotus flowers bloom in the temple ponds in early August. The hot months are July and August, when the temperature seldom exceeds 100° F. In cold weather people pile on clothes layer over layer and huddle about temporary outdoor fires at every opportunity; when it warms up, the layers are removed one by one until summer, when, for everyday working purposes, both men and women are bare to the waist.

The Japanese of Kuma are of mixed physical type. Historically, many Koreans have come into Kyushu, and by tradition the hairy Kumaso were the aborigines of the island. Some men are very hairy on face, chest, arms, and legs, while others are practically hairless in these regions. The type of hair varies from straight to frizzy, though the frizzy type is rather rare and, when it occurs, is considered a minor tragedy, especially in a girl. A great many people have a slight wave in their hair.

The language spoken is a local Kuma dialect of Japanese. The schools teach standard Japanese, and most farmers can speak standard Japanese when speaking to outsiders. Much of the local dialect is giving way to the more standard forms according to the evidence of old people.

A number of foreign words, a small percentage of the number found in cities, have been incorporated into daily speech. Most people do not realize that the words are foreign and are surprised when this is pointed out. Of the extended list of such foreign words current in Tokyo, as given by Professor Sanki Ichikawa,[3] about 15 per cent are found in Suye Mura. Many of the terms used in Tokyo are for foreign products, such as cocoa or apple pie, which are unknown in the countryside.

Of regular words, many are used in everyday speech that are formal or archaic in Tokyo. Archaic words go with many old usages in other fields of life found in the region. A plausible reason for this is that certain usages found there today were current five hundred or a thousand years ago in Kyoto, the old capital, and only reached Kuma a hundred years or so ago. The things that have replaced them in Kyoto and Tokyo have not yet done so in Kuma.

SUYE MURA AND NEAR-BY TOWNS

Suye Mura is one of the nineteen *mura* of Kuma and is located in the eastern part of the county. The southern part of the *mura* lies in flat paddy fields by the Kuma River,[4] the northern on the mountainous border of the next county. Similar communities border it to the east and west. Its area is 1.1 square *ri* or 6.5 square miles, much of which is mountain and forest land. The population is 1,663 people, or 285 houses, the number of houses being the more important count, as nearly all civic duties are by households rather than by individuals. This is especially true of local *buraku* affairs.

Although most place names in Kuma have a meaning (thus Hitoyoshi means "good man"; Taragi, "many good trees"; Fukada, "deep paddy field"), no one knows the meaning of the word Suye, nor does anyone know when

[3] In Inazo Nitobe *et al.*, *Western Influences in Modern Japan* (Chicago, 1931), pp. 142–77.

[4] Those *buraku* not on the Kuma River are on tributaries of it. All rice villages in Japan are on or near some river.

or how the *mura* was originally founded. It has never played any important part in the history of Kuma, and

MAP II

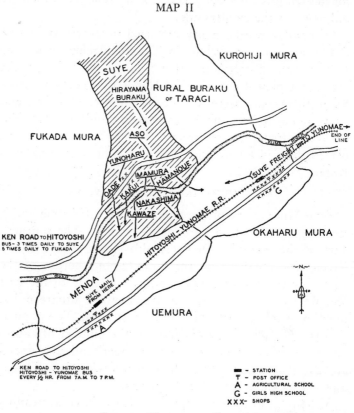

■	- STATION
T	- POST OFFICE
A	- AGRICULTURAL SCHOOL
G	- GIRLS HIGH SCHOOL
XXX	- SHOPS

SUYE AND NEIGHBORING TOWNS

there are people in Hitoyoshi who have never heard of Suye Mura. Nevertheless, the people of Suye are well satisfied with their own *mura* and have recently expressed their local patriotism by opposing a proposed amalgamation of Suye with the neighboring *mura* of Fukada and

Menda; but not too violently, for, as one farmer remarked, if the powers that be decide in favor of amalgamation, it will be done anyway.

Near Suye are two small towns—Taragi Machi (population of 5,000 plus about 2,000 in rural *buraku*) and Menda Mura, with a population of about 5,000 (see Map II). They have increased markedly in population since the building of the railroad. These are the immediate shopping-centers for Suye men to buy farming tools and for their wives in need of manufactured cloth, kitchenware, fancy footgear, and gifts; the towns also serve as a market for firewood and vegetables. Here, also, are the *geisha* restaurants, a form of small-town prostitution. These small towns buy their food from the surrounding *mura* and in return sell dry goods, tools, and hardware, making a nice profit in the process. A Hitoyoshi-Yunomae bus goes through the towns every half-hour from 7:00 A.M. to 7:00 P.M. From Suye, however, the usual mode of transportation is by foot. From the towns come the two fishmongers on daily trips to different sections of the *mura*, a kitchenware vendor, and other peddlers every month or so.

Menda, though technically a *mura*, is actually a small town with many shops. Located there is the only agricultural school in Kuma. The western half of Suye trades there. Letters for Suye come to Menda and are delivered once daily in Suye by a mailman from Menda post office.

Taragi became officially incorporated as a town (*machi*) in 1925. It is a little larger than Menda in population, but much of this extra population is in rural *buraku* much like *buraku* in Suye. In Taragi is the other girls' high school. The eastern *buraku* of Suye trade there.

In Hitoyoshi is the only middle school in the county and

the larger of the two girls' schools. The district court is also at Hitoyoshi.

VILLAGE AND HAMLET

Until 1926 the prefectures of Japan were subdivided into *gun* or counties. *Gun* were then abolished as a political division, thus placing *mura* directly under the prefectural government. There remains the geographical and social county. People are very conscious and proud of belonging to a particular county, and agricultural and business associations are organized on a county-wide basis. There are in Japan 627 counties, and each is characterized by many local customs.

The next political subdivision, then, is the *mura*, commonly translated as "village."[5] It is not, however, the cluster of farmhouses ordinarily meant by that term. Rather, a *mura* consists of several such house clusters, each united geographically and socially in its own little organization (see Map III). These separate social units or hamlets, known officially as *buraku*, are united by a common headman (*sonchō*), village office (*yakuba*), village Shinto shrine (*sonsha*),[6] and often by a common primary school and agricultural association. In this book the English word "village" will be used adjectively only, as in "village office."

Before the Meiji Restoration there were about seventy thousand *mura* in Japan, whereas today there are less than ten thousand. For administrative purposes many groups of two or three *mura* were consolidated, and, as the *mura* now became in part self-governing and self-supporting, it

---

[5] Sansom, however, translates it as "township" (G. B. Sansom, *Japan: A Short Cultural History* [New York, 1931], p. 165).

[6] The *son* of *sonchō* and *sonsha* is a term of Chinese derivation which, when used in Japanese, is equivalent to *mura*.

was often necessary to have a larger geographical unit with greater economic resources. When this occurred, the old *mura*, as included in the new larger political units, were called *ōaza* (see Map III).

Naturally such a *mura* covers a comparatively large area. Except for a common village office, headman, village Shinto shrine, agricultural association, and school each *ōaza* continued to function as a *mura*, much as it did

MAP III

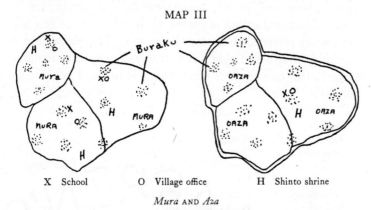

X   School   O   Village office   H   Shinto shrine

Mura AND *Aza*

At left: Three *mura* with constituent *buraku*. *At right:* The three *mura* after amalgamation into a single *mura* with three *ōaza*.

before the consolidation. Usually, besides the main school, each *ōaza* had a branch school.

In popular terminology both *ōaza* and *buraku* are often called *mura*. Some people believe that the *buraku* were once independent communities, and even today each *buraku* is largely self-contained socially with its own unofficial headman and religious center. The village office appoints in each *buraku* or group of *buraku* a deputy (*kuchō*) to perform certain administrative chores such as collecting tax money and attending *mura* shrine ceremonies.

Suye consists of but one *ōaza* (see p. 23). There are eight official *ku*. All members of the *mura* are considered to belong to one of these eight *ku* as far as the village office is concerned. Actually, for social purposes, several of these *ku* contain two or more primary groups or communities called *buraku* each with its own head and own branch of the village agricultural association. Each *buraku* consists of about twenty households and has a name of its own. There are, in all, seventeen such communities in Suye. They are called *mura* by their inhabitants but are sometimes referred to as *buraku* or *aza*. The eight *ku* are officially numbered but, for convenience, are usually named after one of their constituent *buraku*. They are as follows:

Ku	Constituent *buraku*
Oade	Ishizaka, Oade, Kamo
Kakui	Kakui
Imamura	Imamura, Tontokoro
Aso	Kami Aso, Naka Aso, Suanoharu, Yunoharu
Hirayama	Hirayama, Nakanotani, Funeno
Hamanoue	Hamanoue, Tashiroda
Nakashima	Nakashima, Kojo
Kawaze	Kawaze

The *buraku* are further subdivided socially into groups called *kumi*, which function in *buraku* festivals and on some other occasions (see chaps. iv and vii).

Everyone belongs to some *buraku* and to some *kumi*, just as in Tokugawa days every house was a member of some *goningumi*, only today the compulsion is social and economic rather than legal. This point is further discussed later.

Ku and *buraku* refer to settlements of people within a village and are not strictly geographical terms. The geographical subdivisions are called *aza*. In Suye there are over eighty *aza*. Some *buraku*, such as Kakui, consist of but one *aza*, but most *buraku* include several. Many *aza* are forest or paddy field with no houses on them. Each *aza*, like each *buraku*, has its own name (see Map IV).

MAP IV

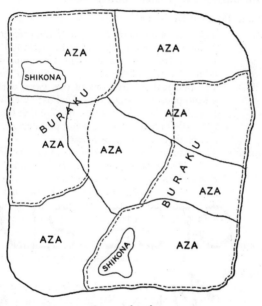

Aza AND *buraku*

There is still another geographical division. Many small areas, usually including only one or two houses, have popular names (*shikona*), not recorded on any official maps.

A certain confusion of terms is unavoidable, as the words *mura*, *aza*, and *buraku* are often used synonymously by the villagers. *Mura* is the term most commonly used for both the *buraku* and the *mura* proper. In this monograph the word *mura* will be restricted to the political unit including several *buraku* as in Suye Mura. *Buraku*, while not very colloquial, is at least accurate[7] and so will be used to refer to the smaller social grouping. For the official *ku*, also sometimes called *buraku* by villagers, the term *ku* will be employed.[8]

To summarize then, Suye comprises:

I. Social and Political Divisions

1 *mura*	The rural administrative unit of the prefectural government in contrast to *machi* (towns) and *shi* (cities). Its unity comes from a common headman, administrative office, school, and Shinto shrine.
8 *ku*	The political subdivisions of the *mura*, with village-office-appointed heads (*kuchō*)whose chief function is to collect taxes. *Ku* contain from one to four *buraku*. Officially known by number but popularly called after one of their constituent *buraku*.
17 *buraku*	The natural communities of about twenty households each. Historically the social and economic unit is this *buraku*. It is significant that it is referred to as *mura* by its inhabitants. It has its own head (*nushidōri*) and takes care of its own affairs, such as funerals, festivals, roads, and bridges, on a co-operative basis.
Many *kumi*	Groups of three to five houses. Their role in *buraku* life is described at length in chapters iv and vii.

II. Geographical

Aza	Geographical units. Used as a basis of landownership. Often uninhabited, but in each many people from various *buraku* own land.
Shikona	Small roughly defined regions with names known to the local people but not written in any official records.

THE ORGANIZATION OF THE *buraku*

The *buraku* has a head (sometimes two or three) called *nushidōri*. *Nushidōri* are elected for about two years at a

[7] It is the term used by Japanese rural sociologists.

[8] The term *buraku* appears to be a recent term adopted since Meiji to distinguish the local group *mura* from the larger administrative *mura*. The administrative *ku* and *kuchō* also appear to be of recent origin in the *mura*.

time by discussion among the responsible house heads of the *buraku*. While for official elections involving governmental matters all men over twenty-five vote, in all local affairs each house has but one vote, a household being the political unit in the *buraku*. Life in the *buraku* is notable for its lack of bosses, and the *nushidōri* is not so much a chief as a caretaker of *buraku* affairs. When a death occurs in the *buraku*, the *nushidōri* is immediately informed; he then informs other people and oversees funeral preparations. If a road is to be fixed or cleaned, the *nushidōri* appoints a day. Any *buraku* property is looked after by him, and in some *buraku* there are special *nushidōri* for boats and special ones for bridges, whose duties are to keep records of the work on bridge-repairing, see that every house does its share, and keep a record of materials bought. A boat or bridge *nushidōri* usually acts in co-operation with the regular *buraku nushidōri*. *Mura* or *buraku* holidays are proclaimed by a *nushidōri*. To do this, he beats on a special wood slab (*bangi*) or beats together two slabs of wood (*hyōshigi*). More recently metal bells have been introduced into some *buraku* for this purpose. There is a special speed and number of beats to indicate (1) fires, (2) a meeting to begin community labor, (3) a meeting to discuss *buraku* affairs, and (4) a holiday.

Formerly *nushidōri* also supervised agricultural matters. During the last ten years, with the formation of the Agricultural Co-operative Association (*sangyō kumiai*) in the *mura* and its branch associations (*kokumiai*) in each *buraku*, these functions of the *nushidōri* have been greatly reduced. He is being replaced by the heads of the branch agricultural associations (*kokumiaichō*).

Agricultural association membership is restricted to farmers. Thus in Kakui, the shopkeepers' *buraku*, only half the houses belong to the branch association, and it is in Kakui that the *nushidōri* has retained the larger part of his functions, the *kokumiai* head being relatively unimportant. In one paddy *buraku*, on the other hand, the *nushidōri* has completely disappeared to be replaced by the *kokumiai* head and a group of elders called advisers (*komon*).

Each *buraku* has in it a wooden frame used to tie up horses when they are bled and have their hooves trimmed. This operation, called *chizashi*, is done thrice a year by a veterinary from Taragi (see p. 118).

In each *buraku* is a small wooden structure called *dō*, usually tile roofed though sometimes tin or straw roofed, which houses some Buddhist diety.[9] The *dō* plays an important role in the life of the *buraku* as a gathering and play place for the *buraku* children. Every day after breakfast the small preschool children under seven years of age as well as a number of fourteen-year-old nurse-maids carrying smaller babies on their backs gather here. They play until noon—then come back again after lunch and play until nightfall and suppertime. The children enjoy running around the building and playing games on the floor. It forms a shelter in case of rain. The children are in nobody's way as the *dō* is left quite unused except two or three times a year when celebrations are held there for the patron deity. The image enshrined gives mothers a feeling that the place is safe for their children.

Young men often sit and talk in a *buraku dō* at night. During the end-of-the-year night watch, when young men guard the *mura* against thieves, those not on duty used to sit in the *dō*. Of recent years they have come to sit in

[9] See chap. vii for discussion of these deities and their significance in *buraku* life.

someone's house where it is warmer.[10] Wandering pilgrims and beggars often spend the night at the nearest *dō*. A wandering peddler or footgear-mender will do his work under the shelter of this little building. Anyone, be he ever so humble, may find shelter in the *dō* and feel he has a friend in the Jizō or Kwannon who resides there.

Rivalry exists between the *buraku* and is expressed in joking remarks and finger-game competitions between men of different *buraku* at parties and by certain ritualized activities in the moon festival of the eighth month (see p. 288). An expression of this rivalry occurred recently when a comparatively wealthy member of one *buraku* gave to it a new fire bell as a memorial to his deceased father. The neighboring *buraku* was immediately seized with a desire for a new bell, although it had a perfectly good *bangi*, and it was not long before they raised some money[11] and erected one. Formerly *buraku* rivalry was more manifest than it is today. The women tell of parties they used to give to women of other *buraku* where each group competed in playing on the other practical jokes of such nature as serving soup with live frogs which jumped out as each guest lifted the cover of her soup bowl.

Buraku lines are to a certain extent giving way to social class lines. These are discussed in the chapter on social classes.

The house clusters forming *buraku* in Suye vary considerably in type. Kawaze and Nakashima are located on the rice paddy plain, across the river from the rest of the *mura*. They are characterized by a greater number of people per house, comparative wealth, close social ties,

[10] Mr. Mogami of Meiji University told me that in some *mura* young men sleep in the *dō* during summertime, using it as a clubhouse.

[11] From the writer because he was considered to be the wealthiest resident.

and common economic interests; most of the families living there have existed from olden times and are thus nearly all related through blood or marriage.

Oade and Imamura are "upland" *buraku*, that is, *buraku* on land not suitable for paddy, yet not in the mountains. They possess little paddy land within their boundaries and have to cross the river to cultivate rice. Kawaze and Nakashima, on the other hand, must cross the river in the other direction to cultivate upland crops such as sweet potatoes, taro, and mulberry—it is also necessary for paddy *buraku* people to cross the river to gather firewood in February.

Kakui and Tontokoro both present sharp differences from the paddy and upland types. They are shopkeepers' *buraku*. In Kakui nearly all the shops of the *mura* are assembled, as well as the village office and the *shōchū* factory. The prefectural road runs through both these shopkeepers' *buraku* (and where it runs through upland Oade it influences the *buraku* toward the shopkeeper type). The shopkeeper *buraku* is not socially unified. The farmers and the shopkeepers are about evenly divided in Kakui, and there are many quarrels and much malicious gossip as a result of their divergent interests. Many of the inhabitants of the shopkeeper *buraku* are immigrants, not born in Suye (see Table 4).

Hirayama, the mountain *buraku*, is the most isolated of all. It is justly noted for heavy drinking, kind hearts, and ignorance. Those families doing farming have long been settled there, but the mountain workers are mostly poorer people who were born elsewhere. Two or three Korean families are among these latter.

Maps V, VI, and VII illustrate three important types of *buraku*—the paddy, the shopkeeper, and the upland. It

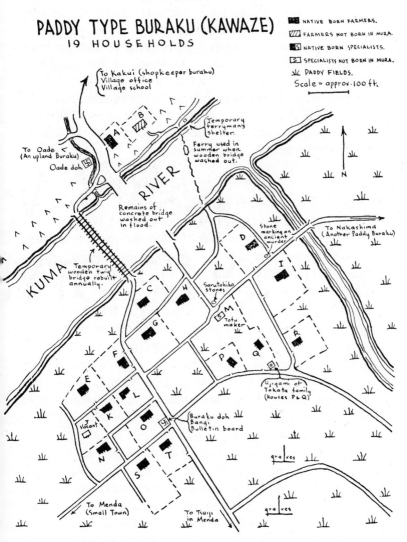

MAP V

PADDY TYPE BURAKU (KAWAZE)
19 HOUSEHOLDS

■ NATIVE BORN FARMERS.
▨ FARMERS NOT BORN IN MURA.
▣ NATIVE BORN SPECIALISTS.
▢ SPECIALISTS NOT BORN IN MURA.
PADDY FIELDS.
Scale = approx. 100 ft.

To Kakui (shopkeeper buraku)
Village office
Village school

Temporary ferryman's shelter.

Ferry used in summer when wooden bridge washed out.

To Oade
(An upland Buraku)
Oade doh

RIVER

Remains of concrete bridge washed out in flood.

Stone marking an ancient murder

To Nakashima
(Another Paddy Buraku)

KUMA

Temporary wooden twig bridge rebuilt annually.

Sarutahiko stones

Tatu maker

Ujigami of Takata family
(Houses P & Q)

Buraku doh
Bangi
Bulletin board

Vacant

To Menda
(Small Town)

To Tsuiji in Menda

graves

graves

N

will be noted that, in the paddy type, the houses are close together and in blocks, the whole surrounded by rice paddies. Everyone is a farmer, most families being native.

Through the shopkeeper type runs the prefectural road, lined on both sides with small shops of various kinds. Scattered houses not on the road are mostly farmers'.

The upland type, owing partly to the rougher nature of the land, is characterized by scattered houses and winding pathways, but, like the paddy type, most of the inhabitants are farmers.

FORMATION OF A NEW *buraku*

In Aso Ku a new *buraku*, Yunoharu, has gradually formed in recent years. In a small uninhabited valley between the next *mura* of Fukada and the main settlement of Aso various poor families, mostly from *mura* other than Suye, have moved in one at a time until by 1935 there were in all thirteen households. With so many households together they became recognized as a separate *buraku* and so regarded themselves. While the present heads of households were born elsewhere, most of their children were born in Yunoharu, the new *buraku*. There is only one family head born in this *buraku*, and he is a *buraku* leader. No regular *nushidōri* ever existed here, as the agricultural association branch came into existence about the same time as the *buraku*. A member of the one native family is the agricultural association head.

When forming this separate section of the Suye Agricultural Association, the people of Yunoharu built a small building to house some of the association's tools. This structure was erected near a rock of queer formation considered to look like a bull's nose and held to be somewhat

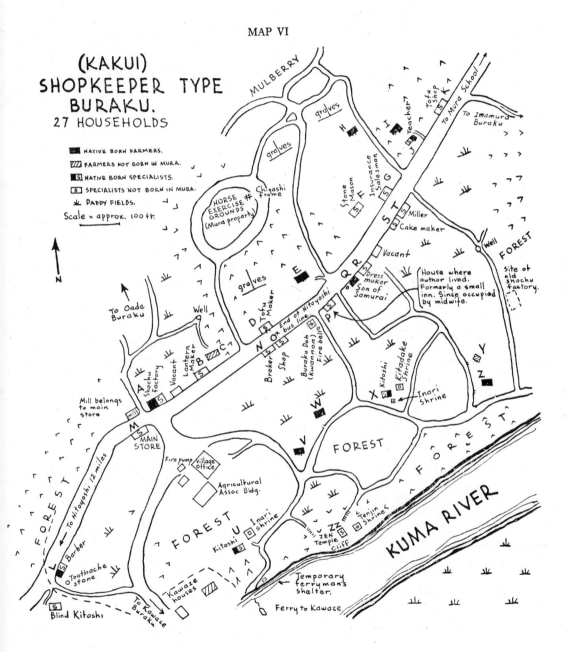

MAP VI

(KAKUI) SHOPKEEPER TYPE BURAKU.
27 HOUSEHOLDS

- ▢ NATIVE BORN FARMERS.
- ▨ FARMERS NOT BORN IN MURA.
- Ⓢ NATIVE BORN SPECIALISTS.
- ⓢ SPECIALISTS NOT BORN IN MURA.
- ⅄ PADDY FIELDS.

Scale = approx. 100 ft.

N

MULBERRY ST

graves

graves

HORSE EXERCISE GROUNDS (Mura property)

Chirashi frame

graves

Stone Mason

Insurance Salesman

Teacher

Tofu Shop

To Mura School

To Imamura Buraku

FOREST

Miller

Cake maker

Well

Vacant

Site of old shochu factory.

Dress maker

Son of Samurai

House where author lived. Formerly a small inn. Since occupied by midwife.

To Oade Buraku

graves

Well

Tofu Maker

End of Hitoyoshi bus line.

Broker's Shop

Buraku Doh (Kwannon)

Fire ball

Kitadake Shrine

Kitoshi

Inari Shrine

Lantern Maker

Vacant

Shochu factory

Mill belongs to main store

mill

MAIN STORE

Fire pump

Village office

Agricultural Assoc Bldg.

FOREST

FOREST

FOREST

Teijin Shrine

Kitoshi

Inari Shrine

ZEN Temple

Cliff

KUMA RIVER

To Hitoyoshi, 12 miles

Barber

Toothache stone

Blind Kitoshi

Kawaze houses

To Kawaze Buraku

Temporary ferryman's shelter.

Ferry to Kawaze

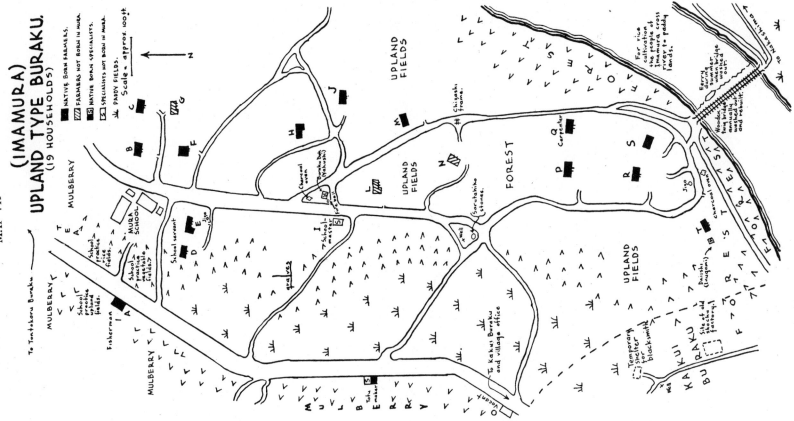

MAP VII

(IMAMURA)
UPLAND TYPE BURAKU.
(19 HOUSEHOLDS)

■ NATIVE BORN FARMERS.
▨ FARMERS NOT BORN IN MURA.
Ⓢ NATIVE BORN SPECIALISTS.
Ⓢ SPECIALISTS NOT BORN IN MURA.
↓↓ PADDY FIELDS.
Scale - approx. 100 ft.

N

To Tentokoru Buraku

MULBERRY

MULBERRY

MULBERRY

School practice rice fields.

School practice upland fields.

School practice vegetable fields.

Fisherman

A

School servant

MURA SCHOOL

E A T

B

C

G

F

H

J

D

E
Jizo

I
School-master

graves

Charcoal oven

Bamboo Dam (Yabushita)

Fire-well

L

M

UPLAND FIELDS

N

Sarutahiko stones.

well

UPLAND FIELDS

FOREST

UPLAND FIELDS

P

Q
Carpenter

R

S

#
Chizashi frame.

UPLAND FIELDS

Charcoal oven

Jizo

T

Daishi (Inugami)

Temporary shelter for blacksmith

Site of old shochu factory.

KAKUI BURAKU

FOREST AREA

To Kakei Buraku and village office

Tofu Maker

B

vacant

For rice cultivation the people of Imamura cross river to paddy lands.

Ferry during summer when bridge washed out

Wooden hay bridge annually washed out and rebuilt.

To Nakashima

sacred. Children play on the platform of this building. A few years ago someone found an old neglected stone Jizō in the woods; he brought it home and put it in the building by the platform where the children play. The building is not actually called a *dō*, nor is any special celebration held for the Jizō in it, but it is already a central play place for young children. The Jizō was put there to act as guardian (not because it is a Jizō but because it is a "person"— Amida or Yakushi would do as well).

The whole settlement of Yunoharu is not twenty years old, but all the inhabitants are farmers and thus have more economic interests in common than the much older but less unified business *buraku* of Kakui or Tontokoro. They have already developed a feeling of belonging to one group, the Yunoharu group. Doubtless the building where the agricultural association tools are kept and in which the Jizō resides and the children play will in a few years become a regular *dō* with an annual celebration in honor of Jizō, just as, for instance, the Kawaze *dō* celebrates Kwannon.

In the field work on which this study is based, the writer concentrated on Kawaze and Nakashima as typical paddy *buraku*, Kakui as shopkeeper, Oade and Imamura as upland, Hirayama as mountain, and Yunoharu as new upland. Except for Hirayama and Yunoharu, all these *buraku* are adjacent. The *buraku* in Aso Ku and Hamanoue Ku and the other *buraku* (Tontokoro, Kamo, Ishizaka, and Kojo) present no particular features not found in the seven selected.

THE CO-OPERATIVE NEIGHBORHOOD GROUP (*kumi*)

There are within the *buraku* certain smaller unofficial groups called *kumi* whose function today will be discussed at length in chapter iv on co-operation. They are probably the survival of older, more formalized groups of Tokugawa days—the five-man group or *goningumi*. The formalized system dates back to a similar system adopted from China during the T'ang dynasty, and, after falling more or less into official disuse, it was revived and reorganized by Toyotomi Hideyoshi in 1597 and carried on through Tokugawa days for administrative purposes.

The *goningumi* system was begun by the government with the object of organizing the villages into a self-governing system. Every five houses formed a group with a headman, and several such groups formed a *mura* under a *mura* headman, through whom the government acted. For instance, in issuing laws or regulations, they were announced first to the *mura* headman, who transmitted them to the *kumi* head, who in turn informed the men of his group.

The five members of each group were held responsible jointly for whatever any one of them did, and in case any member of a group committed a crime and the other members shielded him, if the criminal were discovered by someone else, not only the other members of the group had to bear responsibility for the crime jointly but the headman of the *mura* also had to share in it. This joint-responsibility feature of the *kumi* is the thing best remembered by old farmers today. Evidently, while it provided some with a chance to pass on responsibility, it frequently proved a tyrannical system.

Thus the *kumi* system, while still a functioning organization in the village today both in the form of the *buraku* and in the smaller groups still called *kumi*, was originally organized by the government as a means of keeping the farmer in his place, honest, frugal, and industrious.

The village organization of today is a modification of

forms already in existence in Tokugawa days. Villagers were then governed by a people's representative called *nanushi* or *shōya*. He was subject, however, to orders of a *shōgun*'s representative (*gundai* or *daikwan*). Below the *shōya*, who in rural regions away from the capital had in reality much the same authority as the headman today, were the *kumi* heads (*kumigashira*, *kumichō*) of the village and village councilors (*toshiyori*). The *shōya*, like the modern headman, usually came from an old and well-to-do family in the village. Usually not a *samurai*, he was a true representative, just as today the *sonchō* is usually of an old landed farming family and acts as representative of his *mura* to the prefectural and central governments.[12]

There has been a strong centralizing tendency in the governing of the country. The *kumi* are giving way to the *buraku*, and small *mura* have been amalgamated into larger ones under a single headman. Several provinces have been amalgamated to form a single prefecture under a government-appointed governor. While the *mura* is self-governing, it is responsible to the prefectural government which appoints its schoolteachers, agricultural advisers, and policemen, and it is expected to raise enough money in taxes to meet all *mura* expenses including the schoolteachers' salaries. There are at present (as of 1936) in Japan 9,724 *mura*, 1,693 towns (*machi*), and 129 cities (*shi*).

[12] See also Eitaro Suzuki, *A Plan for a Rural Sociological Survey in Japan* ("Research Bulletin of the Gifu Imperial College of Agriculture," No. 19 [Gifu, Japan, 1931]); Yosoburo Takekoshi, *The Economic Aspects of the History of the Civilization of Japan* (London, 1930); and Sansom, *op. cit.*, pp. 163–71. The fullest descriptions in English of the old *mura* and *goningumi* are to be found in D. B. Simmons and J. H. Wigmore, "Notes on Land Tenure and Local Institutions in Old Japan," *Transactions of the Asiatic Society of Japan*, XIX (1891), 37–270 and K. Asakawa "Notes on Village Government in Japan after 1600," *Journal of the American Oriental Society*, XXX (1910), Part III, 259–300; *ibid.*, XXXI (1911), Part II, 151–216.

AGRICULTURAL PRODUCTS, TOOLS, AND MACHINES[13]

Higo, the old province now called Kumamoto in which Kuma lies, has been described by Kaempfer as a "middling fruitful country affording plenty of firewood and wood for building, and also corn, peas, fish, crabs and other necessaries as much as will supply the wants of the inhabitants."

The fertile plain area of Kuma is an ideal region for rice paddies, so it is not surprising to discover that some of Japan's best rice is grown here. The broad flood plain is one big network of irrigation ditches fed by the Kuma River or its tributary mountain streams. Running the length of the south side of the basin (the Kuma River runs along the north side) is Hyakutaro Ditch, a canal dug in feudal times. This canal, built with forced labor, was very slow in completion, and so many obstacles appeared that finally those in charge concluded that the water-god wished a human sacrifice. After this wish was complied with, the canal was quickly finished and has served ever since to irrigate many acres of rice land.[14] The tributary valleys also afford good ground for growing paddy-field rice. There is no extensive terracing of the land to obtain paddies on hillsides, the upland ground being used for growing mulberry bushes, sweet potatoes, giant radish, and other vegetables as well as wheat and barley, millet and dry rice.

One crop of paddy rice is grown a year. The whole *mura* is sowing it in seedbeds in May, transplanting it forty days later in June, weeding in late June and July, harvesting in October, threshing in November and December. In the fall about half the paddy area is transformed into

---

[13] See also Appen. I, "Economic Base."

[14] The idea of a human sacrifice as necessary whenever any big public works such as bridges, forts, or buildings were undertaken was widespread in old Japan.

RICE HARVEST

In the background are the mountains which surround Kuma County

FAMILY WORKING TOGETHER SEPARATING CHAFF FROM GRAIN
BY MEANS OF A HAND-POWERED WINNOWER (*TŌMI*)

dry fields, and a winter wheat and barley crop is sown, to be harvested in May between the planting and transplanting of rice. The remaining fields are planted with legumes or allowed to lie fallow.

Rice being the main crop, it requires the major portion of a man's labor and a woman's also. Rice is by far the most important product of the *mura* and one of its chief sources of income. It is the rice of *mura* like Suye that feeds the nation of Japan. This is an important economic fact when considered in connection with the moneyless way in which it is produced (see chaps. iii and iv). Thus the *mura* contributes rice to the nation while receiving very little money for it, and what money it does receive goes out of the *mura* again to purchase sugar, salt, fertilizer, and manufactured articles. Increased production in recent years through improved agricultural techniques has been more than taken up by the increased population of the nation, especially in the nonproducing cities. Rice is also, of course, the staple food within the *mura*. Its great importance to the villagers—its social value—is recognized in many ways.

There are special words for rice, as a plant (*ine*), when first harvested (*momi*), when hulled (*gemmai*), when polished (*hakumai*), when boiled (*gohan* or *meshi*), and when talking to children (*mamma*). There is also a general word for uncooked rice (*kome*) as against other grains. Rice that ripens early is called *wase*.

Many different things are made from rice. It is boiled and in this state forms a staple of diet, a man eating two or three bowls with each meal. The general word for food or a meal is the same as that for boiled rice, namely, *gohan*.[15] Similarly, children call all food *mamma*. Candies

[15] Breakfast is *asa(go)han* (morning rice); lunch, *hiru(go)han* (noon rice); and supper, *yū(go)han* (evening rice).

and cakes are made from rice, and the most important ceremonial cake, *mochi*, is made of pounded rice. Rice is used as money within the *mura* and forms the usual gift in the countless calls a woman makes to relatives and on such occasions as funerals, parties, and naming ceremonies. Wandering pilgrims carry pouches to receive the little saucerful of rice most housewives give as alms. The liquor (*shōchū*) so very much drunk in Suye is made from rice.[16] Rice and *shōchū* are standard offerings to the gods and spirits. *Shōchū* mixed with snake skin is used to cure venereal disease. Rice water and rice flour diluted in water are used as infant foods. The great value of rice in the local economy is illustrated by the fact that it is the only thing ever regularly locked up. Furthermore, one must never throw away or be disrespectful to rice—rice thrown into the fire, for instance, is likely to turn into a fireball and whiz out of the house.

Rye (*hadakamugi*), wheat (*komugi*), and barley (*ōmugi*) are grown as winter crops on drained and plowed-up paddies. All three are commonly referred to as *mugi*. This double-crop system was begun at the suggestion of the prefectural office agricultural advisers about ten years ago. Previously *mugi* was grown, but only on upland fields, whereas today about half the paddies are drained and planted in *mugi*. Prisoners and soldiers have rice served with some type of *mugi* in it. Most farming people leaven their rice with a little *mugi* or millet because it is cheaper and is said to be good for the health. It is not considered good to taste and is never eaten alone. Even as a leavener for rice, it is never served to guests. There is, however, a special festival cake, *mugi-dango*, made of *mugi* flour.

[16] Of recent years, beer has come to be drunk in the towns and *geisha* houses, but few farmers ever drink it. *Shōchū*, like *sake*, is drunk warm, so there are people who prefer their beer warm too.

SUNNING GRAIN

POUNDING MILLET—MOTHER AND CHILDREN

Rice and *mugi* are both grown as money crops. Yellow millet (*awa*), on the other hand, is grown mostly for home consumption. Upland (dry) rice, as against paddy rice, is also grown for home consumption. The chief use of millet is as an economical leaven for rice. It is very old, being mentioned in the *Kojiki*, but today does not play an important part in the life of the villager. However, it is considered better and is used more often than *mugi*. Occasionally, *mochi* and rice cakes are colored yellow with millet.

After rice and *mugi*, silk cocoons form the third important item in the agricultural economy of the *mura*. The worms are raised and cocoons sold in three crops, each taking about forty days from hatching to spinning. In early summer the first worms begin nibbling at mulberry leaves. The first cocoons are sold in early June, the second in late August, and the third in early October. No worms are reared in late June owing to the busy rice-transplanting season. Many second-rate cocoons are kept at home—those a little off-color or out of shape—to be reeled by women of the household. During the early spring months before the wheat harvest, when work is slack, the women bring out their looms and weave beautiful homespun fabrics. Silkworm-raising is a minor industry in Suye compared to the intensified sericulture of true silk regions such as Nagano Prefecture, where four crops are raised and where the worms are bred as well as raised by the farmers. In such regions, of course, rice culture plays a correspondingly minor role.

The silk industry, while not new, has expanded greatly in the past few decades as Japan's markets for silk have increased. However, today it is only practiced by about half the villagers—the more well-to-do half with menservants and maidservants and spare upland fields on which to raise mulberry. Two of the largest spinning companies of Japan, Katakura and Kanebo, furnish eggs to the farmers and buy their cocoons when spun. They have organized the farmers into sericultural associations which receive aid and instruction from the company teachers and which receive banquets at company expense from time to time. Thus, the silkworm-raisers have certain privileges in addition to the rather small cash payments for the cocoons.[17]

The two major companies represented in Suye have as heads of their respective village silk associations the village headman and a village councilor, both rich and influential men in village affairs. These men receive many special favors from the companies in the way of gifts and, on their part, explain the company's aims to the farmers and offer explanations when the company hands out a poor batch of eggs or happens to pay a lower price for cocoons than usual.

One of the few examples of rivalry in village affairs is that between these two company associations. They always hold their meetings separately and attempt to outshine each other in production and in parties after the sale of cocoons and even in the type of priest hired to thank the gods for a good year (see p. 228).

The time a farmer is not busy with rice, *mugi*, or silk he may fill in by tending small vegetable patches, cutting grass for his horse or cow, and raising a few chickens. The chickens, incidentally, are a recent innovation in the village economy. Only one farmer in Suye raises more than five or six; most keep only two or three.

---

[17] Like the rice broker, the spinning company obtains the money while the farmer does the work. Whereas the government-sponsored village agricultural co-operatives are replacing to a large extent the unscrupulous broker, there are as yet very few silk co-operatives in Japan.

SORTING SILKWORMS THAT ARE READY TO SPIN, PREPARATORY
TO PUTTING THEM IN COCOON NETS (BEING MADE AT RIGHT)

Househead and his brother making nets, daughter picking up worms, wife at extreme left. The other woman is a neighbor helping.

"Fortune," September, 1936

SPINNING DURING WINTER MONTHS

The two staple vegetables are giant radishes (*daikon*) and sweet potatoes. Besides these, many other vegetables are raised, some of them of recent introduction to the *mura*. (The sweet potato and the cucumber are phallic symbols; the bean and a certain bean-stuffed cake (*manjū*) are female sexual symbols, the latter being synonymous with vulva.)

Tōfu (soy-bean curd) is prepared in the *mura* by several *tōfu*-makers and sold to the rest of the villagers. It is made by grinding soy beans in a stone quern. It is eaten a great deal in soup and is used as a cheap substitute for fish at some social gatherings.

The diet is largely vegetarian, though fish and occasionally chicken accompany a banquet. Plenty of proteins are available in the many foods made of soy beans, especially the soy-bean soup (*miso-shiru*), soy-bean sauce (*shōyu*), and soy-bean curd cake (*tōfu*) (see Table 1).

Food and complexion are believed by villagers to be correlated; a person with light skin is said to eat only white rice, unmixed with wheat or millet. Every festival has its own particular food, and certain foods are recommended for the sick and for the pregnant. One food or another is the usual gift taken when one goes calling on a friend or relative.

A little hemp is grown, the fibers being sold for manufacture into rope and other hemp products. A large variety of trees grow in Japan, many of which are represented in Kuma. For building and general utility the following are the most important in Suye: bamboo, cryptomeria (*sugi*), cypress (*hinoki*), a Japanese variety of oak (*kashi*), various pines and firs called collectively *matsu*, and willow. It is significant that four of these trees (cypress, bamboo, pine, and willow) possess a ritual as well as a practical

TABLE 1

AGRICULTURAL PRODUCTS BY SEASONS*

Spring (Mar.–May)	Summer (June–Aug.)	Autumn (Sept.–Nov.)	Winter (Dec.–Feb.)
Bamboo shoots	*Azuki* (a bean)	*Azuki* and *sasage*	Buckwheat
Beet tops (*Fudansō*)	Bean sprouts	(beans)	Carrots
Broadbean (*sora mame*—mostly turned under for fertilizer)	Carrots	Buckwheat	Chinese cabbage
	Citron (*yuzu*)	Cabbage (*botana*)	*Daikon*
	Cucumber	Camellia nuts (for hair oil)	*Gobō*
Clover (turned under for fertilizer and used for horse food)	Early *daikon*	Carrots	Onion and green onion
	Eggplant	Chestnuts	Pear
	Grapes	Chinese cabbage (*hakusai*)	Persimmon
Dozen shoots	Japanese pear (*nashi*)	Citron	Sweet potato
Fern shoots (*warabi, zenmai*)	*Kaya* grass (for house roofs)	Corn (maize)	Tangerine (imported)
Fuki stems	Onion	Cucumber	Taro
Futsuba (a green—used in Girl Day cakes)	Peach	*Daikon*	*Takana* (a green)
	Plum (mostly for pickling)	Eggplant	*Kwannonsō* (a green)
Garlic (*ninniku*)	Pumpkin	Ginger	*Osogona* (a green)
Gumi berry (mostly eaten by children)	*Rakkyō* (a kind of onion)	*Gobō* (root of burdock)	*Rengesō* (lotus stems)
Honey	Rape seed (*Natane, undai*—for oil)	Grapes	*Seri* (a green)
Kona (a green)	*Shiro uri* (a melon)	*Hechima* (*luffa petola*)	*Tabirago* (a green)
Mugi† (harvested in April and May)	*Shiso* leaves (for pickling plums)	*Konnyaku* (a root)	*Yomena* (a green)
Napa (a green)	Tomato	Millet (*awa, kibi,* and *kokibi*)	[These last seven greens come in spring by the old lunar calendar and are regarded as spring herbs]
Parsley (*Seri*)	Watermelon	Mountain potato (*yama imo*)	
Peas (mostly turned under for fertilizer)	Yellow daisy (leaves of)	Mushrooms	
Sanshō (leaves and seeds)		*Niga uri* (a kind of melon)	
Sazo (or *satogara*‡ —sprout of)		Onion and green onion	
Senmoto (wild grass)		*Osogona* (a green)	
		Persimmon	
		Pumpkin	

* A full description of most of these products and the chief foods made from them, such as tea, *tōfu,* and *shōyu* is given by J. J. Rein in *Japan* (New York, 1888–89), Vol. II.

† Collective term for wheat, rye, and barley.

‡ Called *itadori* in other parts of Japan. Rein identifies it as *Polygonum cuspidatum.*

§ Called *kara imo* and *satsuma imo* in Kuma. The farmer considers *kara* to mean "from" and says one variety is "kara" China and another "kara" America. No one said "kara" Riukiu Islands, as reported by some writers, e.g., Robert Hall and J. J. Rein.

TABLE 1—*Continued*

Spring (Mar.–May)	Summer (June–Aug.)	Autumn (Sept.–Nov.)	Winter (Dec.–Feb.)
Spinach String beans *Takana* (a green) Tea (picked in May) *Tsubana* (flower of *kaya* grass) Turnip (*kabu*)		Rice (harvested in October) Sesame seed Soy bean Sugar cane (wild) Sweet potato§ Taro (*sato imo*) *Toga* (a white gourd) *Toimo* stems Turnip Watermelon White potato	

From River and Paddy

Shrimps Snails (*Tabinna, Tanishi, Shijimigai*, etc.)	Eels Trout (*ayu*) *Funa* Carp and other fish	Shrimps Carp and other fish in ditches when paddies are drained before harvest	

value. Trees grown for their fruits are camellia (nuts used for hair oil), a kind of palm (for fiber), mulberry (leaves for silkworms), tea bush, chestnut, peach, pear, persimmon, and plum. Mulberry wood has special values; for instance, a teacup made of it acts as a disease preventative. Maples grow in the hills and are admired for their red leaves in autumn. Trees and shrubs admired for their beauty when in bloom include azalea, cherry, peach, plum, *jinchō*, and *nanten*. *Nanten* is usually grown by the toilet and has a certain ritual purificatory value. The *sakaki*, used in Shinto rituals, grows in the hills. There are many flowers both wild and cultivated of which some of the commonest are iris, goldenrod, various asters and chrysanthemums, lotus, violets, and *Higan bana* (*Lycoris radiata*). Bouquets of most of these flowers when in bloom are placed by household and wayside shrines and sacred spots. The crimson *Higan bana* is a curious exception to this, never being offered to the gods.

Horses and cows are kept, but they are used only as beasts of burden. The animals are backed into their stables, where they spend all their time when not working. Milk is considered dirty and is only drunk on doctor's prescription. The chief times these animals are used is at rice-planting and transplanting (May and June) and at wheat-planting (November). There are no pastures for livestock to graze on, so all hay and grass must be cut by hand and brought to the animals in their stables. Before feeding straw or grass to them, a farmer chops it up into small bits on a hand chopper. Livestock is also fed on rice and wheat bran. Because of their military value, farmers are encouraged to breed horses, and for every equine birth registered at the village office in a *baseki* (horses' record, similar to *koseki* for men) a farmer is given two yen.[18]

A few goats are kept partly as pets and partly for their milk, which is taken as medicine. Some dogs are kept as pets. Cats serve a useful purpose in catching mice. A few rabbits are kept as pets and occasionally sold. Both dogs

[18] Many government-sponsored activities can be traced to military expediency. Much of a recent economic reconstruction movement to encourage farmers to produce more crops both in quantity and in variety is more for the purpose of strengthening the position of the country than to enrich the farmer. A recent law, which affects *shōchū* manufacturers, makes alcohol a government monopoly and has as its basic reason the desire of the government to have control of all production of alcohol, valuable in wartime.

and cats eat rice. Many people keep various types of birds in little cages as pets.

Pigs are raised for sale to outside dealers by most of the *tōfu*-makers. A piglet is bought for five yen from some city broker, fed on *tōfu* waste and general garbage (very scanty in a farmer's house) for about a year, after which time the broker comes back and buys the grown pig for from fifteen to twenty yen. The pigs are taken to larger cities for sale. The *shōchū* manufacturer also keeps pigs, feeding them on bran and *shōchū* waste.

Changes in diet have been few. While pigs are raised to sell to cities which have taken up pork and ham as food, the villagers never think of eating pig meat themselves. An increased variety of green vegetables is the most notable change in recent years and a few new types of wheat cakes prepared with soda introduced by the school.

Tools used in farming are still, for the most part, of the wooden and iron hand variety, machines being few and of recent introduction into the region. The bicycle and a special rearcar are much used in addition to man and horse for carrying loads.

Grain mills for hulling grain and making flour, run by electricity, gas, or water power, are all privately owned in Suye. The next *mura* has one owned by the *mura* agricultural society, however.

Some people make flour at home on revolving grindstones (*hikiusu*), similar to those used in making the beancurd *tōfu*. Rice is often polished at home on a foot-powered machine called *fumiusu*. There is also a homemade mill similar to the foot mill but powered by water.

Simple wooden tools such as carrying sticks, blunt wooden rakes, and baskets are made at home. Iron tools are today mostly purchased in Menda or through the agricultural association.

In addition to the various sickles, hoes, and mattocks used from old times, several machines have come into use during recent years. The commonest and oldest (twenty years) of these is a foot-powered thresher (*inekogi*) costing about twenty-five yen. Nearly every farmer has one of these. They have replaced the older arduous hand methods of threshing by beating grain against a log or pulling it through a series of spikes. More recently a few gas-engine-powered threshing machines have come into the village and are in part replacing the older foot-powered threshers. Some are privately owned, and some are owned by *buraku* agricultural associations. For separating chaff a hand-powered wooden wind winnower (*tōmi*)[19] is used.

There are special hand machines for making noodles, owned by a few households. Hand-worked machines are also used for removing the excess fuzz from silk cocoons.

Fire apparatus consists of a hand pump, and most *buraku* own such a fire pump. The *shōchū* factory, privately owned, has modern distilling machinery. There are three radios (owned by the school, a broker, and the headman), several phonographs (one at school), and several sewing machines (two at school). Every house has a clock. When in the fields, time is told by the passing of trains. In 1936 a telephone was installed in the village office at the cost of eight hundred yen.

Artificial fertilizer is one of the most important additions to farming life. The first thing a man says in speaking of modern times is the great boon of artificial fertilizer.

[19] An almost identical machine is used in rural China. Many other characteristic Japanese farm tools have their counterparts in China. In fact, all the simple hand-powered grinders, winnowers, etc., seem to have originated on the mainland.

Formerly a man had to go far into the mountains to collect loam and old dead leaves to scatter on the fields. However, every scrap of human manure is used today just as it was then. The school and village office rent out the right to collect their night soil.

From Table 2 it is apparent that the machine age has come to Suye during the present generation. Thirty years ago all farming was done by hand; fertilizer hand gathered; transportation by foot, horse, or boat; and clothing all homespun. In the mountain *buraku* of Hirayama, even today, there is no electricity, and there are no modern engines of any kind.

With machines have come increased contacts with, and dependence on, the world outside Kuma, coupled with a widened horizon of interests. The bicycle has brought the towns closer, and the bus has made Hitoyoshi much more accessible. With the closeness of town and city and with the newer money crops of wheat and silk have come also an increased use of money. Frequently the machines have tended to replace hand labor calling for the co-operation of several households, and in this way have contributed their share to the breakdown of some of the co-operation systems described in later chapters.

THE SEASONS

The seasons play an all-important part in village life. Indeed, even in cities, the Japanese are very conscious of changes of season, and there is much poetry on the subject, each season having its characteristic symbol—the evanescent cherry blossoms of spring, the dragonfly of summer, and the peculiar delicacy of the tall *susuki* grass on the hillsides in autumn, heralding the coming of snow to change a drab village to a faery apparition. In addition to

TABLE 2

Machines in Suye Mura

Machine	Number in Use	Approximate Age of Oldest Machine (Years)
Water grain mill.............	1	20
Electric grain mill (replacing old individual water wheels, foot-pounders, etc., many of which still exist, especially in the the mountain *buraku*)	3	7
Foot-powered rice thresher.....	1 per farm household	20
Gasoline engines.............	7 (3 private, 4 owned by *buraku* agr. assoc.)	10
Gasoline-engine-powered threshing and hulling machines now replacing foot-powered machines, especially for wheat...	18 (8 private, 10 owned by agr. assoc.)	10
Cocoon fuzz remover..........	1 per silk-raising household	10
Cocoon netmaker.............	1 per silk-raising household	15
Udon-maker.................	30	9
Ropemaking machine (replaces older hand methods and with it co-operation of several houses in ropemaking bees)...	60	20
Hair-clippers.................	100	30
Bicycles.....................	160	25
Bicycle rearcars..............	47	10
Motorcycles	1	2
Automobiles.................	0 (1 in Fukada)*	
Sewing machines.............	4	30
Radio.......................	5	5
Phonograph..................	20	30
Telephone...................	1 (in village office)	1 (1936)
Electricity came 11 years ago Ice cakes† in Taragi 3 years ago Bus 2 years ago (6 or 7 years ago a service began and stopped for lack of trade) Railroad to Taragi and Menda 12 years ago		

* Owned by a doctor. There are, however, several in Taragi and Menda.
† A kind of popsicle, costing one sen each; popular in summer.

PREPARING RED JUICE FROM *SHISO* LEAVES FOR
PICKLING PLUMS—A SPRING OCCUPATION

Pickling bucket in foreground. Salt is in basket at right, resting on an unused grinding-stone.

LINE FISHING IN THE KUMA RIVER

the seasonal nature of sowing and harvesting the summer grains, there is a set season for making most village products. A year's supply of hair oil is pressed in spring before the work of wheat harvest and rice-planting begins. About the same time, plums are pickled and *miso* made for the ensuing year. A year's supply of *shōyu* is prepared in the heat of summer after rice-weeding and before the harvest. The floods wash out bridges in early summer which are replaced by a co-operative ferry service until just before fall harvest when villagers set to and build new ones. *Kaya* grass for roof thatch is cut in autumn and put away to be dried until the next year when, just before rice-planting and just before harvest, new roofs are made and old ones repaired. In spring, in summer, and in autumn, the horses of the village are "cured" at *chixashi*, and at each change of season there is a *buraku* gathering to which a priest comes and makes talismans to put at *buraku* entrances to ward off evil spirits. The relation of the seasons and the festival calendar is discussed in chapter vii.

Each season has its characteristic clothing just as does each age-grade and each sex. Even the games the children play are seasonal—girls bounce balls in fall and juggle beanbags in spring; boys chase dragonflies and walk on stilts in summer. Daily greetings are conventionalized on a seasonal basis. In winter one greets a fellow-villager with "It is cold"; in summer with "It is hot"; and during the rainy season with "It is raining." Such greetings are much more frequent than "Good morning" or "Hello."

Such important social events as weddings bow to the seasonal nature of village life, occurring mostly in late autumn after the rice harvest is in. The only aspects of life in the *mura* not affected directly or indirectly by the seasons are those works of fate—birth and death.

A lunar calendar is used by farmers in the *mura*, and all local holidays and festivals are observed according to this calendar. *Buraku* rest days are on the first, eighth, fifteenth, and twenty-fourth of the lunar month. Many festivals fall on the first or fifteenth. *Buraku* meetings and parties are usually arranged for one of the *buraku* rest-day dates, when no one will be busy; and even the school, which is run by the Gregorian calendar, bows to local custom inasmuch as its young people's school (*seinen gakkō*) is held on *buraku* rest days—days when young men and women will be free to attend. The newer agricultural pursuits, such as winter wheat and increased sericulture, and the introduction of the Gregorian calendar with Sundays as holidays for the village office and school, are tending to break up the older rhythms of *buraku* work and recreation. People are too busy, they say, to do more than make a few special cakes for various festivals which in the old days called for three holidays in a row. This will be further discussed in chapter vii; meanwhile, Table 3 outlines the principal seasonal occupations of Kuma farmers, as Table 1 outlines the seasonal diet.

VILLAGE SPECIALISTS

Practically everyone in Suye is a farmer; there are, however, some specialists and shopkeepers.

The most ancient type of specialist is probably the carpenter. There are usually two or three in each *mura*, each of whom has served an apprenticeship under some master-carpenter before setting up locally as an expert. When a house is built, the carpenter is a necessary man in directing the building of the framework and the honored man at the feast that follows.

The stonecutter makes gravestones and foundation

TABLE 3

Yearly Round of Labor in Suye*

Jan.–Feb.	Mar.–Apr.	May–June	July–Aug.	Sept.–Oct.	Nov.–Dec.
Wood-cutting Charcoal Blacksmith (visits village to repair tools) Vacant paddies readjusted Some bird-shooting Snow and frost	Charcoal Roads repaired Roofmaking Hair oil made (women) *Weaving* (women) *Baskets* (men) Fern shoots gathered Some vegetables planted Mulberry fields fertilized Wheat fields tended Shellfish collected in paddies (women) Spring *chizashi* (April)	*First silk crop* (May) *Azuki* beans planted *Rice-planting* (May) *Tea-picking* and drying Wheat harvest Irrigation ditches repaired *Rice-transplanting* (June)† Bamboo shoots gathered Potatoes transplanted	*Second silk crop* (Aug.) *Rice-weeding* (July) *Shōyu-* and *miso-making* (women) Fishing (men) Pickling plums (women) Millet-sowing First eggplant and cucumber (end of Aug.) Summer *chizashi* (July) Very hot weather	*Third silk crop* (finished before rice harvest) Millet harvest (Oct.) *Rice harvest* (Oct.) Mushrooms (Oct.) Tubmaker visits village (Sept.) Fishing (Sept.) Roofmaking Wood bridges rebuilt (before rice harvest) Charcoal Persimmon harvest Clover seed sown in paddies just before harvest Autumn *chizashi* (Oct.) before rice harvest	*Rice-threshing and hulling* Potato harvest Rice and millet harvest continued Taro, sweet potato, cabbage, and *daikon* harvest Some bird-shooting (Dec.) Frost
A season of comparative leisure	*No intensive labor*	*A very busy season*	*Very busy season until rice-weeding is finished*	*A busy season*	*Busy with harvest and threshing*

* Seasonal activities italicized are the most important. † After cocoons are sold.

stones for buildings. In the old days he made household necessities such as foot rice-grinders (*fumiusu*) and bathtubs, now replaced by iron and cement ones bought in town.

Another important specialist is the cakemaker. Like the carpenter, he learns his trade through apprenticeship elsewhere, then comes to Suye to do business. The cakemaker, beside furnishing cakes and candy to children, is important for the making of the formalized cakes (*rakkan*) used at naming ceremonies, weddings, and funerals.

There is no blacksmith in Suye. For the necessary work a man is hired from the next *mura* every spring; he sets up a temporary forge and works a couple of weeks on work brought him by villagers. He receives his pay in rice. The carpenter, on the other hand, is usually paid in money. Other visiting specialists are a tubmaker, a tinker, and a fishmonger. This last is a very important person in connection with the numerous banquets which occur in the village and at which fish is always de rigueur. The fishmonger's role in village life will be further described in chapter iii.

There are three women specialists. One of these is the midwife of which there are two in the *mura*. They have attended some school of midwifery and so are legally entitled to their trade. As the carpenter holds the place of honor at a housebuilding celebration, so the midwife is given the place of honor at a baby-naming ceremony. Another woman specialist is the seamstress. She has a sewing machine to mend shirts and make working clothes for men. Usually a woman who sews *kimono* (always sewn by hand) is different from one who sews work clothes, as she is, as a rule, of higher social rank. There are no professional *kimono*-makers in Suye, but the wife of one of the village

THE CAKEMAKER (KAKUI)

TŌFU SHOP (KAKUI)

This woman makes *tōfu* daily. Her shop carries a few tinned goods, some candy, beer, *geta* thongs, etc. It is a favorite gathering-place for people to sit about and talk.

office clerks helps women with their sewing and takes orders for *kimono*. Most women make their own clothes, having learned sewing at school.

Some widows and farmers' wives, usually of the poorer families, make *tōfu* as a means of increasing the family income. Such a family usually has only a little farm land, otherwise the wife would not have the time to devote every morning to making and selling *tōfu*. A *tōfu* shop often sells a few other edibles such as soda water, candy, bottled beer, canned fish, beef, and pineapple. Only a few people such as visiting officials or schoolteachers ever purchase the canned and bottled goods. Each *buraku* has a *tōfu*-maker, and the *tōfu* shop is often a center for people to sit about and gossip, and here young men often gather at night to talk.

Most of the carpenters, stonemasons, and blacksmiths make a living at their trade. Other specialists, such as the five or six expert roofmakers of the *mura*, are, however, primarily farmers. Several roofmakers are hired, paid in rice, and fed by the man having his roof fixed. At other times roofmakers are ordinary farmers. The barber runs a barber shop and also does farming on a fairly large scale. His wife raises silkworms. Similarly, the Buddhist and Shinto priests combine farming with their specialty. Some praying priests (*kitōshi*) do farming also, but one blind priest is so prosperous as a *kitōshi* that he does nothing else.

Other small farmers do river fishing on the side during the summer months. This is a time-consuming occupation, and, as a rule, only poor farmers without much land to take care of or shopkeepers who are not busy do much fishing. Two men make a living at fishing while their wives make *tōfu* or *manjū* cakes.

In the mountain *buraku* are some people who raise mushrooms and bees and make charcoal or do lumbering as a side industry. Some poorer ones make their whole living as hired labor for Hitoyoshi capitalists by cutting trees and making charcoal. The two or three Korean families in Hirayama are among these.

Some farmers keep a cart horse and four-wheeled wagon (*basha*) and so make extra money by transporting loads for people in the neighboring towns. Whereas some people in towns are exclusively wagon-drivers, in Suye there are only part-time wagoners.

Of another type and class from farmers and village specialists are the small shopkeepers. These people in their economic way of life and consequent money consciousness are more like their brother-shopkeepers in the near-by towns than like other farmers. It is significant that not one single shopkeeper in Suye is a native. The shops are all located on the prefectural road that goes through the *mura*. Shopkeepers, as a rule, do some farming on the side but do not follow many of the customs of the farmers.

The only factory in Suye is a *shōchū* factory. Formerly there were several *shōchū*-makers in Suye, but, since government regulation, there is only one, located in Kakui, the business *buraku*. The government imposes strict standards and a heavy tax so that small manufacturers are now excluded from the business. It is worth noting that the family of the *shōchū*-makers is one of the richest in the *mura*, and the young (twenty-nine) head of the family is one of the very few men to have gone to college from Suye.

Rice and wheat need hulling, and for this purpose there are several millers, all nonnatives. They run electric or water mills which have largely displaced the older hand methods used in the home. The richest general storekeeper also owns an electric-powered mill in Kakui.

Shopkeepers make an honest living, and, though known to count pennies, they are not objected to by the farmer. The broker, on the other hand, is considered to be, as he often is, dishonest. Brokers come from almost any background. They are usually men who lack scruples and are clever enough to outwit their fellow-villagers. Working without capital, they arrange to collect debts, getting a commission from creditor for collecting and from debtor for persuading the creditor to reduce the debt; they buy and sell at profit pieces of land or houses; and they buy up *kō* (see chap. iv)and speculate in rice. *Mura* brokers are naturally small fry in comparison with their city brothers, but they indulge in the same luxuries of *geisha* and *sake*. The important and at the same time unpopular position of the broker is a result of the need for a go-between in all important transactions of life such as marriage or business. The broker fills the need in business.

Another nonfarming type, and also nonnative, is the schoolteacher. Schoolteachers (ten in Suye) are more aloof from the *mura* than the shopkeepers and more economically independent of it. Schoolteachers are transferred from place to place every few years by the prefectural education bureau. They have had more education than any of the farmers and consequently are more literate and have a different mental outlook from that of the farmer; they are full of conscious nationalism and the uplift spirit. This comes out strongest, of course, in the schoolmaster. Their salaries, like other school expenses, come from village taxes, though the village has no voice in their appointment.

The only other special group is that of the village officials. These men vary a great deal. Some are farmers who have become officials; many are rather like brokers by nature only more honest. Like the brokers, these men visit the *geisha* of the near-by towns while ordinary farmers practically never have any connection with *geisha* unless it is to sell out one of their daughters.[20]

The business *buraku* of Kakui (and similarly of Tontokoro) has the largest number of specialists and the smallest number of pure farmers. The number of shopkeepers has not increased with the years. If anything, there are fewer shops selling special goods than there were fifteen or twenty years ago. This is due to the railroad and the rise of the near-by towns as shopping-centers. The work of such specialists as the blacksmith has been reduced owing to the great increase in manufactured articles for sale in the near-by towns.

The paddy *buraku* of Nakashima and Kawaze and the mountain *buraku* of Hirayama have the fewest specialists but the most farmers. Upland *buraku* are intermediate. There is no prefectural road in Kawaze, Nakashima, or Hirayama. In such upland *buraku* as Imamura and Oade the few business people, shopkeepers and brokers, are located along the road as it passes through the *buraku*. Such experts as carpenters and roofmakers exist in any *buraku* regardless of other specialists and shopkeepers.

The role of money in the household economy varies with occupation. Of an ordinary farmer's living expenses, about 50 per cent is paid out in money—other necessities are grown or made at home. The biggest single item is rice. All farmers grow their own. Shopkeepers, on the other hand, have to buy their rice with money. Of their total living expenses, about 90 per cent is paid out in money. In a farmer's household straw footgear and straw grain mats are all homemade. Women weave not only silk garments

[20] Girls have gone out as *geisha* from three or four of the poorer households in Suye.

TABLE 4*

SPECIALISTS OF SEVEN *buraku*

Buraku	Households	House Heads Native to Suye Mura† No.	%	Houses with Farming as the Main Occupation No.	%	Houses Which Also Raise Silkworms No.	%	Tōfu- and *manjū*-makers	Cakemaker and Shop	Matmaker	Basketmaker	Carpenters	Stonemasons	Roofmakers	Well-Diggers	Millers	Wagon-Drawers	Mountain Workers (Charcoal, Mushrooms, etc.)	Fishermen	Midwife	Shopkeepers (Including *shōchū* Factory)	*Shōchū* Salesmen	Brokers	Patent-Medicine Agent	Officials in Village Office	Schoolteachers	School or Village Office Servants	Healing-Spring Proprietor	Shinto Priest	Buddhist Priest	Healing Priests (*kitoshi*)	Other Specialists‡	Total Number of Different Occupations
Kawaze (paddy)….	20	17	85	19	95	16	80	1			1		1						1			1	1		1								8
Nakashima (paddy).	27	20	74	26	96	22	81	1				2		1			1						1	1	1								8
Oade (upland)……	21	17	81	17	81	15	71	2						1					3						1		2		1		1		9
Imamura (upland)…	19	15	79	16	84	13	68	1				1		2	1		2		1						1	1			1	1			11
Kakui (upland—shops)…………	27	14	52	11	41	12	44	3	1					1	1		2	1			1	4	1	1		1	3			1	3	2	6	22
Yunoharu (upland—new)…………	13	3	23	12	92					1				1														1			1		5
Hirayama (mountain)	25	20	80	20	80	3	12							1				5														4
Total or average	152	106	70	122	80	81	53	8	1	1	1	3	2	6	2	2	4	5	5	1	4	2	3	1	3	4	3	1	1	1	4	6	34§

* Most specialists in this table also do farming, notable exceptions to this being shopkeepers, midwives, brokers, *tōfu*-makers, and cakemakers.

† If head is adopted to native house from a different *mura*, he is listed as native.

‡ "Other Specialists" (all in Kakui) are lantern-maker, seamstress, barber, conscription insurance agent, a sericultural adviser, and an unemployed son of a *samurai*. Two specialists not in the seven *buraku* above are an arrow-maker and a pear-orchard proprietor.

§ Total number of *different types* of specialists in the *mura*.

but cotton ones also, purchasing the cotton thread in Menda. Men make baskets, tool handles, and other farm utensils. While much fertilizer is purchased through the agricultural association, a great deal is also obtained by carefully saving all human excretion.

Formerly a farmer's living costs would probably have included less than 10 per cent of money expense, but today he must pay cash in shops in the towns, for electricity, and for such things as tobacco, medicine, sugar, and salt.[21]

Most farmers own some land including the land on which their house stands and also rent some. There are 32 pure landowners in the *mura*, 112 who are both landowner and tenant, and 71 who are purely tenants. There is no single big landowner in the *mura*, a wealthy farmer possessing only two or three *cho* of land.[22]

Five types of *buraku* are illustrated in Tables 4 and 5: (1) paddy (Kawaze and Nakashima), (2) upland (Imamura, Oade), (3) business (Kakui), (4) new settlement (Yunoharu), and (5) mountain (Hirayama).

In regard to the number of households, Nakashima and Hirayama each have a few more houses in actual fact, but those households have been omitted which are not considered by the main part of the *buraku* as a part of them— i.e., the omitted houses do not co-operate in *buraku* affairs. It is notable that the isolated houses are always of poorer families who are not natives of Suye.

In population the notable point is that the paddy *buraku*, being richer, can afford more servants and hence have more people per household than the other *buraku*. Yunoharu, being a region of poor families, has very few per house, for many young people are working out as servants.

[21] For further details see Appen. II.

[22] One *cho* is equivalent to 2.4 acres.

The paddy *buraku* also have the highest percentage of natives, the business *buraku* the least. The business *bu–*

TABLE 5

POPULATION AND WEALTH OF SEVEN *buraku*

Buraku	NUMBER OF HOUSEHOLDS	POPULATION*		HOUSES WITH ONE OR MORE SERVANTS		HOUSEHOLDS IN WHICH ONE OR MORE MEMBERS HAVE RECEIVED EDUCATION BEYOND SUYE MURA SCHOOL†		HOUSEHOLDS WHICH SUBSCRIBE TO A NEWSPAPER		AVERAGE HOUSE TAX (TO NEAREST 5 YEN)
		Total	Average per House	Total	Per Cent	Total	Per Cent	Total	Per Cent	
Kawaze (paddy)	20	138	6.9	9	45	9	45	2	10	40
Nakashima (paddy)	27‡	194	7.2	9	33	8	30	4	15	30
Oade (upland)	21	114	5.4	4	19	6	22	2	10	15
Imamura (upland)	19	119	6.3	7	36	6	31	3	16	20
Kakui (upland—shops)	27	150	5.5	8	30	9	33	7	26	15§
Yunoharu (upland—new)	13	58	4.5	0	.....	0	.....	0	.....	5
Hirayama (mountain)	25‖	153	6.1	4	16	1	4	0	.....	15
Total or average	152	926¶	6.1	41	27	39	26	18	12	20

* Figures include servants.

† Higher education usually consists of three or four years of high school or agricultural school. Only one man (from Kawaze) has been to college.

‡ This figure does not include five houses near Taragi which are not considered to be part of Nakashima socially.

§ Kakui is relatively low because many of its constituent specialists are landless and so have no fixed assets. (House tax is based on income plus fixed assets.)

‖ This figure does not include four mountain workers not considered to be part of Hirayama socially.

¶ Total population of *mura* is 1,663.

raku has the greatest variety of occupation and so has the fewest farmers.

Besides the people living in it, there are specialists who visit the *mura:* (1) the blacksmith in spring; (2) the tub-maker in summer; (3) the *chizashi* (horse) doctor in spring, summer, and winter; (4) the tinker in summer; (5) the mender of wooden footgear (*geta*) in summer; (6) the ice-cake peddler in summer; (7) the kitchenware peddler monthly; and (8) the fishmonger daily. There are also miscellaneous itinerant peddlers, sellers of medicines, pilgrims, etc. They usually visit only those *buraku* along the prefectural road.

Mura UNIFIERS

As the *buraku* have been described as primary social units, it may appear that there is no great cohesion among them in the form of *mura* unity. There are, however, several institutions on a *mura*-wide basis, most of them forming also links between the *mura* and the nation. The most important of such unifying organizations are the village office, the village school, the Buddhist temple, and the village Shinto shrine.

THE SHINTO SHRINE AND BUDDHIST TEMPLE

The Shinto shrine, in which resides the patron deity of Suye Mura, serves as a protection to the health and well-being of the inhabitants of the *mura*. Most official ceremonies at the shrine, performed by the village Shinto priest, are attended by village officials only, so that, while theoretically one might expect the Shinto shrine to have a great influence over the social life of the villagers, it actually enters but slightly into their everyday life. The Buddhist temple is more important in this respect as the Buddhist priest is a necessary functionary at all funerals

and memorial services. Temple services and lectures are
rather infrequent, but, when they occur, people from all
buraku attend. Because of the predominant influence of
the Shinshū temple in the next *mura* of Fukada, the local
Zen temple, with a membership of only fifty households,
is less of a unifying influence than it might otherwise be.
The influence of the temple is probably weaker than it
once was, while that of the shrine is gaining ground. Formerly there were Shinto shrines in almost every *buraku*,
but after Meiji these were amalgamated into one for the
whole *mura*. This is in line with the whole trend toward
greater centralization of government and serves both to
unite the *mura* and to bring it into closer contact with the
nation—to replace local, provincial loyalties and ideals by
a spirit of nationalism and feeling of oneness with the Empire. In regard to both the Shinto and the Buddhist practices, the household and neighborhood deities play the predominant role in daily life. The whole matter of Buddhism
and Shinto in the village organization is further discussed
in chapter vii.

VILLAGE OFFICE

In most *mura* the village office and school are in the
same *buraku*. This was formerly true in Suye, but some
years ago the village office was moved from upland Imamura to business Kakui as being more central and convenient. Its yard includes a wooden building with four
rooms, the village office or *yakuba* proper, a small wooden
house for the Kakui fire pump, an old stone-and-plaster
fireproof records building, and a fine new stone agricultural association building.

In the village office work the headman, assistant headman, treasurer, agricultural adviser (*gite*), and two clerks.
The headman's office is considered to be an honorary one,

with a salary of only five hundred and forty yen a year. Owing to entertaining and other extra expenses incidental to his position, it is necessary to be rather a rich man to fill the office. He is elected by twelve village councilors who in turn are elected by the villagers. The term is four years but can be prolonged indefinitely. In his official capacity he helps to settle disputes and tries to encourage the well-being of his constituents. The assistant headman with a salary of three hundred and sixty yen a year is also elected. Both these officials have farms taken care of by their wives, children, and servants. The clerks are appointed by the headman. Their salaries range from thirty-six to forty-five yen a month, depending on length of service. The monthly salary increases one yen a year.

The *buraku kuchō* who act as village office deputies are paid by the village office eight to eleven yen a year, depending on the size of the *buraku*.

There are two menservants whose duty it is to run errands and to serve tea to visitors, also a regular midmorning and midafternoon tea and pickle to the staff. They receive seventy sen a day. For the frequent parties at the *yakuba* they go to buy the *tōfu*, prepare the soup, and serve the food, later joining in the drinks.

The village office collects a house tax (*kosūwari*) from every house in the village. From this money village expenses are paid, such as village officials' and schoolteachers' salaries, upkeep of certain public buildings, and some of the Shinto priest's salary. The central government and prefectural government both give aid in road- and bridge-building, as well as some school expenses.[23]

Vital statistics and the all-valuable *koseki* are kept at the village office. The *koseki* is a man's official family rec-

[23] For speeches on taxes see Appen. III.

ord kept at the place of his official residence. In it are recorded births, marriages, and deaths. When a child is
born, the father goes to the clerk in charge of village records and officially registers its birth in his *koseki*. The
child is put down as (1) child of such and such parents or
(2) bastard of so and so, father known, or (3) bastard of so
and so, father unknown. When a man marries, the seals
of both families involved are required. The bride's name
and parents' names are put down. The date of the registration is recorded but not that of the marriage. Thus,
since a marriage is often recorded only after the pair have
been married a year or more, it is frequently impossible
to tell just when the wedding actually took place. If a
girl is married, her name is blotted out of the *koseki* of her
father, and the same is done when a man is adopted out or
when a man or woman dies. The *koseki* is always kept in
one's home village and is a valuable record for the police
and the military. If a man commits a crime in another
mura, it is recorded not in that *mura* but in the *mura*
where his *koseki* is kept. By means of the *koseki* the authorities know who is due for conscription. If a person takes up
permanent residence in another *mura* or town, he can have
his *koseki* transferred.

Valuable as a *koseki* is, there are things it does not tell:

1. Any marriages or adoptions which are dissolved before being recorded.
2. Later marriages, divorces, and deaths of a son or daughter adopted
   or married out are not recorded because such sons and daughters are
   blotted out of the *koseki* and entered into their adopted family's
   koseki.
3. Deaths or divorces in the family before the *koseki* is established in
   a new center are not recorded in the village office to which the *koseki*
   is transferred.
4. Population of the *mura*. Many people live elsewhere without removing their *koseki*, and many have moved into the *mura* without

transferring their *koseki*. This is partly rectified in the latter case by means of temporary records of nonresidents. Often a man having lived twenty years in Suye is listed on such a "temporary" record Some people, such as the Korean mountaineers in Hirayama, are not even on this temporary record, and, possibly because of this, their children do not attend the village school. On the other hand, they do not have to pay any house tax.

The clerk of the *koseki* also looks after conscription and school matters.

There is a clerk of taxes and maps. His knowledge of landownership is essential to the related task of estimating taxes, and through him any disputes over landownership are settled. The treasurer takes care of all actual income and outgo of money.

The agricultural adviser is partly employed by the village office, partly by the agricultural association. He is actually appointed by the prefectural office, so is not a native of the *mura*. His education is superior to that of most of the villagers, as he has been to an agricultural college or some equivalent training school for agricultural advisers. His duty is to advise and instruct farmers in the agricultural association, a co-operative organization for joint buying of fertilizer and farm supplies, selling of farm products, especially rice and wheat. It is through him that agricultural improvements come into the *mura* such as the use of improved fertilizer, growing of salable side crops, and increased co-operative buying and selling. The new economic reconstruction movement uses the agricultural adviser as a spearhead in each *mura*. A successful adviser must be intelligent, but not to sophistication; progressive, but not so much so as to antagonize the people he is there to assist. Most of the agricultural advisers in the Kuma region are just such happy combinations.

The agricultural association is a local branch of a national organization. It is a farmers' co-operative organization working in harmony with the government agricultural policy. Most *mura* have one. There are four divisions: (1) co-operative buying, (2) co-operative selling, (3) credit, and (4) co-operative utilization. Only the first three are active in Suye. The utilization association covers such things as an association store or grain mill. Fukada, the next *mura*, has such a co-operative utilization association.

In the association building are stored grains to be sold through the association when the best price comes. Meanwhile the farmers are given a down payment. From its office can be bought the association magazine, *Ie no Hikari* ("The Influence of the House," "Home Companion"), a cheap, twenty-sen magazine of fiction and agricultural advice. More people in the *mura* (sixty houses) read this than any other periodical. Rubber work shoes (*jika tabi*), soap, and some medicines are also purchased at the association office.

The credit association acts as a village bank. Anyone may deposit money here. Most young men do so. To borrow, one must be a shareholder, which means a fairly well-to-do person. The amount borrowed depends on the number of shares held and on the approval by the village headman and association head. In Suye the assistant headman is also the association head.[24]

Each *buraku* has a branch association (*kokumiai*).[25] The chief function of these branch associations is to encourage progressive farming, as noted above. The branch associa-

[24] It was for the use of the agricultural association that the new telephone was installed in the village office in 1936.

[25] Some communities have local *kokumiai* without having an official *mura* agricultural association.

tions with their classmates from all the *buraku* of Suye. Here they all receive a common education in the standard Japanese dialect, in official history and ethics as well as practical agriculture and a smattering of the sciences. Through the school a child becomes a citizen of the *mura* and the nation as well as of his own small *buraku*.

Some *mura* have a meeting hall for village gatherings such as lectures. In Suye there is no public meeting hall so the school auditorium is used instead. Here everyone comes for *mura* gatherings of all kinds. The school building itself serves as a meeting place for all inter-*baruku* affairs. Here the whole *mura* gathers to see school athletic meets, school plays, and the annual inspection (*tenko*) of military reserves. On this occasion all the women of the village don Patriotic Women's Association white aprons and shoulder bands and act as hostesses to the visiting military, while men returned from barracks and also those who did not go line up for inspection and drill by the visiting officers. The inspection is followed by strong "national policy" speeches to the soldiers and special lectures on the same subject to the women, couched in simpler language that farmers' wives might understand. School children also line up for inspection and listen to speeches. Thus once a year the village has its attention drawn to war. No one is exempt from *tenko*—not even the Buddhist priest. This, like school uniforms, has a strong leveling influence. A priest in the drab uniform of a private presents a very different appearance from the same man in his robes of office. This effect is not lost on the villagers. For instance, in the course of conversation following a memorial service some days after a *tenko* in Suye, the guests commented on the Shinshū priest's poor appearance in uniform. Thus it is impossible for even a Buddhist priest to gain too strong an ascendancy over the local people.

Both the silkworm-raising associations of Suye hold meetings in the school auditorium with subsequent drinking parties; here lectures of all kinds, often of two or three hours' duration, are given and patiently listened to by men, women, and babies of all *buraku*.

In every classroom is a world-map or map of Asia which shows Japan in red as a very small land indeed, compared to the mainland nations of Asia. Manchukuo is colored pink, but even this pink area is not so large. In a perfectly bland manner some villager, on looking at such a map, will suggest how nice it would be to appropriate a bit more of China. Charts of various nations' military strength, always emphasizing the smallness of Japan in comparison to these others, are hung in various schoolrooms. These maps and charts illustrate to the farmer and his child how essentially reasonable it is for Japan to enlarge, and how unreasonable are those nations that object. The effects of the school on the individual are further discussed in chapter vi.

The village office and school observe Sunday as a day of rest. This is not a native custom, however, and the *mura* as a whole goes right on working. The school and village office do business according to the Gregorian or "new" calendar, while the farmers follow the "old" or lunar calendar. Calendars must, by law, print the dates of the Gregorian system in large letters, those of the old in small; but regardless of this it is the small dates on the lunar calendar that are followed in most farmhouses. Occupation is closely correlated with seasons—the old festivals must be by lunar calendar to fall in their proper seasonal place. As already noted, this lunar calendar is beginning to break down, especially in regard to the festivals which come in conflict with new agricultural activities.

In addition to the regular *mura* unifiers just described,

there are certain occasional events which serve to bring people of all *buraku* together and make them conscious of their membership in the larger organization of the *mura*. If a new public building, such as a village office or school is finished, the whole *mura* participates in the completion ceremonies. If an important bridge is completed, the oldest man in the whole *mura* must be the first to cross.[26]

POPULATION, IMMIGRATION, AND EMIGRATION

The population of Suye is 1,663 persons, or 285 households, of which 788 are male and 875 female.[27] In the statistical tables which follow data gathered by the author are given for a little over half of the total, i.e., 926 people living in 152 households. This comprises the same seven *buraku* already included in Tables 4 and 5.

During the past few years there has been little change in gross population, any excess of births over deaths being taken care of by emigration. Movements of population appear to be from the mountainous *mura* of Itsuki and Youra south into Fukada and Suye (see Map I). Those who leave through poverty go to the mines in Fukuoka or to the munitions factories of Yahata. Girls who work in spinning factories or as servants or those sold into prostitution go either to near-by towns or to any large city.

Table 6 shows the mobility of the population during the past decade. It may be observed that, to some extent at least, excess population of the village is taken care of by emigration. The table also indicates the rapid rise of Yunoharu with five new families settling there during the

[26] This particular custom is evidently identical with the usage in rural China (see J. H. Gray, *China: A History of the Laws, Manners and Customs of the People* [London, 1878] II, 104).

[27] Village office figures for 1933.

last ten years. Aside from this new community, the *mura* shows an excess of emigration over immigration of about eight to five. The well established do not move. Most im-

TABLE 6*

Population Movements in and out of Suye Mura during the Ten-Year Period 1925–35

Buraku	New Im-migrant† Residents (Families)	Changed Residence (Families)	Emigrants‡									
			To City		To Mines		To Man-chukuo		Became School-teacher		Where-abouts Un-known	
			M	F	M	F	M	F	M	F	M	F
Kawaze (paddy)...	2	3	1	1	1	1	2	...	...	...	2	...
Nakashima (paddy)	2	2	...	2	...	...	...	...	1	...	...	...
Oade (upland).....	...	2	...	...	2	1	...	...	...	...	...	...
Imamura (upland).	1	3	2	2	...	...	...	...	...	...	1	...
Kakui (upland—shops)..........	2	4	4	...	...	...	...	...	1	...	1	...
Yunoharu (upland—new).........	5	1	...	...	...	...	...	...	...	...	...	...
Hirayama (moun-tain)..........	1	1	...	...	1	...	...	...	...	...	...	...
Total........	13	16	7	5	4	2	2	...	2	...	4	...

* Figures do not include the temporary migrants: servants coming in or conscripts and students and servants going out. Movements from one *buraku* to another within the *mura* are not shown.
† For origin of nonnative families in Suye see Table 7.   ‡ Individuals.

migrants are poor landless people or shopkeepers who have come to Suye because "they heard" that it was a good place. If successful in Suye, they eventually acquire some land and become permanent residents. More often they stay a few years, then move on, not having gained a solid foothold in the village. Frequently a man who works in Suye as a servant decides to stay and establish a family there. Emigrants are usually poor people or certain dissatisfied misfits. The total population of the *buraku* tabulated is over 900, whereas the number of people who have moved in or out during the last ten years is about 140, of which 60 were through marriage or adoption, leaving only 75 or so true migrants over this long period. Aside from those coming in from neighboring *mura* through marriage and adoption, immigrants consist mostly of people from the near-by *mura* of Itsuki, from the Islands of Amakusa, and from the counties of Shimomashiki and Yatsushiro, all north of Kuma (see Table 7). From Suye there were no emigrants to America, though from neighboring *mura* there were a few.

The figures do not show the temporary migrants—servants, conscripts, and students. These people, by leaving the *mura* and later returning to it, add to its range of interests and its social relationships. Similarly, temporary residents such as schoolteachers bring national views into the ken of *mura* affairs. Every two or three years a new teacher arrives to replace one who leaves. Servants usually work one or two years, then return home or set up branch families of their own. The number of servants in the seven *buraku* and the number of servants and students temporarily out of the village are tabulated in Table 8. It will be noted that menservants outnumber maidservants by about three to one.

An interesting side light cast by Table 8 is that no servants went to Hirayama from other *buraku* of Suye. The reason for this is that Hirayama is considered wild and mountainous by people of the other *buraku*, and, on the other hand, people from these *buraku* would not make good workers in the eyes of Hirayama people. Hence, what outside servants they have come from the mountainous *mura* of Youra to the north and the more rural *buraku* of Taragi to the east.

TABLE 7

PLACE OF BIRTH OF NONNATIVE HOUSEHOLD HEADS
IN SUYE MURA (AS OF 1936)

Buraku	Kuma County	Kuma-moto Prefec-ture	Kyushu	Outside Kyushu	Total
Kawaze (paddy)	. . . .	2	. . . .	. . . .	2
Nakashima (paddy)	3	3	1 (Miyazaki)	. . . .	7
Oade (upland)	2	1	1 (Kagoshima)	. . . .	4
Imamura (upland)	1	2	1 (Kagoshima)	. . . .	4
Kakui (upland—shops)	4	6	3 (Miyazaki, Fukuoka, Nagasaki)	. . . .	13
Yunoharu (upland—new)	4	3	1 (Miyazaki)	2 (Wakayama, Tokushima)	10
Hirayama (mountain)	1	. . . .	4 (Fukuoka, Kagoshima— 2, Oita)	. . . .	5
Total	15	17	11	2	45

An important factor in the range of *buraku* relationships is that of marriage and adoption into and from the *buraku*. By this means, houses of one *buraku* have relatives not only in other *buraku* of the *mura* but also in most of the neighboring *mura*.

Table 9 shows the source of wives and adopted sons in Suye. Except for the mountain *buraku* of Hirayama, where 50 per cent of the marriages are endogamous, all the

TABLE 8

TEMPORARY IMMIGRANTS AND EMIGRANTS—SERVANTS
STUDENTS, AND CONSCRIPTS

	FARM AND HOUSEHOLD SERVANTS									STU-DENTS AND CON-SCRIPTS		TOTAL TEMPO-RARILY OUT OF *mura*†	
	Same *buraku*		Into *buraku*				Out of *buraku*							
Buraku			From Different *buraku*		From Different *mura**		To Different *buraku*		To Different *mura**					
	M	F	M	F	M	F	M	F	M	F	M	F	M	F
Kawaze (paddy)......	...	...	5	...	9	...	...	...	...	1	3	1	3	2
Nakashima (paddy)...	3	...	4	2	3	1	1	...	...	1	2	...	2	1
Oade (upland).........	...	1	1	...	2	1	2	3	3	1	...	...	3	1
Imamura (upland).....	...	1	2	1	5	...	2	...	...	1	2	...	2	1
Kakui (upland—shops)	...	...	...	3	4	...	4	...	1	...	2	...	3	...
Yunoharu (upland—new)...............	...	...	...	...	...	...	4	3	...	3	...	...	...	3
Hirayama (mountain).	1	...	...	...	3	3	2	1	...	...	2	...	2	...
Total...........	4	2	12	6	26	5	15	7	4	7	11	1	15	8

* None out of Kuma County.

† To be compared with third column—number of servants in Suye from other *mura*.

buraku show a very marked tendency toward exogamy, and those in-marriages which do occur are mostly special cases such as marriage to an immigrant into the *mura*, the marriage of a widow or divorcee, or a common-law marriage.

TABLE 9

PLACE OF BIRTH OF BRIDES AND ADOPTED SONS

Buraku	From Same buraku		From Other buraku in Suye Mura		To the North — Youra (Adjacent to Suye)		To the North — Itsuki (One mura Removed)		To the East — Taraga (Adjacent to Suye)		To the East — Kurohiji (One mura Removed)		To the East — Mizukami (Two mura Removed)		To the East — Yunomae (Two mura Removed)		To the South — Menda (Adjacent to Suye)		To the South — Kume (One mura Removed)		To the South — Okaharu (One mura Removed)		To the South — Uemura (One mura Removed)		To the West — Fukada (Adjacent to Suye)		To the West — Kinoue (One mura Removed)		To the West — Places More Than Two mura Removed		Total		From Outside Kuma	
	M*	A*	M	A	M	A	M	A	M	A	M	A	M	A	M	A	M	A	M	A	M	A	M	A	M	A	M	A	M	A	M	A	M	A
Kawaze (paddy)	2[i]	2[jb]	10	2	1			4	6		1								1			2		1	1		3	1				12	9		
Nakashima (paddy)	2[i]	4[bjf]	8	8	1		1	1	3		1						4	1	1		2				2		1				16	2	1	1
Oade (upland)	5[iicd]	1	4[i]		3	1			3	3				1		1	1						1		5	1♀	1				14	7		
Imamura (upland)	2[ii]	2	4	1				1	4	4	5		1		1		2				2				2	1			1		18	6		
Kakui (upland—shops)			3[i]	1		1	2	1	1			1	1		1		1		1	1			1		4			1	3	1	15	6	1	
Yunoharu (upland—new)	1[x]																		1		1										2			
Hirayama (mountain)	10[i]	4[i]	1			5	4		1				2				1								3						11	5	1	
Total	12[y]	7[y]	28[y]	12	10	5	3	15	17	1	9		2	1	2	1	9	2	3	1	7		2	3	16	5	4		4	1	88	35	4	1

* M = women coming in through marriage; A = adoptions—all male unless otherwise indicated.

a An urban center. Brides and sons mostly from rural buraku of.

b One a bastard of mother before her marriage, hence adopted out.

c Common-law marriage.

d Wife was a divorced woman.

f Younger sister adopted by elder brother.

i One married to an immigrant.

j One a junyōshi, i.e., younger brother adopted by an older brother.

x Wife resident of Yunoharu but born in Kume.

y These total figures omit all special cases such as noted in foregoing footnotes. Only in Hirayama is there any large amount of marriage within the buraku—all the others are largely exogamous.

♀ Female.

The *mura* as a whole is also largely exogamous, only a little over 20 per cent (excluding Hirayama) of all the marriages tabulated being within the *mura*. Of the remaining 70-odd per cent, all but a fractional percentage come from within Kuma County, i.e., within fifteen miles of Suye. Of those rare cases of a bride or adopted son from outside the county, none comes from beyond the confines of Kumamoto Prefecture or Miyazaki, the adjacent prefecture to the east—at most one hundred miles from Kuma. These more distant marriages and adoptions are usually arranged by some relative of a Suye family who happens to be living in that region. Frequently several married women in a *buraku* will be from the same *mura*, and there is one extreme case where three sisters were married into a *buraku* one after the other. Kawaze, for instance, obtained most of its women from a section of Taragi, Imamura from Kurohiji, Oade and Kakui from Fukada, and Hirayama from Youra. In all cases the favored region is the closest region to the *buraku* outside the *mura*. This situation is partly the result of the fact that after the first marriage social relations between a family in a Suye *buraku* and the given outside *mura* have been set up, thus facilitating further marriages. And for the same reason it is easier to arrange marriages between daughters of the *buraku* and sons from the same outside *mura* so that often one can trace a series of exchanges of women between the two communities. This relationship is sometimes further strengthened by the custom of cousin marriage (see p. 88).[28]

While most men living in Suye are natives of the *mura*, nearly all the women are nonnative. This situation affects the social life of a *buraku* in several ways. The women are

---

[28] The same remarks apply to adoption, the two chief sources of adopted sons being Itsuki and Fukada and, for Hirayama, Youra.

not so close with one another, and they have no opportunity to form same-age associations and friendships from
childhood. This subject will be further discussed in the
chapter on co-operation.

Just as few servants from outside the *mura* work in
Hirayama, so few Hirayama brides come from other *buraku* of Suye but rather from within Hirayama itself or
from the adjacent *mura* of Youra.

Regular immigrants to the *mura* establishing new households there come from greater distances, some of the settlers in Yunoharu coming from regions outside Kyushu.
They are tabulated in Table 7.

CHANGING RANGE OF THE VILLAGERS' WORLD

The world of an inhabitant of Suye Mura is, first of all,
his own household. Here he eats and sleeps with other
members of the household who share his labors and recreations. The household as a unit co-operates in rice-growing,
sericulture, and ancestor worship. The next most intimate
group of which he is a member is the *buraku* or more especially that section (*kumi*) of it in which he lives, and the
neighbors with whom he co-operates in rice-transplanting.
Everyone in the *buraku* knows everyone else very well,
most of the male inhabitants having been born there. The
buraku is united by many group activities. The next larger
area of acquaintance consists of neighboring *buraku* which
are, in some instances, in the next *mura*.

All these connections and relationships are personal,
face-to-face ones. The next wider acquaintance of the villager is with the neighboring towns. With the town he has
an occasional rather than an everyday contact, and the
connection is largely economic, the farmer going there to
buy tools or materials or to sell some farm produce. A

common occasion for visits to neighboring towns is some festival. Whereas in the *buraku* and inter-*buraku* contacts a man knows and is known by everyone, in the town he is a stranger and has personal acquaintance with only a few people; his contacts with the town are more impersonal so that his visits to a town festival have more the characteristics of a holiday trip; he goes as a spectator in search of amusement, whereas in his participation in his local *buraku* or *mura* festivals a peasant forms a part of the festival and feels himself part of the group he is in.

More intimate external relationships exist, however, among people from different *buraku* and *mura* related through marriage and adoption. These people are in other *mura* rather than in the towns, and they come into action as a group whenever an occasion arises for the extended family to unite, for instance at a wedding or a funeral. The inter-*buraku* and inter-*mura* relations are probably little changed today from what they were a hundred years ago. The relations with the towns, on the other hand, have become much closer especially because of the new railroad line to them which has increased their importance as trade centers, and the bicycle, which has made them more readily accessible.

The connections of people with Hitoyoshi, the big town or small city twelve miles away and the old county seat, are rather infrequent. Many farmers never visit Hitoyoshi from year's end to year's end; village officials and certain shopkeepers and rich farmers, on the other hand, have business which takes them frequently to Hitoyoshi and sometimes even to Kumamoto, the prefectural capital. Whereas formerly a trip to Hitoyoshi was an all-day affair, today the bus covers the distance in forty-five minutes. Two or three people a day go from Suye on the bus.

Beyond Kumamoto the people of Suye have no direct contact. Knowledge of Tokyo comes by newspaper and hearsay, economic and political relations through the village office, small towns, and the prefectural capital. One exception to this is the conscript soldier. While most conscripts receive training in Kumamoto City, some are occasionally sent to Tokyo as Imperial guards, to Formosa or to Manchukuo. The returned conscript is one of the important factors in the widening range of the villagers' world.

A few girls go to work in factories, and some become prostitutes. Occasionally, a son leaves Suye to work in a city. These people, while no longer of Suye, often correspond with relatives and thus create a personal connection between people in Suye and the various cities of Japan. The visits of peddlers such as the all-important fishmonger, the gossiping clerks of the town shops, and the daily trips of the mailman from Menda all play their part in bringing news to the *mura* and in making contacts with the rest of the county.

Once a year the older school children are taken by their teachers on trips to Kumamoto or Kagoshima in order to let them see something outside Kuma as part of their education. The farmers are very much in favor of these trips, feeling that, when the children grow up, they will have but few opportunities to travel.

The newspaper has come to the *mura* of recent years and is subscribed to by about one household in ten. It is delivered by a boy from a magazine shop in Menda. More households subscribe to the National Agricultural Association magazine, *Ie no Hikari*, than to a newspaper.[29] These

[29] The women's magazines, such as *Fuji* and *Shufunotomo*, so much read in urban Japan, have very few subscribers on the farm.

papers and magazines provide news and views of the world at large.

In 1935 the farmers of Kuma were very conscious of the world-depression. Many a banquet was curtailed and festival celebration reduced because of *fukeiki*. As far as the farmers themselves were concerned the depression appears to have hit them through the drop in silk prices as a consequence of the depression in the United States. While silk is a secondary crop in this region, it is a primary source of cash income, and many a household used to make enough from silk cocoons to send children to high school or even to college. To account for the drop in silk prices, representatives of the big companies told their village silk-association members various tall tales, among others that American girls, being lazy, did not care to wash their stockings so that now they bought only cheap rayon hose which could be thrown away as soon as they became soiled.

Through the silk industry almost every little village in Japan is tied to the world-market. Thus, while rice is the staple crop and chief means of subsistence in Suye, it is the price of silk that determines whether the village is prosperous or not. It is the cash paid for cocoons, through the big silk companies, that has much to do with the encroachment of a money economy into the countryside. The silk-company representatives are the intermediaries in silk between the village and the world, just as the grain broker is in the field of rice.

Another aspect of the silk industry is the recruiting of girls from villages to work in the spinning factories. These girls, aged sixteen or seventeen, go for a few years to the city, then come back home to be married. Frequently, on their return, they are unhappy in the village and hanker after city ways. Even if satisfied on returning to the farm, they are no longer so provincial as they once were.

The idea of belonging to a nation and an empire is of recent date. Formerly all loyalty belonged to the local *samurai*, whose loyalty in turn went to the feudal lord. Today schools emphasize loyalty to Japan and the Emperor rather than to any local region, and this attitude is further encouraged through the village Shinto shrine and occasional governmental officials who lecture in the *mura*. On the whole, the villagers' range of personal contacts with and impersonal knowledge of the world outside the *buraku* is much greater today than it was fifty years ago. It is, for instance, by no means so isolated as it was in the days of the Tokugawa, when a farmer was tied to the place of his birth and knew little and experienced less of life outside his own little *mura*. Today there are several families whose native land is not Kuma but some outside region, and many people emigrate from Suye to other regions. Through the price of silk, the village is becoming aware of a world outside Japan.[30]

[30] Since 1937 the war with China has also, doubtless, had similar effects on village life.

CHAPTER III

FAMILY AND HOUSEHOLD

THE primary social unit in *buraku* life is the household. This household includes the small family, perhaps a retired grandfather or grandmother, and one or two servants to help in the household and farm labor. The size of a *buraku* is reckoned by the number of households, not by the number of people, and participation in *buraku* co-operative affairs such as funerals or bridge-building is per household, not per capita. People and things of the house are referred to as *uchi no* (of the house), as, for instance, mother of the house, bicycle of the house, cow of the house.

The small family consists of master, wife, eldest son (own or adopted), eldest son's wife, any unmarried children of the master, and eldest son's children (own or adopted). A larger relative group includes members not living in the house. This extended family consists of siblings of male members of the house and children of the master who are married or adopted outside the household. This extended family comes together on the occasion of weddings and funerals. Members living near by help one another at such work as roof-fixing or housebuilding.

Living in the house with the small family may be a retired (*inkyo*) father or mother, or both, of the master. Sometimes a younger unmarried brother or a sister who has left her husband may live in the house. These extra people are included, with the small family, in the household. Such people, like members of the small family, are also referred to as "of the house," e.g., *uchi no bāsan* (grandmother of the house).

The more well-to-do families have a manservant and a maidservant who may come from the *mura* or more often from another *mura* (see Table 8). A servant is frequently a nephew or niece of the master or his wife. They are hired by the year, and their salaries, in sacks of rice, are paid to their parents. They are included in the household, eating with the family and working side by side with members of the family in the field. Not infrequently after a manservant and house daughter have worked together for some months, an unexpected pregnancy occurs. Since in many ways the servants are thus included in the life of the family, it is necessary to include them in the unit of the household which may now be defined as the small family plus relatives and servants living in the same house.

Within this social unit of a household the master's (*koshu*) word is law. As he decides, so must the members of the household act. He is first to take a bath, first to be served with food or *shōchū*, and he has a special place to sit by the fire pit. All farming income goes to the head who dispenses it as he sees fit to other members of the household. Even income from sericulture, which is chiefly woman's work, goes to the head. On the other hand, anyone may act as deputy of the head. Thus, in various *buraku* undertakings such as road-repairing, a head's son or wife or servant may go in his place.

The wife is given money for household expenses as she needs it. She in turn buys new clothes at New Year's and Bon seasons for the servants. The head gives pocket money to servants when they go on a holiday to some festival. A son, as he needs money, usually asks for it. An adopted son or a daughter-in-law, however, does not ask directly for money. As one man explained, they feel embarrassed to do so. A good head will realize when an adopted son or daughter (for a bride is really such) needs money and will give it. It is on just this point of spending money that trouble often arises between an adoptive child and his family of adoption. It is a common cause of disadoption and divorce, though rarely given publicly as such. It is usually said and accepted that a young man or, more often, a bride "became sick" and "went home."

The selling of daughters as *geisha* and prostitutes is a prerogative of the father. A recent law says a girl's consent must be obtained, but in practice this is a mere formality. A girl is in no position to refuse her consent.

Recent laws which have made it possible for women to own property have only resulted in aiding their husbands who are in debt. When the creditor comes, the man divorces his wife and puts his property in her name and is thus penniless himself. The creditor is balked. Later the man may, and usually does, remarry his divorced wife.

ADOPTION

For many centuries in Japan the family name has been very important. Mr. Hozumi has described this aspect of Japanese social organization in his book, *Ancestor Worship and Japanese Law*. The value of the family name and the importance of the memorial tablet of the ancestors probably came into Japan with, or was greatly strengthened by, Confucianism in the sixth and seventh centuries.

In the event of no sons the problem of perpetuating the family name and of taking care of the ancestral tablets when one dies is solved by adoption.[1] A more practical need for a son is to help work in the house and provide sustenance for the old people. This custom of adoption is common in Suye. When a married couple is childless, they will usually adopt some young boy. Often he is a nephew, most often a brother's son. It is always preferable to keep property within the extended family. Indeed, so much so is this the case that sometimes a girl relative is adopted, then a husband adopted for her.

Occasionally, if the married couple have some children, but all are girls, a son may be adopted who later either marries one of the girls or marries some entirely different girl. Or the parents may wait until one of the daughters is of marriageable age and then adopt a husband for her.

In still another instance a man may have a son who is sickly and who possibly may not live, so, to be on the safe side, a son is adopted. Or he may have only two or three children and, disliking to see his daughter married out, adopts a husband for her. Or if her husband has financial troubles after marriage, the father may adopt him as a second son. However, to adopt a son or a husband for one's daughter when there is already a son in the family is rare. Such a situation, being very disfunctional, usually creates friction in the family.

There is a remarkable number of childless couples in Suye, so adoption is very common.

Who gets adopted.—If a man has several sons, he usually lets the younger ones be adopted out. If, beside the eldest son, there are one or two not adopted out when time for marriage comes around, these second sons will form branch

---

[1] When a man dies, a posthumous name is given him by the Buddhist priest. It is this name on a wooden slab or *ihai* which is kept in the butsudan and receives offerings from time to time, especially at Bon.

families. An adopted son or daughter's husband is called *yōshi*.

An interesting variation of this is *junyōshi*, or younger-brother adoption. Often a childless man has some younger

YOSHI:-

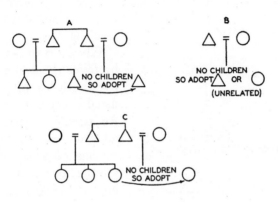

JUNYOSHI:-

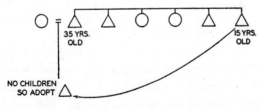

FIG. 1.—*Yōshi* chart

brother fifteen or twenty years younger than himself. In such a case the logical thing for him to do is to adopt as son his younger brother. The younger brother will then live in the elder brother's house with him as his son (see Fig. 1).

A first son is rarely adopted out. In case of poverty or close friendship he will sometimes be adopted out, in which case he usually retains his original surname, and through his children his adopter's surname is perpetuated.

Often in genealogies one finds apparent first sons adopted out. They always turn out to be bastards of the mother before she was married (see Fig. 2).

ACTUAL GENEALOGY

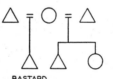

BASTARD
ADOPTED OUT

GENEALOGY GIVEN THUS:—

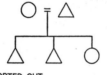

ADOPTED OUT

FIG. 2.—Chart showing adoption of bastards.

When a man is adopted, he takes the name of and lives with his adopter and usually becomes his heir. As already stated, he is adopted because his adopter has no sons. As with a bride, an adopted son or husband takes the Buddhist sect of his adoptive home. One of the reasons for adopting him is that he may look up to and pay respects to the house ancestors.

There is no special ceremony of adoption, but, as a rule, the two fathers concerned, real and adoptive, exchange cups of *shōchū*. Legally the adoption is put in the village records. The boy leaves the *koseki* of his own father and enters that of his adoptive father. An adopted son retains some connection with his own family, however, by attending its weddings and funerals and by calling in case of fire or flood. This is similar to the manner in which a bride retains connections with the house in which she was born.

An adoption can be dissolved just as a marriage can,

and this is often done. Hence, like marriage, an adoption is not immediately recorded in order to save unnecessary trouble of recording separation if it occurs. Thus adoption, like marriage, is a trial arrangement for the first year or so.

Besides favoring a relative, the good qualities looked for in an adopted son are similar to those looked for in a bride or groom—health, diligence, respect for elders, and good family.

An adopted son has all the rights of a real son. A boy, however, does not always particularly care to be adopted out. Certain strains inevitably crop up. There is the financial one as noted above, and there is the difficulty of becoming adapted to the ways of a strange family. For this reason it is considered better to adopt a boy of ten or twelve rather than one of eighteen or twenty.

In connection with population drifts (p. 68) it is interesting to note that many adopted sons are from Itsuki Mura just north of Suye. Often a second son in Itsuki comes to Suye as a servant and then becomes adopted or establishes a branch family there.

The family system is patrilineal in pattern but, through the customs of adoption, often matrilineal in practice. Inheritance is ideally from master to eldest son. If this is impossible, then an eldest son is created by adoption or adoptive marriage.

NAMES

The family name is always given first, then the personal name. Before Meiji ordinary farmers had no family names. They were called only by personal names, sometimes qualified by the region in which they lived: "Iwao" or "Iwao of Oade." This habit is carried on today among the villagers. Often they will be unable to recall a man's family name but can always give his personal name and where he lives.

Today many people in a given *buraku* have the same surname, though often no family relationship is recognized. This is most marked in Hirayama, where two surnames, Hirata and Hirano, account for twelve of the twenty-five households. Common names in other *buraku* are Aiko and Tsunematsu. One explanation of this phenomenon is that many farmers took the same surname after the Meiji Restoration. But why they did so is not certain. Some of these same-name groups are associated through certain religious ceremonies (see chap. vii).

In ordinary family life a person is addressed according to his relation to the children. A man will be called "father" (*totsan*) or "grandfather" (*jiisan*); a woman, "mother" (*kakasan*) or "grandmother" (*obāsan*). Children call non-relative friends of the family "uncle" or "aunt," and all old people are called "grandfather" or "grandmother." Married couples address each other in the same manner, but there is a special term—*anata*, which means "you." This term is rarely used in everyday speech. Lovers use it when addressing each other as do all young married couples. They do not do so in public until a few years after marriage. It has more of the connotation of "thou" or "dear."

People often avoid a name altogether and use some term such as "the over there grandmother," i.e., the old woman who lives across the road; "the *ne-ne* grandfather," the old man who always says "Ne." People are very bashful about giving their own names. If a person is asked in a group what his name is, he will smile and perhaps ask someone else to tell it.

Siblings frequently all have names with the same first syllable or two, such as Masatoshi, Masayoshi, etc.

In addition to relatives who come together for family events such as naming ceremonies, weddings, and funerals, a man and woman may have some close friend (*tsukiai*) who is almost a relative inasmuch as he helps in case of calamity, and comes to a funeral.

There is an emphasis on age, both in the society as a whole and in the family. This is especially true in the case of men. Boys and men of the same age are close friends, those of the same age being called *dōnen*. The age factor is so strong, indeed, that it is a common occurrence for cousins to be closer friends than siblings.

The kinship terms reflect the emphasis on generation and lack of emphasis on sex. Thus, with siblings one can say "elder sister" (*nēsan*) or "younger sister" (*imōto*), "elder brother" (*niisan*) or "younger brother" (*otōto*); but there is no way to say simply "sister" or "brother." One can only say *kyōdai*, meaning sibling. The age factor is also reflected in the custom of *junyōshi*.

Most hard work is performed by men between the ages of eighteen to forty, termed collectively *seinen* (commonly translated as "young men"). Men from forty to sixty, while doing plenty of work, act as advisers to the *seinen*. It is this older group which, with the *nushidōri*, decides and directs all *buraku* affairs.

A first-son's family of orientation and family of procreation are in the same house. A second-son's family of procreation, on the other hand, is always in a different house and often in a different *mura*. Further, a second-son's family of procreation is frequently of lower social status than his family of orientation. To be a first son (*chōnan*) is to be fortunate. It is the first son who inherits the head-ship of the house with its attendant social status and mate-rial wealth.

There is one advantage second sons (*jinan*) have. More well-to-do families will frequently give a second son more education than the first. The first son must stay in Suye to inherit the name and the property of his father, but the second son may emigrate to a town, or follow some other occupation, and thus he has more choice of occupation than his elder brother.

A daughter is the least desired child and the least for-tunate. She must accept whatever family of procreation fate offers. Unlike a second son, however, she stands an even chance of entering at marriage a household of higher social status than the one of her birth. When the firstborn child is a daughter, people will say politely, "That is fortu-nate—now, when the son is born, there will be a nurse-maid to carry him about."

A man's wife usually comes from a *buraku* other than his own. Thus, while most men are born in the *buraku* in which they live, most women are from other *buraku* or *mura*. This accounts in part for the strength of the *dōnen* (same age) tie among men who have grown up and gone to school together and its weakness among the women, most of whom are strangers to one another before the age of eighteen.

Cousin marriage is frequent, though it is being discour-aged by more educated people on the questionable theory that it is biologically harmful. There is no stated prefer-ence, but parallel cousin marriages appear to be more com-mon. Furthermore, the cousins are almost always children of brothers. This is a reflection of the solidarity of the men in a *mura* and of the lack of it among the women. Two brothers are more likely to be living in the same *mura* than two sisters. More important is the fact that it is the head of a household who actually decides any family matters. Thus, it is easier for two brothers to arrange a marriage of their children than for two sisters, who would have to persuade their respective husbands who might have nothing at all in common.

Except for one or two feeble-minded persons, there is almost no adult in the *mura* who is not married. A widow usually remarries, frequently a younger brother of her late husband. Similarly, a widower may marry the younger sister of his late wife. A woman who has had a bastard frequently marries a widower.

THE HOUSEHOLD

In Suye a farmer's house is much more than a mere shelter against the elements. Here the entire household lives together; here dwell the spirits of the ancestors in the Buddhist alcove (*butsudan*); and here, in some smoke-blackened corner of the kitchen, are the homely deities of good fortune, Ebisusan and Daikokusan. Here also are the household gods who look after the kitchen, the well, and the toilet, respectively.[2] Houses possess an age and character which is lacking in more urban centers. Like almost everything of consequence in the *mura*, a house is the result of co-operative labor by the members of the *buraku*.

The ordinary house is a one-story thatch-roofed cottage with walls consisting of sliding screens with here and there a bit of mud wattle. Doors of wood slide to at night, supposedly as a protection against burglars but actually more as a matter of form and as a means of gaining privacy. If the whole family is out for the day in the fields, these doors

[2] See chap. vii, section on popular gods.

will be partially closed. No one would think of entering another man's house if no one were at home to receive him.

An ordinary farmhouse has about three rooms. The *daidokoro* is the most-lived-in room. It is next to the kitchen and has in or near the center a square fire pit (*irori*) over which hangs an adjustable hook (*jizai kagi*) holding an iron teapot or, at mealtimes, a broad soup tureen (*nabe*). This is where any casual caller, and there are many, is received and served tea by the mistress of the house.

The best room of the house is the *zashiki*. Here are the finest mats (the poorest ones being in the *daidokoro*) and here is the *butsudan* and the alcove called *tokonoma* by which is kept the Shinto-god shelf. Any family treasures might be kept in the *tokonoma*, especially some old family pictures. Guests of honor at a banquet are always seated before the *tokonoma*, and it is a frequent occurrence for two guests to quarrel politely, each urging the other to sit farther "up" in the room, i.e., nearer the *tokonoma*.

In addition to these two rooms, there are various bedrooms and a dirt-floored kitchen. The kitchen is not an integral part of the house, its roof being more of a lean-to than a part of the main house roof.

Since everyone uses the floor to eat and sleep on, there is very little furniture in the house. Cushions are provided for guests, and sometimes a cushion is kept in front of the fire pit for the head of the house (see Fig. 3).

The master of the house sleeps in the main room (*zashiki*) with his wife. If there are children, the master sleeps with the next youngest child while the mother sleeps with the baby. When the baby is asleep, the man visits his wife, a situation which gives rise to many jokes. All the older children sleep together, usually in one of the sleeping-rooms (*nema*) or in the *daidokoro*. Grandparents

HUNTING, FINDING, AND KILLING LICE IN
THE *BURAKU DŌ* (KAKUI)

FARMER'S WIFE IN HOT-WEATHER
WORKING ATTIRE

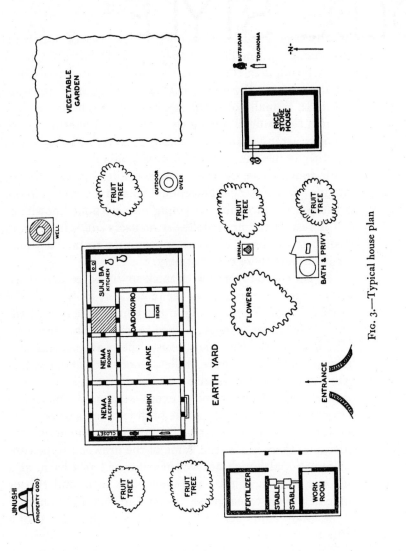

Fig. 3.—Typical house plan

usually sleep separately, each with one or two of the grand-
children, as no one likes to sleep alone. If there is a newly
married couple in the house, they have a separate room—
usually a *nema*. Big houses keep a maid in a small separate
nema. In a small house she sleeps with the children. Very
often in the summer, owing to a shortage of mosquito nets,
sleeping arrangements are changed, everybody crowding
together under the number of nets available.

All rooms have sliding screens (*shōji*) opening to the
outside. A maidservant sleeping alone in a separate room
is thus easily accessible to young men without knowledge
of the rest of the household. A manservant, who lives in
a room in the barn, also has opportunity to take a young
maid servant there clandestinely.

The floors are covered with thick six-by-three-foot straw
mats (*tatami*), necessitating the removal of footgear before
entering. Nearly everything in the house—the *tatami*, the
sliding doors, the arrangement of rooms—is standardized.

In addition to the main house, there are several outhouses—barn, bathhouse, toilet, woodshed, and outdoor
oven—and rich houses also have a rice storehouse. The
bath is heated by firewood every afternoon about five
o'clock. The labor of filling the bath (women's work) with
buckets from the nearest well and of heating it is considerable; there is also the value of the firewood to be considered. So, although nearly every house has a bath, as a
rule one woman lights a fire under her bath, and two or
three neighbors come to use it, then the next night another
of the group lights her bath, and so the work and cost of a
bath are rotated.

The evening bath plays an important role in the household life, especially of the women. After the menfolk have
bathed, the women will take their turn. If a woman has,

as she may well have, one or two younger children, they all sit in the tub together. This intimate association every evening creates a strong social bond within the family between the mother and her children. While a woman has but little formal status in the home, there is a very strong emotional tie between a mother and her children. The bonds formed by a boy in early youth by sleeping together and bathing together with his mother are never completely lost by later experience in a patriarchal social organization. Frequently, two or three women will bathe together, one being in the tub at a time, the others standing by and talking. There is a warm intimacy about these evening chats at the bath which keeps close the relationships between the women of three or four neighboring households and helps to make up for the social bonds they lack by being born in different *mura*.

The house yard is as important to everyday life as the house itself. This space of bare flat earth is where the household grain is periodically dried in the sun; here in slack seasons a man sits to make baskets or his wife to reel silk. The yard is the only available place for all kinds of women's work such as pressing nuts for hair oil or rolling tea leaves. Somewhere in every yard is a flower garden, and also, as a rule, a vegetable patch. From these gardens come flowers for the household gods and vegetables for the household soup.

The land area, including house and outhouses and its adjacent fruit trees, garden, fishpond, and vegetable patch, is called *yashiki* and has a different tax rate from regular farm land.

In accordance with the advice of praying priests (*kitōshi*), farmhouses ordinarily face south. Barns and outhouses are all to the south or to one side of the main house,

it being considered unseemly to have any structures hous-
ing waste products or animals north, i.e., "above" the
dwelling-place of the owner.

Fire is a constant hazard in the *mura*, and the house is
constructed so as to reduce this hazard to a minimum. The
bathhouse is usually across the yard from the main house
and thus presents no danger when firewood is placed under
it for the evening bath. The kitchen is dirt floored, and
the stoves are placed by the outside wall, i.e., away from
the mat-covered floors of the main part of the house. The
only real danger of fire comes from the fire pit and this is
more dangerous to small babies, who may fall in and lose
a hand or a foot, than as a source of conflagration.

In paddy *buraku* all houses are rather close, so that what
goes on in one house cannot be kept secret from the next.
Even in upland *buraku* houses tend to be located in clusters, frequently of relatives. These clusters of households
often use the same well, share a common hair-oil press,
exchange labor at rice-transplanting, and take turns at
using one another's bath. It is such clusters of houses that
usually form the small co-operative units called *kumi*.
Contiguous living in which privacy is lacking and in which
public opinion is strong characterizes life in each *buraku*
and gives the *buraku* a geographical unity to strengthen
or complement its social integration.

The house has remained constant in structure more than
any other aspect of village life. It appears to have done so
for centuries. Certain basic features of the house, such as
a separate lean-to for kitchen with dirt floor, and separate toilet and bathhouse, are essential for hygienic and
safety purposes.

In ordinary daily life the whole household is together for breakfast, lunch, and supper, sitting together around the fire in the evening. During work, for some things such as harvest, the whole household works together, but frequently the women do such work as silkworm-rearing and washing clothes, and the men do such work as making charcoal, separately.

The predominance of a unified household in eating, working, and sleeping is in sharp contrast to the way in which it acts in public. Man and wife are never seen to walk down the street talking together. The man will go alone or with a group of men, the wife alone or with some other women. To *buraku* affairs, both communal work and parties, man or wife or son or daughter goes, but rarely two from the same house. Brother and sister are almost never seen together in public. Both man and wife, however, usually come to strictly family affairs such as weddings and funerals, though even here men and women are seated on opposite sides of the room.

The household is pre-eminently the woman's domain. Here she lives most of her life and does most of her daily work. The house is the scene of banquets, prepared by women, and much of the village gossip goes on in the kitchen or by the doorway.

The housewife and her daughter-in-law prepare the soy-bean soup and cook the rice daily. The simple boiling of rice is actually one of the most difficult jobs of a housewife. Most men are utterly unsuccessful on the rare occasions they attempt it, and the uninitiated invariably burn the rice or have so much water in that the grains become soggy before the water is boiled out. There is a popular verse giving the proper method of cooking rice:

Saishō toro toro naka bombo	Little fire, little fire, big flame, big flame,
Guzu guzu yutokya hi wo hiite	Bubble, bubble, take out the big fire
Osan ga naku tomo futa toruna	Even though Squeezix cry, don't take off the cover.

The making of and caring for clothes is women's work. A man's mother and sisters usually weave at home his silk clothing for marriage. All mending is performed by a man's wife and female children. Some women's *kimono* and some work clothes are made by professional *kimono*-makers and seamstresses. This is especially true of occidental-style school dresses.

All dress is standardized. Fashions do not change rapidly in Suye. Yet with this there is a great variety in types of dress. A different costume is made for work and for parties, for young people and for old, for men and for women, for winter and for summer. Except for the newly introduced European clothes, however, all forms of clothing follow the *kimono* pattern, i.e., of a wrap-around garment held together by a cloth belt or *obi*. Formerly farmers were prohibited by sumptuary law from wearing the finer silk clothes, but today the only restrictions on dress types are custom and financial condition.

European dress is worn for working purposes, as it is found more convenient. School children and school masters wear rather drab black European uniforms, and certain shopkeepers and village officials wear European suits, especially in summer. Women, who sometimes wear a simple European dress in summer for house work, always resort to *kimono* for holidays and social events. *Kimono* with long sleeves and long skirts are admirably fitted to life in a house without furniture. Where men must work in Western-style buildings such as the school or village office, they wear European suits as being more practical.

Everyone in the family does some work. Old people help look after the small children and do simple handwork such as making straw rope, mending *geta*, and sweeping out the yard; children help their parents in whatever is being done and often carry a young sibling on their backs. Young people of fifteen or over do regular work along with their parents.

In farm work man and wife are equal, so that in a farmer's household a woman has a comparatively higher status than in a shopkeeper's house. If a man did not get along with his wife on the farm, his own income and food supply would be endangered. Every member of the household works not for himself but for the house, and, even if a member leaves home, he is expected, if successful elsewhere, to contribute money to his house. This co-operative unity of the household affects many relationships. In marriage, for instance, it is essential for the bride to be not only a good worker but also to be willing to forget her old home, to turn all her loyalty to the home of her husband. Similarly, in case of adoption of a son, it is desirable to choose a young boy and, whenever possible, a relative. Because the household is a unit, anyone from a house may represent it in *buraku* co-operative affairs—not only the head. The house head, like the *buraku* head, acts as adviser and director and bears responsibility for the group of which he is the leader. The household, as a working unit, is thus the basic co-operative group, and all other co-operation within the *buraku* depends on these constituent household groups. The unity of the household was even

stronger in the old days than it is today, and today the
unity is stronger in the farming *buraku* than in the "business" *buraku*. (*Buraku* co-operation is described in chap.
iv.)

Many home industries are being replaced by dependence
on shops for manufactured goods. Whereas formerly practically all cloth was home woven, today many housewives
go to Menda drapers for their fabrics. Whereas formerly
many items such as footgear and tools were made at home
by men, most of these are now purchased with money.

Electricity has so far affected the *mura* chiefly by replacing kerosene lamps with electric bulbs and water-
powered grain mills with electrically powered ones. The
electric mills have indirectly affected household activities
inasmuch as many houses now find it worth while to take
grain for grinding to the professional miller instead of
pounding it up at home. The extra leisure brought about
by these changes in household industries is more than
taken up by the heavier farm programs followed today.
The increased dependence on money crops and on the
shops and small towns for manufactured articles are com-
plementary factors in the changing conditions of the household economy.

Whereas formerly, in government elections, a household
had only one vote, exercised by the head, since 1925 any
man over twenty-five may vote. Similarly, whereas only
the head could inherit or own land and property, today
adult men, and in some cases women, can independently
own property. While most of these changes are purely
legal and have but little effect in *buraku* life, still they
exist and, in one or two instances, have been a basis for
division within the household.

PARTIES AND BANQUETS

The farmer of Suye has plenty of hard work to do—work which gives to the peasant and his wife horny hands, bronzed faces, and a remarkable docile patience. But work with the earth is different from work with a machine. A man can always sit down to smoke his pipe and chat a while; his wife can pause to suckle her baby. Work with the soil also makes a man conscious of fertility and of sex. Peasants the world over are notorious for their broad and earthy humor, and the Japanese peasant is no exception.

As the year goes round and work periods wax and wane, many opportunities arise for *buraku* people or groups of relatives to gather and have a good time with plenty to eat and drink.

When a newcomer arrives, he must hold a face-showing party (*mishiri*) for his *buraku;* if he is going away, he holds a farewell (*wakare*) party for his *buraku.* At a naming ceremony there is a small party; at a wedding a series of three big ones; at a funeral helpers and relatives each have a separate feast.

No community work is ever done without a party at the end. After the *buraku* has worked together to build a bridge, a party is held; after working to prepare things for a funeral, drinks are served. The same is done after rice-transplanting, after road-building, after housebuilding, and after roof-building. After the work and the evening bath, a party of the workers begins. Any ceremony, however minor, nearly always winds up with some drinking. These parties are always given in someone's house, and the preparations are always done by the women. The fishman from Taragi, a man on a joking relationship with most of the village housewives, is called in for supplies and expert assistance. All morning preparations for the party go forward, and neighbors, especially two or three young women, are usually asked to assist at this, later helping as serving girls.

One never receives a party for nothing; one either gives labor, as in the case of a funeral, or brings a gift of some kind, as in case of a farewell party. For ordinary banquets the usual gift which a person is expected to bring is a small square lacquered box (*jūbako*) of rice and about a pint of *shōchū*. These are brought wrapped up in a *furoshiki* (colored cloth used for wrapping up parcels).

On arrival at the host's house a man leaves his *geta* outside. If wise, he will put them in some out-of-the-way corner because later many drunken people will be going in and out to urinate, and they will not waste time looking for a particular pair of clogs. A man often goes home from a banquet in some one else's footgear.

On stepping into the *daidokoro*, the guest bows low to whoever is there to receive him—master, wife, or servant girl. If the guest is a woman, her two hands will be placed on the floor before her knees, and she will bow her head so low as to touch the floor. If a man, his hands will be placed on the floor about a foot apart, and he will bow until the back of his head and the back of his neck are in a horizontal plane.

Then the maid, daughter, or wife will bring him a tray on which is a teacup and a dish of pickle or some beans. She will set the tray before the guest, give him a slight bow, and pour tea from a little aluminum teapot. She will then leave him with the teapot. After conversation with other guests in the *daidokoro*, the guest finishes his tea, perhaps has a second and a third cup if he has walked a long way and is thirsty. Then, when the girl comes to take away his tray, he presents his *furoshiki*-wrapped load of rice and *shōchū*. This has been beside him all along, but the girl will look surprised, bow low, and mumble profuse thanks.

The guest is now asked into the *zashiki* where the banquet is to take place. His host tries to seat him by the *tokonoma*, the most honorable place in which to sit. He will refuse, then other guests will urge him on, and, after some dispute, he ends up not in the place of honor and not at the bottom of the line. The village headman as the highest man socially will, if a guest, be seated in the place of honor at any ordinary party; next in honorableness is the schoolmaster. Then come village councilors and older men; next, younger men; and, last, women.

At each place will be a tray with chopsticks, soup, raw fish, and a little thimble cup (*choku*) for *shōchū*. There will probably also be a gift box of food to take home (*orizume*), containing attractively arranged colored food and pieces of fruit. This has been prepared by the Taragi fishman and contains deep-sea fish, served only at banquets.

When all guests are assembled, the housewife will come in, bow, and apologize for having "nothing to serve." The host will seat himself before the guest of honor, pour him a cup of *shōchū* from a peculiar jar with a spout called *gara*, ask him to drink, and hand the cup to the guest, who will drink and return the cup. Then he will do the same with the next guest and so on all around the room. At a big party some neighbor's daughter usually comes in to help serve food and drink; she will pour out the *shōchū* for drink exchanges, following the host as he moves down the line. This exchange of drinks is a gesture of good will, and one never refuses a man's offer when he passes the cup in token of friendship. The essential part of a wedding

ceremony consists in just such an exchange of drinks between bride and groom and between bride and groom's
father. Similarly, an adopted son and his adoptive father,
a master and his new apprentice, exchange cups as a sign
of the new social bond between them.

Other guests now begin to circulate as did the host,
and before long there are as many people on the inside
line as on the outside. The host's wife usually appears before long to exchange drinks with each guest.

There are many games to encourage drinking. In the
country they are played only by men, though in towns
geisha may also play them. One is a guessing game (*nanko*)
played with three pebbles or broken chopsticks; others are
very quick finger games—complicated varieties of *jan ken
pon*. One of them, *kuma-gen*, is local to Kuma.

Some parties men alone attend. The party plays *ken*,
gets drunk, and goes home. But often women also attend
or come in later. After such a party has been in progress
for some time and plenty of *shōchū* has been imbibed, a
samisen is produced and played by a daughter of the house
or some neighbor, or by some older woman, and soon good
fellowship finds expression in song and dance. While both
men and women can sing, some are known as better singers, i.e., knowing more songs than others. Someone, either
man or woman, will get up to dance. The dance is often
a representation of some task such as weeding—one of the
hardest, most tiring jobs of a rice farmer—or it may illustrate some sad story or be a parody of a drunkard or anything peculiar, such as the writer's long-legged gait. Before long, however, the dances acquire a sexual character.
Some good housewife will take the floor and perform a
dance, jerking her hips forward to the refrain of some very
free verses. A stick may be used by a man as a phallus

DRINK EXCHANGE (*SAKAZUKI*)

Here the farmers of Hirayama are acting as hosts to the agricultural adviser who has come to discuss a proposed horse-powered rice mill for the *buraku*.

BANQUET AT HOME OF FIRST BON

The hostess is facing her guests. This is a somewhat poor house in Yunoharu. Note the rice stored on dirt floor in the background. The time being summer, the fire-pit at left is covered with a board.

and a song sung in its praise; a cushion folded adroitly or a *gara* covered with cloth may also be used for such dances. These performances invariably bring roars of laughter from the assembled company, and, after a particularly good dance, a person is offered many drinks of congratulation. While they are being enjoyed by everyone present, children peer in at doorways to enjoy the sport, and between dances a woman may sit down to nurse her youngest baby.

When a man has had sufficient *shōchū* and is thinking of departing, he goes out into the *daidokoro* and sits by the fire pit where he is served tea and rice. Eating rice is an indication that one is through drinking. In fact, the men of Suye say that they cannot drink after having eaten rice.

While the guest is eating, some woman of the household will wrap up his *jūbako* and *shōchū* bottle in his cloth *furoshiki*. In the *jūbako* will be put all food not eaten at the banquet plus the *orizume* or gift box of fish. After rice, the bowl is rinsed and the last grain swallowed by pouring tea in the rice bowl and drinking it off.

The departing guest now bows to his host and hostess, whichever is on hand, thanks him or her for the nice party, and starts off home. Often three or four men will leave in a group and, instead of going straight home, stop in at one or two houses along the way and have another drink. Such impromptu callers are called *heyorigyaku*.

The work of giving a party falls mostly to the women of the household. They order the fish from the fishman, who is a great help to the household in giving a big party. He comes early, delivers the needed fish and *orizume* which he has previously prepared at home. He helps lay out the room for the guests and helps serving girls by refilling *gara* with *shōchū*. Furthermore, he later joins the guests, exchanges drinks, sings songs, and dances.

When the party is over, the women sweep out the room, then usually go to bed. The dishes are cleaned the next morning, and those borrowed for the occasion returned with some small thank gift (*orei*). If a neighboring young girl helped at the party, she also helps clean up the next day. A few days later the housewife will call at her house and present her with new footgear or some cloth as a return gift.

These parties, drunken as they are, almost invariably make for better friendship. By exchanging drinks together, people's friendliness with one another is renewed. The opportunity to dance and sing gives a person so desiring a chance to express himself. It is only very rarely that a quarrel occurs during such a party—and then it is usually caused by some perennial hard-to-get-along-with (*yakamashii*) person.

Most parties occur in the winter when there is no work on hand. Others come after periods of intensive work such as rice-transplanting. While today there are many banquets, villagers all speak of the years gone by when there were more and bigger feasts. Of recent years undue expenditure for such purposes has been discouraged by the government through the agricultural association and the headman. The school also instils a new self-consciousness and modesty concerning sex so that those people with more education tend to be less frank in speech and action.

SONGS AND DANCES

The songs of Suye, all of them as familiar to the singers as the old *buraku dō*, create a strong feeling of unity among the singers. This is emphasized by the rhythmic clapping that accompanies the singing. The dances, just as familiar, just as homely, give a man or a woman a

BURAKU SENDING OFF ONE OF ITS MEMBERS
(IN THIS CASE THE AUTHOR)

BURAKU WOMEN PRACTICING A DANCE FOR A SCHOOL-OPENING
CEREMONY AND CARNIVAL (*RAKUSEISHIKI*)

chance to express himself or herself before the group. During the ordinary humdrum daily life there is scant opportunity for self-expression, but at these drinking parties anyone who feels the urge may display his abilities. In the dances the folk, especially the women, show a remarkable sense of mimicry and satire.

Besides parties and banquets certain festivals used to be characterized by special songs and dances. In many parts of Japan this is true of Bon, but in Suye the Bon dance has died out, and only a few old people know any verses of the local Bon song. The reason it is kept up in cities such as Tokyo is probably, in part at least, commercial.[3]

For occasions such as prayers for rain each *buraku* formerly had a special song and dance with costumes and special rituals—but these have mostly disappeared also, though they are still occasionally seen when some big event such as the opening of a new school or village office building takes place. On such occasions different *buraku* of the *mura* prepare dances and perform them during the day of the festival.

At village parties younger girls about seventeen or eighteen serve *shōchū*, and one of them plays a *samisen*. The *geisha* in the towns do the same. However, in the villages it is the older men and women who dance, not the young girls, who are much too bashful. Young women would not think of indulging in the dances of their mothers.

A few examples are given here of songs sung in Suye. These songs, as well as the dances, are evidently very ancient. The texts, given in the local dialect, vary some-

[3] The government suppressed many rural Bon songs because of their extreme sexual nature, just as it destroyed many a wayside phallic stone. The almost forgotten Bon song of Suye possesses its share of sexuality, and it is possible that the old Bon dance as a public performance outdoors was suppressed by the government. The religious significance of Bon is given in chap. vii.

what from singer to singer, but most of the popular ones are fairly uniform. However, a singer leading the singing may frequently add some topical or humorous verse of his own. Each district in Japan has its own body of local song. Some of these local songs, such as *Ohara bushi*, have become famous all over the nation; others are unknown outside their native milieu. The songs sung at parties are true folk songs inasmuch as they are anonymous, known to all the singers, and frequently added to or varied to suit the situation. Some are simple descriptions of scenery, others sentimental love songs. The favorite local song of the region—*Rokuchōshi*—has been used as a trade name by the Suye *shōchū*-maker, which boosted the sale of his product because of the popularity of the name.

Modern popular songs have scarcely penetrated to Suye as yet. One best seller of 1936 was learned by a prominent young man on his visits to Kumamoto. He used to whistle it as he walked down the road, and it was not long before the nursegirls by the *dō* were singing it to one another. At a party, if anyone knows a new song or dance, it is always in much demand. Such "new" songs and dances, however, are often merely old folk products from other regions.

KUMA *ROKUCHŌSHI*
(Kuma Six-Tone Song)[4]

Kuma de ichi ban	In Kuma the best (beauty spot)
Aoi san no gomon	Is the gate of Aoi shrine
Gomon gomon to	
Mae wa hasuike	With lotus pond in front
Sakura baba	And the cherry-tree riding ground.
Yoi yasa koi sasa.	

[4] This is the special local song of Kuma and as such is sung on the least provocation. For complete set of annotated folksong texts sung in Suye see author's *Japanese Peasant Songs*, Memoir 38, American Folklore Society, 1943.

Koko wa Nishimachi
Koyureba Demachi
  Demachi Demachi to
Demachi koyureba
Sakura baba
  Yoi yasa koi sasa.

Here's Nishimachi,
Beyond is Demachi,

Beyond Demachi
The cherry-tree riding ground.

Kuma to Satsuma no
Sakai no sakura
  Sakura sakura to
Eda wa Satsuma ni
Ne wa Kuma ni
  Yoi yasa koi sasa.

On the boundary of Kuma and
  Satsuma
(Grows) a cherry tree
With branches in Satsuma
And roots in Kuma.

THE COUNTRY HEADMAN[5]

Inaka shōya dono
Jōka kembutsu
Miyare yoisa
  Asa asa asa no hakama
Ushiro dako
Mae hikkaragete
Gombo zuto yara
Yama-imo zuto yara
  Shakkuri shakkuri
Shasha meku tokoro wa
Ara ma shōshuna
Torage no inu ga
  Shōya don shōya don shōya don
Uchi kamo shite
Hoe mawaru
      Yoi yasa

A country headman
Sightseeing in the castle town.
Look at the hemp skirt, the hemp
  skirt,
Tucked up behind,
Hanging long in front;
What with *gombo* in straw wrap-
  ping,
What with mountain potato,
Hobble de hoy, hobble de hoy.
Strutting along
Ara ma! What a funny sight!
Ferocious dogs
The headman, the headman, the
  headman,
Are biting,
Are barking all around.

DRINKING WITH ONE'S LOVER[6]

Ippai totta
Oshōchū wo
Kuro jokkya

A full cup taken
Of wine.
Into the black jug

[5] A *Rokuchōshi hayashi*, i.e., a song from the *Rokuchōshi* cycle which is spoken very rapidly in a special voice and rhythm to occasional bangs on the *samisen*.

[6] A *Rokuchōshi hayashi*.

Nawashite	Pour it,
Shiro jokkya	Into the white jar
Nawashite	Pour it.
Sama to futaide	Together with one's lover
Yattai	Giving,
Tottai	Taking,
Suru tokya	How does it feel?
Kokoro wo	
Doshta monkya	
Ha ha ha	

THE NEEDLES OF THE GREEN PINE[7]

Aoi matsuba no	Needles of the green pine,
Shūte uriya are	When dying,
Karete karete	Even in falling
Karete ochiru mo	Fall down
F'taridzure	In couples.
Yoi yasa	

COUNTRY WRESTLING
(*Dokkoise*)[8]

Dokkoise dokkoise wa	*Dokoise, dokoise* is
Inaka no sumoyo ye	The country wrestling.
Okitsu motsuretsu	Getting up and becoming entangled
Matamo dokkoise	Again and again, *dokkoise*.

OTHER *dokkoise* VERSES

Dokkoise no	If eggs are tended,
Tamago wo	They become chickens.
Sodatsurya hioko	If chickens are tended,
Sodatsurya toki uta wo	They crow in the morning.

Maru tamago mo	Even round eggs
Kiriyo de sh'kaku	Can be cut square.
Mono mo īyo de	Things that are said
Kado ba tatsu	Can be very sharp.

[7] Sung to tune of *Rokuchōshi*.

[8] *Dokkoise* is a type of song found in many parts of rural Japan. In Suye it is regarded as local. This description of country wrestling as a parody of the sex act always causes much laughter when sung.

MY OLD LADY IS A WOMAN[9]

Yūcha s'man batten	I beg your pardon, but—
Uchi no kaka unago	My old lady is a woman;
Kesa mo hagama de	Even this morning in a basin
Bobo aruta	Her *bobo*[10] she washed.

A FAREWELL SONG[11]

Sama to wakarete	On parting from my lover,
Matsubara yukeba	When I go through the pine grove
Matsu no tsuyu yara	Whether it is the pine sap
Namida yara	Or my tears (I cannot tell).

CHIEF OCCASIONS FOR BANQUETS AND PARTIES

AT EXPENSE OF HOST

Naming ceremony...........Relatives and friends invited

Wedding.................First day relatives; second day important people of *mura;* third day *buraku* (one person from each house)

Funeral..................(*a*) Relatives; (b) *buraku*

Memorial services including Bon.....................Relatives

Face-showing party on arrival in *buraku*................*Buraku*

Farewell party on departure..*Buraku*

Soldiers' farewell and return parties..................*Buraku* and relatives

New Year's................Relatives

AT EXPENSE OF ALL MEMBERS

After various co-operative undertakings...............*Buraku; exchange-labor groups*

[9] Sung to tune of *Rokuchōshi*.

[10] A humorous folk term for a woman's genitals.

[11] There are many songs sung on the occasion of a farewell party. This one is sung to the tune of *Rokuchōshi*.

AT EXPENSE OF GOVERNMENT OR BUSINESS COMPANY

Parties after government lectures at school............	Everyone present or one from each house in the *mura*
Parties after lectures by spinning company officials at school....................	All members of the company-sponsored sericultural association

Except for these parties and excursions to various shrine and temple festivals, there is practically no recreation. The periodic festivals which occur in near-by towns and *mura* afford opportunities for good times. Young people especially make a point of dressing up to walk the few miles to such festivals. Of recent years, these have been increasingly commercialized in the towns with side shows and circuses, while in the *mura* the local festivals have tended to disappear. Formal entertainment whereby people sit passive while someone amuses them is rare. The two forms of it occasionally met with in Suye are the *naniwabushi* and the movies.

The *naniwabushi* is an old Japanese type of amusement. A man sings and recites to the accompaniment of one or more musical instruments some tragedy, comedy, or epic. Some of the story is told as a narrative, much of it in dialogue, the teller vividly impersonating the different characters' voices. Often such *naniwabushi* travel from place to place during the winter. Two came to Suye in the course of a year; one stopped at the barber's house, got a very small attendance; the other did business at the school auditorium with a good-sized audience. At the school admission was ten sen for adults, five sen for children. Voluntary contributions were made at the barber's house. *Naniwabushi* visit Suye less often these days than in former years.

A more recent type of amusement is the movie. Movies come to the *mura* two or three times in summer. A small movie-house owner of Taragi comes over and shows the films in the evening either at the school or in some vacant space outdoors. They are long, often historical, dramas of feudal times, with many a sword battle. Admission is ten sen, five sen for children. In Menda and Taragi are small movie houses showing pictures three times a week. Occasionally some villagers, mostly young people, go. Compared to the songs and dances of the villagers at parties or special celebrations, the movies are unimportant. They are, however, becoming more common as the years go by.

The radio owned by the broker is always turned on but rarely listened to. The one at school is used chiefly for radio exercises. When the 1936 Olympic games were broadcast, less than five young men bothered to go to the school to listen at 9:00 P.M.

For men there are the *geisha* restaurants. Village office clerks and brokers are usually the chief rural patrons of the Menda restaurants, such entertainment being too costly for a farmer.

CHAPTER IV
FORMS OF CO-OPERATION

INTRODUCTION

TWO outstanding features of *buraku* life are co-operation and exchange. Co-operation is the voluntary working together of a group of people. This implies that there is no "boss"—no person who forces the people thus to work together. For co-operative work there must be some motive, some compelling cause other than an altruistic common good, some hard fact such as economic necessity. With a wet rice crop which demands a large amount of labor at transplanting time some method of obtaining extra help is imperative. It could be hired, but until recently this was not practical. So some form of co-operation is necessary. An exchange of labor is one solution of the problem. Similarly, a community without money cannot hire people for public works such as road-building or bridge-building, and so some form of co-operation is again necessary. In Suye this takes the form of all the households in a *buraku* working together at regular intervals to perform such jobs. This joint working of the community not only gets the work done, but keeps the people together by uniting them in a common task and afterward in a common drinking party.

Before Meiji the peasants were little better than serfs. They had to contribute so much rice per year to the lord of Sagara in Hitoyoshi who had a granary in Suye for collecting its harvest. No money to speak of was in circulation, and rice was the staple currency. In the *mura*

rice is still used as money for local purchases, in co-operative credit clubs, and as payment for local workers
and servants. Rent is a percentage (usually about 50) of
the rice crop.

Today the feudal lord is gone and is replaced by money
taxes. This requires that rice still be grown in large quan-
tities and sold in order to pay the taxes. The *mura* have
become self-governing units with their own headmen.
Mura boundaries have been rather arbitrarily drawn, as
noted in an earlier chapter, but the *buraku* communities
are still much the same as they were a hundred years ago.

Physical aspects of life have changed with the introduction of new machinery for farming, artificial fertilizer, and
winter wheat as a money crop; but the social organization
is not so radically changed, and the old co-operative forms
still persist. The lack of bosses or chiefs in local social
forms is very marked. It is possible that strong expression
of character was discouraged by the lords of Sagara.

The importance of the household as a co-operative unit
and the more informal modes of co-operation between
houses for baths and for banquets have already been discussed. The five most important forms of co-operation in
Suye, in addition to the household, are: (1) rotating responsibility by groups (*kumi*); (2) civic co-operation; (3)
helping co-operation (*tetsudai*, *kasei*) in housebuilding,
emergencies, and funerals; (4) exchange labor (*kattari*);
and (5) co-operative credit clubs (*kō*).

ROTATING RESPONSIBILITY—THE *kumi* SYSTEM

Many *buraku* religious celebrations are managed by
small groups of three to five households called *kumi*. A
board (*bancho*) is kept on which are listed the names of all
buraku members, in groups of twos and threes or fours and

fives. These are the *kumi*.[1] On the back of the *bancho* is written the business with which these *kumi* are concerned. Thus in Imamura a *bancho* of Yakushi[2] *dō* is kept. Each year there is a celebration on Yakushi Day. One year one *kumi* is in charge, next year another *kumi*, etc. It is the duty of the *kumi* in charge to clean up the *dō* before the day of celebration. Then on the day itself they must sit all day in the *dō* and serve tea and beans to visitors. The *bancho* lists house heads' names, but *kumi* work is done by their wives, mothers, daughters, or female servants. Usually two of the three or four *kumi* members on duty take charge in the morning, two in the afternoon.

During Yakushi Day all members of the *buraku* and many outsiders come up at one time or another to the *dō*, throw a copper sen up toward the image of Yakushi, hold hands together, bow head, mutter a ritual prayer two or three times and retire. An occasional worshiper claps hands Shinto style. Then the visitor is given tea and beans by the *kumi* members in charge, who also exchange some conversation with him. When finished, the visitor leaves a copper on his tray as payment for the tea and beans.

At the end of the day the coppers given to the god are all collected and given to the *buraku nushidōri*. He looks after the money for the *dō*, and it is used to make repairs on, or to buy new things for, the *dō*. The coppers given for tea are kept by the women as a return for the tea and beans which they contributed. Thus a fair exchange takes place. The *bancho* is taken to the house of that member of the *kumi* whose turn it is next. It hangs on the wall of

---

[1] The term *kumi* simply means "group" in Japanese. However, as the word "group" is vague in English, and as I shall restrict the term *kumi* to the groups here described, it seems advisable to use the native term.

[2] See chap. vii for discussion of Yakushi and other deities found in *dō*.

the house, often in the *daidokoro*, until the next year.
Then, when Yakushi Day comes round again, there is no
question as to whose turn it is. There is no head of a
kumi. Indeed, the whole purpose of the *bancho* system is
to shift responsibility and work each year to a different
group.

All *dō* are not celebrated the same way, however. In
Kawaze, for instance, on Kwannon Day's eve (Kwannon
goya) the *kumi* in charge comes, offers *shōchū* and some
cakes, and lights a few candles. Any other *buraku* members who are to come bring their jug of wine and offer
a cup to the god. Then people on hand exchange drinks,
talk, and enjoy the moonlight.[3] When people are feeling
good, songs and dances are frequently performed—technically for the god, actually for enjoyment.

The next day, Kwannon Day proper, a party is held in
the house of one of the *kumi* members whose turn it is.
Each *buraku* member is expected to contribute ten sen for
food and *shōchū* costs whether he attends the party or not.
Thus, if only a few actually come, there is more *shōchū*
for those present. A square of *tōfu* is served each person,
shōchū being served as long as it lasts. Mostly older men
attend who talk and play *ken*. The party is not a boister-
ous one. Most *buraku* parties held at common expense
after some *buraku* ceremony or work serve *tōfu* instead of
fish as *tōfu* is cheaper. Fish is seen rather at banquets
provided by a single household as, for instance, a wedding
feast.

Both the eve (*goya*) and festival day (*matsuri*) parties
are smaller than they used to be and not so widely practiced—only about half the *buraku* of Suye still observe

[3] Most of these celebrations take place on the fifteenth of a lunar month, i.e.,
at full moon (see chap. vii).

them. Like many of the old religious occasions for a gathering and a party, they have gradually diminished of late years. Often this is because farmers are busier than they used to be. Furthermore, the agricultural adviser and the village headman frown on "vain" expenses.

During the seven days of autumn Higan (equinox) the thirty-three Kwannon *dō* of Kuma serve tea and beans to pilgrims. The *kumi* system is used in each *buraku* where there is a Kwannon *dō*. The *buraku* in this case is divided into seven *kumi* so that a different *kumi* serves each day of Higan week.

It is said that one of the lords of Sagara many years ago decided that in Kuma thirty-three Kwannon *dō*[4] should be built, scattered all over the region. Then during Higan pilgrims could make a visit on foot to all of them, the trip usually taking a week. Some people cynically suggest that the lord introduced this custom in order that his agents, in the guise of pilgrims, could inspect the condition of the rice as it stood just before the harvest and thus judge what each *mura* should contribute to the lord's granaries. At any rate, there are today the thirty-three numbered Kwannon *dō* and, in addition, two or three of most numbers so that every *mura* has two or three Kwannon *dō*. Pilgrims still make the rounds during Higan and must be served their tea and beans.

From Suye no one went on this trip in 1935, but in previous years various people have gone. Some make the trip by bicycle. Usually a group goes together, as people do not like to make trips alone. At each *dō* visited they bow before the Kwannon, throw in a copper, and mumble repeatedly "Namanda" (an abbreviated form of *Namu*

[4] Evidently in imitation of a more important series of thirty-three Kwannon in Japan (see Kaempfer, *History of Japan* [3 vols.; London, 1727], II, 339).

jutsu). Most of the groups of pilgrims sing special
s verses called *goeika*. At the end of this the local
on hand give them tea and beans and exchange
conversation. Often some old professional pilgrim
es along and talks at length on the benefits of religion.
the whole the number of pilgrims who make the trip
ch year is on the wane.

All *buraku dō* are taken care of on the *kumi* system,
and a few small Shinto shrines are thus looked after. Most
of these *kumi* were founded, as a rule, on a geographical
basis. In upland Imamura, where little change in the location of families has occurred for many years, a *kumi* is
still often composed of two or three adjacent houses. In
Kakui, the business *buraku*, however, there has been much
moving around, people leaving the *buraku* and coming into
it. Hence a given *kumi* may be composed of households
widely scattered. Indeed the very *bancho* is lost for the
Kwannon *dō* celebration at Higan in Kakui with the result that there is much confusion as to who should take
part in a given *kumi* and which is to start serving first.

There is a *kō* (see p. 138) called Ise *kō* which works on
the *kumi* system. There is no *bancho*, but a book is kept
of members and *kumi*. *Kumi* consist of about three families each.[5] On the sixteenth of the first and ninth months
by lunar calendar the family whose turn it is holds a
party for all *buraku* members. One person from each
house comes and gives about fifteen sen (the amount varies
with the *buraku*), most of which is used up for food and
shōchū expenses. On first coming into the house, a person
goes to *tokonoma* where a *kakemono* of Amaterasu-o-mika-
mi is hanging, throws up a copper before it, claps hands,

[5] It will be noted that there are different series of *kumi* within a *buraku* for
different occasions.

bows, and goes back to the bookkeepers to give his money. Later all the offering money is also collected, and the amount noted in a book by the *kō* leaders. If any money is left over from the expenses of the party, it is sent together with offering money to the great national shrine at Ise. A party is held with *tōfu* and much *shōchū*. Then the *kakemono* is taken down, rolled up, and ceremonially handed to a member of the next *kumi*. Everyone, feeling fine by now, gets up and in a gay procession marches to the house of one of the members of the *kumi* receiving the *kakemono*. Here more *shōchū* is served, in this case at the host's expense. The *kakemono* is then kept in this house until the following meeting, when the same thing happens all over again, and the sacred *kakemono* moves on to the next *kumi*.

The *kumi* and *bancho* system is used also for other forms of co-operation. One of these is the strictly *buraku* affair of *chizashi*. As already mentioned, each *buraku* has a wooden *chizashi* frame. Three times a year—in spring, summer, and autumn—a horse doctor from Taragi comes to the *buraku* to fix up the horses and cows. All the *buraku* members owning cows and horses bring them to the *chizashi* stand. By turn the animals are persuaded or pushed into the wooden frame and tied up. Then the horse doctor makes a cut in the gums and in the rump and takes a hot iron wrapped in a rag and rubs it over the horse's body. These operations are said to improve its blood circulation. The hoofs are then trimmed. Farm horses go shoeless in Suye, only wagon horses being shod.

At the end of the day a small party is given by one of the houses with the doctor seated in the place of honor. Food costs are as usual defrayed by ten sen or so from each house. The doctor is paid in rice once a year, some-

A *KUMI* OF WOMEN SQUEEZING CAMELLIA NUTS FOR HAIR
OIL—A SPRING OCCUPATION

The oil drips into a basin below the wedge block

CHIZASHI—THE "CURING" OF HORSES IN SPRING,
SUMMER, AND AUTUMN

time in the late fall. The standard rate is one *shō* (a little over one and a half quarts) for horses, five *gō* (half a *shō*) for cows. If the price of rice is high, the doctor makes a bigger profit than if it is low. In some *buraku* everyone owning a cow or horse pays the price whether he has his animal doctored or not, in other *buraku* only those who have the cure pay for it. Each *buraku* has a *bancho* and *kumi*. The *kumi* in charge organize the party the day of *chizashi*, collect money, and buy food. The party rotates from *kumi* to *kumi*. When the *buraku* is ready to pay the doctor, a day is chosen, and the doctor gives a big party to which members of the *kumi* in charge from each *buraku* go, taking the rice payments they have collected from other *buraku* members with them. Kawaze, the richest and in some ways the most progressive *buraku* agriculturally, has discontinued the *chizashi*.

Kawaze has an irrigation *kumiai* or association including Kawaze landowners, two from Nakashima and some from adjacent land in the *buraku* of Shoya in the next *mura* of Fukada. It has a *bancho* with *kumi* of four to five people each. Annually the irrigation ditches must be cleaned and repaired, and it is the duty of the *kumi* in charge to select a day for doing this work and to inform other *kumiai* members. The wives of the *kumi* members serve food to the workers, and a party is held in the home of one member of the *kumi* in charge when the work is finished.

In Imamura there is a *bancho* with *kumi* of two or three families each to be responsible in turn each year for re-building the bridge. Instead of a permanent bridge *nushidōri*, as in some *buraku*, here each *kumi* in turn acts as *nushidōri*. The men of the *kumi* arrange a day for the job and get timbers and other necessaries assembled. The *kumi* women serve food to the *buraku* workers at midmorning and midafternoon and also prepare for the party—expenses of which are defrayed, as in other *buraku*, by a contribution of about ten sen from each *buraku* member.[6]

In the spring groups of women, called *kumi*, work together crushing camellia seeds to obtain hair oil. Each brings her own seeds, but all co-operate in pounding heavy wooden wedges into the squeezing frame. Only one or two houses in a *buraku* have such frames, and it is customary for the *kumi* using a neighbor's frame to give her some of the oil obtained. Such *kumi* are permanent from year to year. Formerly there were several varieties of *kumi* of this type (e.g., ropemaking *kumi*), but of recent years these have disappeared with the advent of machines.

Bancho without *kumi* may be kept. In one *buraku* there is a *bancho* with a list of *buraku* members' names on it, not grouped into *kumi*. The *bancho* is passed daily to the next house on the list. The house which has the *bancho* on a given day is responsible for the *buraku*-owned boat. Thus, if there is a flood, someone from that house must go down to the river to see that the boat is not washed away.

For funeral occasions a *bancho* is often kept. On one side is a list of *buraku* members concerned in funeral co-operation; on the other side, a list of rules as to what the bereaved family is supposed to serve to *buraku* helpers and what *buraku* helpers are expected to do. One purpose of this is to avoid competition in giving lavish funerals, thus causing those who cannot afford it much financial trouble in trying to compete.

The night watch kept at the end of the lunar year by firemen is done by a different *kumi* of two or three men each night. Similarly in Kawaze, a night watch is kept by

---

[6] For a description of co-operative bridge-building see p. 122.

kumi at the *buraku* fishpond during the weeks immediately prior to the opening of the fishing season.

In many parts of Japan these small *kumi*, such as the ones involved in *dō* celebrations, have disappeared. In Suye they are beginning to disappear, especially in the shopkeeper *buraku* of Kakui. The *chizashi kumi* have disappeared in Kawaze with the *chizashi*, though the irrigation *kumi* there carries on as strongly as ever.

OUTLINE OF *KUMI* AND *BANCHO*

Religious	Economic	*Bancho* Only
Autumn Higan (33 Kwannon *dō* in 7 days)	Bridge-building	Boat (Imamura only)
	Irrigation	Funeral
	Chizashi (defunct in Kawaze)	
Kwannon *matsuri**	Fishpond watch (Kawaze only)	
Yakushi *matsuri**	Night watch	
Amida *matsuri**		
Jizō *matsuri**	Hair oil (defunct in Kakui)	
Ise *kō*	Ropemaking (defunct)	

* Not all in same *buraku*.

CIVIC CO-OPERATION

ROAD-FIXING

In a small rural community (on land), some sort of paths are necessary. In Suye, except for the prefectural road which runs through it, all paths are primarily for foot travel. If not cared for, these paths become overgrown with weeds, uneven, clogged up by a flood, or in various ways troublesome to the people who are using them daily. So in spring and fall a day is set for cleaning the *buraku* paths. Sometime in April and September every year the *nushidōri* and other householders consult on a good day— a day when people will not be too busy with other work— for cleaning the paths. The arrangement is always for each household to send out one person. In the morning the *nushidōri* rings the *bangi*. Then people with straw brooms and mattocks gradually gather. The edges of the roads are resharpened, grass and brush cut off, and the paths swept clean. In midmorning, people all sit down for a rest and a smoke. One of the families will often serve tea and pickle. By noon the job is usually done.

Each *mura* is required to keep in good condition the sections of prefectural roads that pass through its territory.[7] The prefectural road is fixed annually by the *mura* as a whole, each *buraku* being assigned a different section to work on by the village office. *Buraku* not on the prefectural road tend to shirk their share of this work, so recently a system of prizes was inaugurated to inspire all *buraku* to work equally well. In the evening there is a small road-fixing party, each household contributing ten or fifteen sen for *tōfu* and *shōchū*.

BRIDGE-BUILDING

A bigger job, one requiring more skill and more labor than road-fixing, is bridge-building.

Every year the Kuma River swells to flood proportions sometime in June. This swollen river washes out the frail wooden bridges built to facilitate carrying home rice at harvest time from the paddy fields across the river. So the villagers must use a small boat for a month or so, which is manned in daily turns by someone from each house in the *buraku* concerned. Outsiders pay two sen a ride, which the ferryman of the day pockets.

In September, before the rice harvest, the *nushidōri* consults with *buraku* people on a suitable day to rebuild the

---

[7] This is probably a carry-over of the old feudal system of forced labor on public works.

bridge. Some men go off to the forest to gather wood, bamboo, and tough vines and take them to the riverside.

On the appointed day, about 7:00 A.M., one person from each house in the *buraku* turns up. If the bridge serves two *buraku*, members of each *buraku* work on a separate section of the bridge. Those who did not go to cut wood on some previous day will contribute straw for rope or matting for the bridge. Each person sets to work doing something. There is no boss, yet all gets done without confusion. Some men chop logs into proper shape and fit them into each other; other men split bamboo with the aid of a wood cross or make up the foundation baskets. Women and old men make straw rope. Girls and young men make up sections of cross-twigs with the aid of this straw rope, no nails being used in making these bridges. This gathering-together of the *buraku* in community labor is a good opportunity for talk and jokes.

By noontime all the main framework of the bridge is in place in the river, and everyone goes home for lunch. Two hours later the job is underway again. By now some of the women and older men have dropped out, their share of the bridge work being done.

The bound-twig sections are now put in place, and matting laid over them and tied in place with bamboo strips and mountain vine. When the bridge is finished, a curiously made double vase of freshly cut bamboo is filled with *shōchū*. This is put out in the river bed by a post near the water. It is an offering to the water-god to appease him so that he will not harm users of the bridge. After finishing work on the bridge, everyone goes home, takes off his work clothes, bathes, and dresses in some cool cotton *kimono*.

The women have not been idle in the afternoon. A

drinking party must be held after any such undertaking as this, and they help to prepare for it. Soon after the bath all workers gather at some house chosen by agreement, where a little fish or *tōfu* will be eaten and considerable *shōchū* will be drunk. This is paid for again by the contribution of ten or fifteen sen per house. If two *buraku* work on the bridge, their after-bridge-building parties will be held separately in their respective *buraku*.

And so the work is finished. A bridge has been built at no cost in money. The expenditure in labor, besides giving the *buraku* a bridge, has offered an occasion for the *buraku* to work together, talk together, party together. By the end of the day this common labor and talk and party have reinforced the solidarity of the group. The bridge is yearly washed away; the *buraku* yearly reunited.

This type of co-operation is done for all *buraku* enterprises such as building a new road, putting up a new bell tower, building a *dō*. In this latter case outside help may also be asked, and it will be repaid with a·party. In one *buraku* a concrete bridge has been built so that the annual gathering to build a new bridge no longer takes place. Plans are underway for another concrete bridge so that before many years this occasion for the *buraku* to work and drink together will be gone.

Buraku DANCES PERFORMED IN CASE OF DROUGHT

A variety of civic co-operation is the dancing of *buraku* dances in case of drought. People of all *buraku* assemble at a sacred waterfall in Hirayama, and each group performs its special dance in honor of the god who dwells there in the hope that he will bring rain. Only a few *buraku* still retain these dances. Formerly each *buraku* had a special dance *nushidōri* whose office was hereditary, and special parts in the dance were also hereditary. At the opening ceremonies of big buildings, such as a school, *buraku* frequently perform their dances. In return they receive money from the onlookers which is usually spent on *shōchū*.[8]

HELPING CO-OPERATION (*tetsudai*)

Formerly every *buraku* had a housebuilding and roofmaking co-operative association (*kake* or *kō*). Today, however, most *buraku* no longer have roofmaking *kō*. When a roof is to be made or repaired, roofmakers are hired and paid in rice, food, and a celebration party.

Housebuilding is still co-operative. When a man decides to build a house, the first thing he does is to invite a praying priest (*kitōshi*) to purify the land and propitiate the the land-god so that he will not object to having his land used and bring harm to the users. Next a carpenter is hired. He may or may not come from the *mura*. He and the housebuilder figure out the size and kind of building desired. Then, after timber has been bought from a nearby town and trimmed, the *nushidōri* is informed. A day is set for erecting the framework—a "good" day on the advice of the *kitōshi* and a convenient day from the point of view of the *buraku*. The morning of that day a man and woman from each house come to assist. The men work at putting the posts and beams in place, while the women help to cook food for the men. On this first day relatives who live not too many *mura* away also come to help. The carpenter supervises the workers and also helps in the work. The housebuilder works with the others.

At ten food is served, at noon lunch, in the afternoon more food. The food is at the expense of the housebuilder,

[8] See also section on song and dance in chap. iii.

and it is somewhat better than people would ordinarily eat. Thus, at noon they will be served hot rice rather than cold; in between meals, beans and tea with pickle, not just tea and pickle.

By late afternoon the whole framework is usually in place, including the ridgepole. It has all been fitted together so neatly that no nails are necessary. Then comes the ridgepole or *muneage* ceremony. In this the carpenter officiates. First some men make the paraphernalia for the ceremony:

1. An arrow of wood to be decorated with black paint. It is erected on top of the building and pointed northeast, the *kimon* or devil's direction; thus evil influences will be avoided.[9]
2. A red and white cloth used as a conventional bow to be fitted to the arrow.
3. Three colored banners also to be put up on top of the framework.
4. One or two folding fans to be opened and nailed to the ridgepole.
5. Straw-wrapped fish to be nailed with the fans. The fish is later taken down and placed in the *tokonoma* and then presented to the carpenter.
6. Hemp to be nailed up with the fans and fish. Hemp is an old Shinto ceremonial article.

The carpenter and the housebuilder, often accompanied by the carpenter's assistant and the brother or son of the housebuilder, go up on the skeleton house, taking with them *mochi* (ceremonial rice cakes), salt, and *shōchū*. Salt and *mochi* are put on the ridgepole. *Shōchū* is also poured into a cup and put there. Then the carpenter claps his hands, bows his head, and prays. The prayers are for the safety of the occupants of the house.

He then drinks a cup of *shōchū* and exchanges drinks with the housebuilder and others. When all this is done, the carpenter stands up with the tray of *mochi* in his hand

[9] An imitation bow and arrow is frequently placed in the rice fields to act as a scarecrow and perhaps to protect the rice from evil in general.

and scatters them, one in each of the four directions, starting with northeast and then at random. By now all the children of the neighborhood have gathered in addition to the workers and women. As the *mochi* are thrown, everyone attempts to catch them at once. The *mochi* are made by the household and relatives of the housebuilder.

Now the carpenter and others climb down from their airy perch. Workers take a bath in their host's bath, the fire of which has been lighted by some girl of the household an hour or so before. While this is going on, indeed before the ceremony, the women helpers have been preparing a banquet for relatives in the *zashiki* and one for *buraku* workers in the yard. Workers receive rice and *shōchū* and some other food; relatives who have come to help from other *buraku* or *mura* get rice, *shōchū*, and fish. They receive superior food because (1) they are relatives and (2) they brought some small gift as well as helped in the work. This division of relatives and *buraku* helpers at a *muneage* feast is much the same as at a funeral. The carpenter sits in the place of honor in the *zashiki* where relatives dine. The division is all quite open and customary. The yard is often right next to the *zashiki*, which in warm weather has no *shōji* in it so each group can see the other but does not, i.e., the relatives' party proceeds, paying no attention to the conversation and the happenings in the yard as if no one were there; in the same way the people in the yard pay no attention to the relatives' party.

If the house to be built is a large one, *buraku* people may come to help a second day. More often, however, one day's help is all that is given. After that the family carries on alone, and except for the roof there is no more labor requiring the co-operation of many men.

For making a roof on a new house, or renewing or repairing one on an old house, the house head calls in several men known in the *mura* as expert roofmakers. Some relatives may also assist, but the two or three experts are the important workers. If it is an old roof, the old straw must be all removed, leaving the naked skeleton of beams and joists, exposing the whole house to the sky. If it rains that day, the household is just out of luck.

By the end of either the first or the second day when the roof is finished there is a small ceremony. Houseowner and roof-fixers go up on the roof, three or five pairs of small flags are set crosswise in the roof, and straw bundles containing special rice cakes (*warazuto*) are thrown down. People below catch these and later hang them on fruit trees, especially persimmon. This is done in the belief that the *warazuto* will cause the fruit tree to bear, especially if a grafted tree.

That evening after the bath a supper is served to the workers followed by a party. The roof-fixers will be paid in money or rice, more often in rice. Other helpers, especially a relative or two who live in the *mura*, will probably work on a *kasei* or voluntary-labor basis. They will receive food and a party plus some small return gift (*orei*) later.

While the entire *buraku* does not come to help with roof-fixing, each person will call either on that day or on the next with a small gift. This call is referred to as "taking tea," but *tōfu* is the standard gift to take, four squares of it. Such calls are made in all cases of minor repairs of a building when the whole *buraku* does not help. Tea, rice, cakes, or fruit might be taken as gifts. In case of housebuilding all friends and relatives from outside the *buraku* call with a gift.

The fact that helping co-operation no longer occurs in roof-fixing indicates that this form of co-operation is on the decline. Even in housebuilding this form has broken down in Kakui because of the fact that some of the buildings have concrete foundations or otherwise require too much work for the *buraku* to do in a day, in addition to the fact that people there are not very good at co-operating anyway.

EMERGENCY AID

In the course of village life many calamities and emergencies are liable to occur. Formerly houses were frequently blown down by wind storms. Today this rarely occurs as houses are more substantially built, but there are still fire and flood. In case of fire everyone, but more especially the firemen (one man between twenty-five and forty from each house), come to the rescue. They do their best to quench the fire. The family is expected to give food and *shōchū* to the firemen. Then, after the whole thing is over, *buraku* people will call, bringing gifts of food and offering sympathy. If it is necessary to rebuild the house, one man from each house will come on an appointed day and erect the framework for the house. If the house head is put seriously in debt by the fire, he may borrow money by starting a *kō* among sympathetic friends.

If there is a flood and a man's house is damaged, the same things occur. If many houses in the same *buraku* are damaged, other *buraku* come to the rescue, send them rice, and help get children to dry land. Again it is the firemen who play a prominent part. The *bangi* or bell is always rung by the *nushidōri* in case of calamity to summon aid. After either fire or flood relatives also call with small gifts and sympathetic words. But in the immediate disaster it is the *buraku* that acts.

Frequently a child is drowned in floodtime. As in other disasters the *buraku* comes to the aid of the stricken family, the men searching the river for the body, the women helping in the house to prepare food and *shōchū* to serve the workers. If the search goes on for more than a day, all the *mura* firemen, each *buraku* in turn, will come out. The afflicted house supplies food and drinks but does not actively participate in the work.

Similarly, in case of a death in the *buraku* the *nushidōri* is informed. He lets other *buraku* people know of the sad event. A woman from each house comes over and sets to work helping in the kitchen. They serve tea and beans to people who make visits of consolation to the family. A man from each house in the *buraku* calls, pays his respects, then goes out in the yard to help prepare funeral things. The *nushidōri* consults with the dead man's family as to what is wanted for the funeral and whether coffin and paraphernalia are to be purchased in Menda or to be homemade. Certain of the *buraku* helpers, usually young men, are appointed by the *nushidōri* to dig the grave and later to act as pallbearers.

The bereaved family does nothing but receive callers. Relatives bring gifts of rice, *shōchū*, and colored cloth for funeral banners. Meanwhile the male *buraku* helpers sit in the yard and make the necessary coffin paraphernalia. The women helpers prepare food for the funeral feast to be given before the trip to the grave takes place.

Just before the funeral, relatives place the corpse in the coffin, having first washed it and dressed it in funeral clothes. Then, with the priest sitting in the place of honor, a funeral feast for relatives begins, to be followed by a funeral service.

While members of the family are feasting and exchanging drinks with the priest, the male *buraku* helpers eat and drink in the yard or barn. They frequently continue their drinking and talking right through the funeral service. This division of relatives and *buraku* helpers is similar to that observed in housebuilding. In each case the relatives receive a better banquet as they brought gifts. The specialist (carpenter or priest) sits in the place of honor.

When the service is over, the *buraku* men go into the house, bring out the coffin, tie it to poles, and put the poles on their shoulders. Then they go, with the relatives, in procession to the *buraku* graveyard. When the procession leaves the yard, the women helpers sweep up the room, then have their meal. After the graveside service the priest leaves soon, to be followed by the relatives. The pallbearers fill up the grave and put certain grave markers in place, talking and joking as they work.

At funerals all *buraku* helpers receive food. For this food they bring a measure of rice each. *Shōchū* and other food are in payment for their work. As a further return for their work they expect the bereaved family to help them when a death occurs in any of their families.

The *nushidōri* makes up a book in which he records the names of all people who came to help and the amount of rice they brought. It is said that this book has no significance and is merely made out to acknowledge the fact that help and rice have been received. The day after the funeral, however, two men of the family call on each family that helped and, without coming in, merely bow and thank them for helping.

Buraku help in case of calamity and funeral is called

tetsudai. The same term is used for voluntary aid given by women or young girls to a housewife in case of a big party. As already mentioned, a *bancho* is kept with directions as to how much and what kind of food and drink is to be served relatives, on the one hand, and *buraku* helpers, on the other. The *bancho* often lists the *buraku* house heads in groups of six or seven, each comprising a *kumi*. If only a child dies, then only the *kumi* need help. If a man dies, the whole *buraku* comes.[10]

Another form of helping co-operation is the help of female neighbors given at the time of a big party such as a wedding or a farewell party. At a farewell party the whole *buraku* participates, as will be further described in chapter vi in connection with the departure of conscripts.

In helping co-operation there is a dichotomy of relatives and *buraku* neighbors—the relatives gathering to celebrate or mourn and the *buraku* neighbors helping to prepare for the event. The local group does the work in order that the relative group may properly observe the occasion.

EXCHANGE LABOR (*kattari*)

The most outstanding form of economic co-operation in rural communities of Japan is exchange of labor for rice-transplanting and, in most regions, various other jobs involving group labor. It is variously called *yui*, *i*, or *kattari*.[11] In Suye it is called *kattari* (usually pronounced *katyai*) and functions most importantly in rice-transplanting.

In early May seedbeds are made for rice. A paddy is

[10] Further description of a funeral is given in chap. vi.

[11] Koichi Koizumi, "On the Custom Called *Yuhi*, as a Type of Labor System in Agricultural Villages," *Report of Imperial Agricultural Association* (Tokyo), Vol. XXV, Nos. 8–10 (August–October, 1935). This series of articles (in Japanese) gives the distribution and varieties of this practice in rural Japan.

flooded, plowed up, harrowed, and then made very smooth with a blunt wooden rake. Either long three-foot-wide strips with footways in between are made or the whole field is left smooth and the seed is planted by making footprints as one goes. The members of the household work together in rice-seed-planting. The seeds sprout into seedlings and after forty days are ready for transplanting. By growing rice in seedbeds and then transplanting it, a greater yield results; and it is easier to keep off harmful insects when all the seedlings are in a small area. Once or twice during the forty days the seedlings are growing all the school children go on an insect-hunting campaign.

The transplanting system applies not only to rice but also to sweet potatoes, onions, and many other vegetables. It is not practiced for wheat, probably because there is no time for this since right after rice harvest the wheat is sown, and, by the time it has sprouted up a few inches, frosts have come. Nor is transplanting practiced for upland rice.

Rice-transplanting is one of the biggest events of the year. It is very hard work, and a large field requires many workers to transplant all the seedlings. At this time the whole *mura* is busy at the same labor so that a *buraku* looks like a deserted village, with a few babies and ancient crones here and there in a vacant yard. Every able-bodied man and woman is out in the fields transplanting.

It is a time of hard work, but the work is social. Ten or fifteen young men and women are lined up across a field. As two linemen lay down a guide line with beads every five inches, the human line bends over rapidly, sticks seedlings into the mud, then stands up, and steps back; the lineman shouts *Hai!* moves the string over five inches, and the human line again bends over and pops in the seedlings.

The monotonous work is relieved by a constant chatter-
ing, often ribald. Stepping back to the end of a field
next to which a patch of beans is growing, a man sings out,
"Next we go into the *mame*" (beans). *Mame* being a conventional symbol for vagina, everybody laughs heartily
and goes on to the next paddy to continue transplanting.

Other workers are taking seedlings out of seedbeds and
tying them in little bundles; still others take these bundles
to the paddy fields to be planted and throw them out on
the mud where the transplanters pick up bundles of seedlings as they need them. The paddies have first been harrowed by young men guiding horses, often with hilarious
shouts. The people pulling up the seedlings are usually
older people, more experienced, as the job requires a little
more skill—one must not tear or break roots or tender
sprouts. The "tender" sprouts are often sharp enough to
cut a worker's hands, however. The line of workers doing
actual transplanting includes anybody and everybody—
the young girls and men, older men and women, servants
and house heads. The linemen are nearly always men, as
this job is considered to be a more technical one.

The work is very arduous; the back gets sore. It is either
drizzly rainy weather or the June sun beats down merci-
lessly, but there is compensation in the sociability, the
lively conversation, the jokes. The midmorning and afternoon meals of fifteen minutes each give a little rest. At
noon people go home for lunch and often take a short nap.
In the evening *shōchū* is served, but not too much. A real
party comes only when all work is finished.

In each *buraku* there are several houses on good terms
with one another, often related, usually of about the same
economic and social level. This group of houses co-operates
at rice-transplanting time. They agree to all work first

TRANSPLANTING RICE SEEDLINGS

TRANSPLANTERS EATING A MIDMORNING LUNCH

on one man's field, then all on the next man's, etc., until all fields have been transplanted. Each year the fields of a different member of the group are done first.

The principal of exchange is people and days. Thus, if household A has two people work on household B's field two days, household B is expected to produce its equivalent on A's fields—this may be three people one day and one person another day or any other combination to equal two people working two days. Sex is not involved. The workers from house B may be male or female, servants or members of B's family—just so long as the labor of household A is returned. A man with a horse counts as two workers. The person whose fields are being transplanted on a given day supplies food and *shōchū* for that day. The work of household A is called *kattari;* the return labor of household B, *kattari modoshi.*

When four or five families work together in one *kattari* group, the figuring is on the same basis. This requires a book to check days and workers. It also requires good faith among the members of the group; and for this reason, farmers say, *kattari* is practiced less today than formerly. Since money economy has come into the village and people have become more individualistic, working *kattari* is not so simple. If you deal with someone not a relative or close friend, he may try to skimp on the labor he contributes. Kakui, the business *buraku*, has the least *kattari* work of all. Kawaze, a rich *buraku* uses much contract labor (see below). But most of the upland and mountain *buraku* (e.g., Imamura, Oade, Hirayama) still practice *kattari.* Practically all these *buraku* are divided into four or five *kattari* groups each. *Kattari* groups remain constant year after year.

People with only a little land of their own hire themselves out at transplanting season. A person with a large area of fields often hires several people in addition to the *kattari* group. Thus, some worker during transplanting season will work one day for one man, another day for another. Both men and women, especially poorer people who have little land of their own, thus obtain temporary employment during transplanting season. Such work (*yatoi*) is paid daily in a fixed amount of rice. Very often this work is done as payment in exchange for some favor received earlier in the year from the man whose field is being transplanted. Then the work is not *yatoi* but a form of helping co-operation (*kasei*).

Relatives are most trusted and almost always help one another on a *kattari* basis at transplanting time, just as they do *kasei* at housebuilding or other work. Whereas *kattari* proper is practically always within the *buraku* consisting of neighborhood groups, relatives come from other *mura* to help, and the person helped goes back later to help his relatives.

It is also possible for a person to belong to more than one *kattari* group and, besides belonging to some small *kattari* group, to hire himself out to a contractor or private transplanter.

Thus a line of twenty or so workers in the paddy field may consist of two or three members of four or five families working *kattari*, plus two or three people hired on a daily basis (*yatoi*), plus two or three people helping in return for some past favor (*kasei*).

While *kattari* functions chiefly at transplanting time, some groups also exchange labor for transplanting sweet potatoes, weeding rice, and several other agricultural pursuits.

At the end of the transplanting period the *kattari* group

holds a party at the house of one of the members. All contribute ten or fifteen sen for *tōfu* and *shōchū*. To this party come both men and women, and there is much song and dance to celebrate the end of the hard work. Some special cakes (*ohagi*) are put at the *tokonoma* for the gods.

A modification of the *kattari* system is the *kokumiai* (branch agricultural association) co-operation developed in the paddy *buraku* of Nakashima. Everyone in the *buraku* works on the fields of one man one day, another man another day until all are finished. The first man is chosen by lot. If all his fields are not transplanted the first day, the untransplanted part is left until a second round. At the end of the period, about two weeks, a reckoning is made. Those houses with only a few fields received less aid than they gave and those with large fields, of course, received more help than they gave. The exact amount in days and people is figured out, then the people with large fields pay money to the *kokumiai*, and this is given to the owners of small fields. At the end of the time it takes to do the whole *buraku*'s fields a big drinking party is held. The system, only a few years old, was begun by one of the more educated men who had heard a lecture on the subject. This method of work insures that all work is done by *buraku* people, no money going out of the *buraku*. The keeping of money in the *buraku* and in the *mura* is a point much stressed in Suye.

There are other forms of obtaining labor at rice-transplanting. One of these is hiring temporary labor as already mentioned. Another rather recent method is through a contractor. A contractor, usually from town, comes to a landowner and says, "I will transplant your fields for so much per *tan*." Then he will hire labor himself for money and do the job. If weather is good, he makes a handsome

profit. It is worth noting that the landowner after transplanting holds a party for the contractor and any relatives
who helped, but does not include in this party the labor
hired by the contractor. (During work the laborers bring
their own food and are served only tea and pickles by
the landowner.) The contractor, as a specialist, is given
a place of honor at the party given by the landowner.

With the contract labor system two classes, capital and
labor, are created in *buraku* life. The implications of this
will be discussed later.

CO-OPERATIVE CREDIT CLUBS (*kō*)

One of the most widespread and important forms of economic co-operation is the co-operative credit club called
kō or *kake*. This appears to be a variety of similar credit
clubs existing in China.[12]

ECONOMIC *kō*

If a man is in need of money, due most often to debt
or sickness, he is likely to form a *kō* to raise the desired
sum. The man in need asks one or two of his friends to
help him by forming a *kō*. The amount of the *kō* is tenta-
tively decided upon. At the first general meeting all members pay the man in need a given amount. At this time
permanent *kō* heads (*kōchō*), usually the organizers of the
kō, are chosen and rules of running the *kō*, how often meet-

---

[12] *Kō* is defined in the dictionary as a club or association, but in Kuma it
usually has the more specific meaning of mutual aid club. Masajiro Takikawa
in his article on Japanese law in the *Encyclopedia of the Social Sciences* refers to
kō by the terms *mujin* and *tanomoshi*. As to the age of the institution in Japan,
he writes that "its origin can be traced back directly to the Kamakura period; a
document of 1275 from the monastery of Koyasan referring to *tanomoshi* is the
first recorded evidence of it." Accounts of a similar institution in China may be
found in Daniel H. Kulp, *Country Life in South China* (New York, 1925) and
H. T. Fei, *Peasant Life in China* (London, 1939).

ings are to be held, etc., are decided. Formerly *kō* were called *kake* in this region, and some still are. *Kōchō* were then called *kake nushidōri*.

Either money or rice may be used. I shall describe the working of a *kō* in money for the sake of clarity. If a man needs, say, 160 yen, then a group of, say, twenty friends can each contribute 8 yen toward the loan. This is repaid by him at the rate of 10 yen at stated intervals, in all twenty times. Thus, he pays 40 yen as interest on the loan. The *kō*, consisting of twenty lenders and the original borrower, meets as a rule twice a year thereafter in the eleventh and twelfth months by lunar calendar. At the meetings they each make a secret bid on a slip of paper. The man who bids lowest receives 10 yen from the original borrower and any other member who had already won, plus the amount he bid, say 4 yen, from each of the other members. People who have won cannot bid at future meetings and must pay 10 yen each time.

Usually people bid high at first, desiring not to win, and bid low toward the end. For example, in a *kō* of twenty-one members the bids might run as follows:

At the first meeting: everyone (twenty people) pays 8 yen to man in need—160 yen.

Second meeting: man who was in need pays 10 yen and others pay lowest sum bid, say 6 yen (19 × 6 + 10 = 124 yen to the winner).

. . . .

Sixth meeting: five men pay 10 yen each and others lowest sum bid, say 5 yen (15 × 5 + 50 = 125 yen to winner).

. . . .

Nineteenth meeting: eighteen men pay 10 yen and others lowest sum bid, say 1 yen (1 × 2 + 180 = 182 yen to winner).

Twentieth meeting: nineteen men pay 10 yen and others lowest sum bid, say 0 (1 × 0 + 190 = 190 yen to winner).

. . . .

Last meeting: twenty men pay 10 yen, and the other automatically wins 200 yen.

Toward the end bidding may often be zero or even minus. If minus, the winner pays each of other men who have not already won the amount of his minus bid. In *kō* using rice the bidding is high when rice is expensive and low when rice is cheap. There is also a lottery type of *kō* where one draws lots instead of bidding. In such *kō* one might, for instance, pay eight yen before winning and ten yen thereafter.

A large *kō* of forty or fifty members may last over twenty years. If a member dies during this period, his eldest son usually inherits the rights and duties of membership. A son-in-law or widow less often inherits. While the interest the original borrower pays is high, he never has to pay out any large sum at once.

The reason members of a *kō* meet in the eleventh and twelfth months by lunar calendar is that at this time the harvest is just finished and everyone has rice on hand. Furthermore, this is the slack season when the harvest is over, and the work of the new year has not yet begun.

Kō using money are called *kōgin* or *kanekō* (money *kō*). They are reckoned by the number of yen paid by members after they have won, e.g., ten-yen *kō*, five-yen *kō*. *Kō* using rice are called *komekō* or *komegake* (rice *kō*). If the rice is unhulled (*momi*), the *kō* is called *momigake*. They are reckoned by the number of *to*[13] of rice to be paid each time. Thus, when all members pay one *to* at each meeting after having won once, the *kō* is called "one-*to kō*" (*ittokō*).

A *kō* may be for as much as two hundred yen, or forty *to*, though this is rare in the Suye region; five or ten yen is more common. *Kō* using rice are more common than money *kō* in the *mura*. In towns the money *kō* are more common.

[13] One *to* equals 0.51 bushel.

MEASURING OUT RICE AT A RICE *KŌ*

CIVIC CO-OPERATION IN BRIDGE BUILDING (IMAMURA BURAKU)

Kō of the bidding type are called *rakusatsu;* of the lottery type, *fudakō,* which means paper-slip *kō,* since paper slips are drawn. The winning slip has a square hole cut in it. The winner usually pastes this on a post in his house as a memento.

The four basic types of *kō* are:

Rice (*komekō*)...............	Bidding (*rakusatsu*)	
	Lottery (*fudakō*)	
Money (*kōgin*).............	Bidding (*rakusatsu*)	
	Lottery (*fudakō*)	

The meeting takes place at the house of a man who won the bid or lottery at the previous meeting. He is paid when the members come to the meeting at his house. At a *kō* meeting the business of the day comes first. If a rice *kō,* rice is measured out under supervision of the *kō* heads and checked in a book; if a money *kō,* the money is paid in. Although at a rice *kō* payments are usually in rice, sometimes its equivalent is paid in money. In some *kō* the members meet always in one house, and, when this is done, the host does not have to pay anything toward the *kō.* After payments the bidding or drawing of lots takes place followed by food and drink. A *kō* party, like other parties, begins in the middle of the afternoon and is finished around seven or eight. As no one is more honorable than anyone else, seating arrangement is usually decided by lot.

People come to these meetings in informal *kimono.* The food served is not especially rich, but the drink is usually abundant. The host of the day is expected to supply *shōchū.* The host's daughter and maidservant or some neighbor's girl help to serve. As a rule, only men attend, though occasionally a widow may replace her husband.

The first and last meetings have special names. The first meeting (*hokki*) is taken up with making rules for running the *kō*, making up a record-book, and deciding how much the *kō* shall be for. At the last meeting (*man-ki*), however, there is no real business on hand except drinking and feeling sorry that the twenty years or so of the *kō* are finished. The man for whom it was begun may present the company with a gift, say some fish delicacy, to add to the usual feast. The heads check over the books for the last payments, and the *kō* is finished. At such a meeting there is likely to be more drinking than usual.

Kō members, while not restricted to one *buraku*, are usually all from within the *mura* or, if from another *mura*, they are from a *buraku* adjacent to Suye. If a member lives in some more distant *mura*, it is usually true that he lived in Suye when the *kō* began and has since moved. In the very expensive *kō* (50 or 100 yen), however, the situation is different. Only a few men in a *mura* can afford to belong, and consequently the members are from several neighboring *mura*. Schoolteachers are not members of *kō* as they are not permanent residents and are thus cut off from one of the stronger social ties of the *mura*.

It is possible for two people to have one membership. Sometimes, if a man decides to leave a *kō*, he may sell his membership, and thus it is possible for some men to have two memberships in the same *kō*.

The village brokers always join *kō* with an eye to the profits. They have various tricks to gain more than their due. For instance, if a man has not yet won but wants cash, the broker will offer to buy his membership for an immediate lump sum which is, however, less than the man would win in the *kō* if he waited. It is possible for a broker to buy a whole *kō*. This is managed by approaching members who have already won and offering to take over their obligations to the *kō* for a consideration. If he can manage to get big enough sums from these men and to give small enough ones to the others who have not yet won, he ends with a fat profit. In actual practice, however, a broker never succeeds in more than partially buying up a *kō*.

Occasionally, a *buraku* as a whole will have a membership in a *kō*. Some *buraku* belong to three or four. Money gained in this manner will be put in a *buraku* fund administered by the *buraku nushidōri* or it may be spent on some *buraku* undertaking. In such a case all *buraku* members, whether individually members of the *kō* or not, contribute their share, e.g., one twentieth of dues of a member if there are twenty people in the *buraku*. When the *buraku* wins, the individual members get nothing back as the whole sum goes into the *buraku* fund.

In selecting members for a *kō*, the leaders select men who can afford to join and whom they consider to be good and responsible people. However, after ten or fifteen years a once honest man may start defaulting on his obligations. He may sell out to a broker, or, worse, he may refuse to pay his dues after he has won. Most *kō* involving ten-yen payments or more require that a man put up some land as a mortgage. This is officially registered as a mortgage by the heads. Then, if the member defaults, his land is taken and sold, and the proceeds divided among the members who have not yet won. In the old days, a generation or so ago, such registration was never done in Suye.

There are three types of *kō:* (1) registered, (2) semiregistered, and (3) nonregistered.

1. *Registered.*—All large *kōgin* are registered, i.e., twenty-five yen and up. Often ten-yen *kō* are also registered. For this the original borrower registers some land or property, e.g., house (property must be insured) as surety for debt. A debt bond is made out to the head as creditor. All this is done at the registry office in Taragi town.

In case the debt is not paid, the debtor agrees to give

over some such surety as a house. Other members, when they have won, must also register indebtedness and surety, each time for fifty yen less than the previous man in case of a fifty-yen *kō*.

If a member dies or defaults and the head gets the property, he must divide it among members who have not yet won. If he tries to keep it, *kō* followers can take the case to court. This, however, never happens in Suye because *kō* heads are carefully chosen for their integrity.

Sometimes, however, someone can bribe a *kōchō*, register a poor piece of property as surety, pay a few times, and then default, leaving the *kō* with a loss. Sometimes when the price of rice is low the value of the surety is less (to money *kō*) than when it began; in such a case sometimes a person defaults to his profit and the *kō*'s loss. This procedure, regarded as unethical, has been followed by a broker, a Shinto priest, and a few others in the *mura*.

2. *Semiregistered.*—For *kō* of five to ten yen a surety is not put up, but guarantors are named. In this case no registration is made, but the arrangement is official to the extent of affixing stamps and making the document legal.

3. *Nonregistered.*—Small *kō* up to five yen are usually not registered at all. Of course, records are kept by *kō* members of payments, membership, and winnings, but all this is done quite privately. These same private records are also kept by the registered *kō*.

There is one form of *kō*, the temple (*tera*) *kō*, which is more of a county than a *mura* affair. It is formed ostensibly to repair some temple or to buy some new thing for it such as a bell. The meetings are held at the temple usually once or twice a month. Payments vary from two to seven yen, and membership is from five hundred to a thousand. At the first meeting or two no one wins. Then, when a large capital is accumulated, a bidding meeting may alternate with a lottery meeting, individual members receiving as much as three thousand yen. If at a bidding meeting bids are low, several people win. The winner each time is expected to donate fifty or sixty yen to the temple, thus justifying the title "temple *kō*." In such a large *kō* the managing committee is very important, and all the complications involved open the path to graft on the part of the *kō* heads. One way to obtain graft is thus: Each month people pay dues which go into a fund, then every three months a number is called and it wins a large number of yen, but not so much as has been collected by the managers. The managers pocket the difference. As a result temple *kō* often get into trouble with the law. Several Suye people belong to such *kō* in Hitoyoshi.

In cities such as Kumamoto regular *kō* companies exist. They have complicated rules, and there are governmental laws concerning them.

A somewhat different type of economic *kō* from those described above is the now extinct one for house- and roof-fixing. It was mainly a *buraku* affair. Members gave certain materials agreed upon and a day of labor any time a member needed a new barn, or roof, or some extensive repair to a building. In one round of twenty years or so a man could call for aid but once. When doing so, he informed the *kake nushidōri*, who in turn informed other members. A book was kept by the *nushidōri*, and a circle put by the name of each member as he made use of the *kake*. Often several years would elapse before some member would require aid.

If such a *kō* were purely for roof-fixing, it was called *kaya kake*. All members would help another member to build a new roof, and each would contribute as much *kaya* straw as could be encompassed by a given length of rope. The *kake* was called a one-*jō* or two-*jō kake* according to the length of the rope. Sometimes wheat or rice straw was used instead of *kaya*.

There is today a *minnagake* by which all members of a *buraku* help one another to build. This differs from the *kaya kake* type in that the members do not supply any materials. These house and roof *kō* appear to have been chiefly a means of keeping a record of housebuilding and roof-building labor exchange to see that no one gave more than he received and vice versa. In these and other economic *kō* only one member of a household, the head, belongs.

It is easy to see the important part *kō* play in the economy of the *mura*. There is almost no one who does not belong to some *kō*. Most middle- and upper-class farmers belong to several; a rich man may belong to as many as twenty, while a poor farmer belongs to only two or three. One of the first things done at harvest time is to put aside the rice needed for *kō* to which the house belongs. The more well-to-do men join a *kō* to get rid of debt or to buy up land, while poorer people may have a *kō* begun to defray some unexpected expense, such as sickness or a funeral. This is the traditional purpose of a *kō*— to meet unexpected expense.

Some rich men join a *kō* rather as insurance against a rainy day than because of any immediate need of cash. Such richer men receive the most profit from a *kō*. They can afford to wait until the last meetings before winning, thus paying in least and taking out most. From this results a situation whereby the more substantial members of the community act as bankers to their less substantial neighbors.

Most farmers have debts amounting to a hundred yen or more. There is nothing dishonorable in a debt as such. But to have a *kō* debt and be unable to pay it is very dishonorable indeed. So much so in fact that one man who was in that predicament hanged himself and another sold two of his daughters into prostitution. In the latter case the *kō* members had agreed to accept a somewhat reduced payment after the sale of the first daughter and were distinctly annoyed when, with the balance of his money from the sale of the second girl, the man began to make repairs on his house.

More money is tied up in *kō* than in banks, village credit association, and postal savings put together (see Appen. I). Money *kō* did not exist in the old days. With them has come an increasing interest in *kō* as a speculation for profit rather than as aid to some neighbor in need.

OTHER TYPES OF *kō*

In addition to these primarily economic *kō*, there are many varieties, some for minor economic purposes, many for purely social purposes. All these more sociable *kō* are of the lottery type and are unregistered. As in other *kō*, the drawer of the lucky *fuda* or paper slip has the next meeting at his house at which time he is paid and at which time he furnishes the *shōchū*. A *kō* of twenty-five members may drink eight *shō* at one meeting. Each member gives ten or fifteen sen for food, usually *tōfu*. Membership usually runs to around fifteen or twenty people.

One common type of *kō* is the *kasa kake* or umbrella *kō*. Umbrellas are of oiled paper and are much used. If caught in the rain, a man steps into the nearest house to borrow one; so a good supply of umbrellas at all times is necessary. Even in going out to weed or carrying pails of fertilizer to the fields on a rainy day one carries an umbrella. *Kasa kake* are begun by umbrella dealers in Menda and are usually *buraku* or part *buraku* affairs. They meet monthly, each person giving fifty sen to the dealer, or bimonthly, each man then giving one yen. The winner of the lucky slip has the privilege of receiving four or five umbrellas or sunshades from the dealers. Similar to the umbrella *kō* is the shoe *kō* in which winning members are expected to buy shoes with their winnings.

In the livestock *kō* (*chikusan kō*) the winner is supposed to buy new livestock or trade in old animals for better, but actually the *kō* is more for sociability. Members pay two yen or, if they have won before, two yen and forty sen. The forty sen is called "interest." Only more well-to-do farmers have livestock, so to form a *kō* it is necessary to include several *buraku*. It meets three or four times a year.

There are *kō* of a purely social type, quite unrelated to financial gain. The most important of these is the *dōnen kō* or *kō* made up of men of the same age. This group meets four times a year, usually in the second, sixth, ninth, and twelfth months by the lunar calendar. Young men form a *dōnen kō* shortly after returning from the barracks at the age of twenty-two or twenty-three. As men grow older, they frequently amalgamate two or three different ages, e.g., sixty, sixty-one, and sixty-two years. Dues are two yen a meeting and two yen twenty sen for those who have already won. The chief point of a *dōnen kō* meeting is for men of the same age to get together for a happy drinking party. Occasionally, a *dōnen kō* is made up of classmates rather than men of the same age (which is almost the same thing).

If the son of the house is host to a *dōnen* group, the

parents remain out of sight. If a member dies, all the other members attend the funeral if it is a young man, or pay a call of condolence if it is an older man. They also come to the *chanomi* party after the wedding of a member.

Wagon, or *basha*, *kō* are social *kō*, membership being restricted to wagon-drivers. It meets once a month, the members paying one yen and fifteen sen interest for winners.

There are many people in Suye who come from the mountain *mura* of Itsuki either to work as servants or to form branch families, or to be adopted as sons and husbands. Some of these people have formed a social *kō* among themselves called Itsuki *kō*. It was supposedly begun to aid an Itsuki man and is for two yen. There is only one such *kō* in Suye.

There is a sericulture *kō* (*yōsan kō*) with seventeen members. The dues are three yen, and winners pay seventy sen interest. The meetings are held three times a year— once after each silkworm season. It was begun by a man who had three silkworm-crop failures in a row. There is only one such *kō* in Suye.

Corresponding to the *dōnen kō* are the women's *kō*, also primarily sociability clubs for singing, dancing, and drinking. Being of the same age is not important because there are not enough native women of the same age to form a *kō*. Girls of the same age group marry out into different regions, and women who come in as brides do not necessarily form their friendships within the age group. Occasionally, a small group of women married within the *mura* will meet for a *dōnen* drinking party, but no special *kō* is run. The women's *kō* are of the lottery type; dues vary from fifty sen to three yen depending on the group. For those who have won there is a ten- or twenty-sen interest. Fifteen or twenty sen are contributed for food; *shōchū* is partly contributed by the hostess, partly brought by the members. It is worth noting that a man, usually the husband of the hostess of the day, is at the meeting. He keeps the books and is seated in the place of honor; meetings are four or five times a year.

Sometimes a women's *kō* is called a bedding (*futon*) *kō*. In this case the winner is expected to use the money to buy new bedding materials.

A variety of the women's *kō* (ostensibly a religious society) is the Kwannon *kō*, a social gathering of women at the Zen temple in Suye which also houses an image of Kwannon. Each member brings a measure of rice and twenty sen in return for which the temple furnishes *shōchū* and food. The priest gives a talk and collects money offered to Kwannon. It meets on New Year's Day and once during the summer.

Some *buraku* meet twice a year, in the first and ninth months by lunar calendar, to hold an Ise *kō*, another semi-religious group. This has been described under *kumi* (see p. 117). It is the only *kō* where *kumi* are involved and is strictly a *buraku* affair.

In the small purely social *kō* for one or two yen there are no regular heads, and no permanent books are kept. There is simply a check of names at each meeting to see that everyone gives his one or two yen as the case may be.

Kō meetings occur with seasonal frequency. The economic *kō* are all bunched in the two or three months after the rice harvest. *Dōnen kō* usually meet three to five times a year—in periods when farm work is not so urgent: (1) around New Year's time; (2) spring Higan (equinoctial) holidays; (3) July, after transplanting and weeding are finished; (4) autumn Higan; and (5) just after harvest. Favorite times of meeting of women's *kō*, as one woman described it, are: the third month—flowers are in bloom, a good time to drink *shōchū* and look at flowers from inside the house; the sixth month—rice-transplanting is just finished, so people take a rest; the twelfth month—to celebrate the end of the year. Such a meeting is termed *shiwase* (end-of-year party) *kō*.

Kō, such as umbrella or wagon-drivers', that meet monthly skip the very busy months such as June when transplanting is going on.

CLASSIFICATION OF *KŌ*

I. Social and economic varieties of *kō*

  A. Primarily economic
    Rice
    Money
    House
    Roof

  B. Partly economic, partly social
    Livestock
    Umbrella
    Bedding
    Shoe
    Silk

  C. Purely social
    Same age
    Same region
    Women's

  D. Partly social, partly religious
    Kwannon
    Ise
    Tera

II. Territorial varieties of *kō*

  A. *Buraku*
    Umbrella
    Shoe
    Ise
    House
    Roof

  B. *Mura*
    Kwannon
    Livestock
    Same age
    Itsuki
    Women's
    Rice
    Money

  C. County
    Tera
    Big money and rice

The many forms of co-operation—*kumi*, *kō*, *kattari*, civic, labor, and aid in time of emergency or death—all serve as integrating forces, especially in *buraku* and *mura*, and sometimes among relatives. On the whole, co-operation is a function of the local group, either *buraku* or *kumi*, as distinct from the extended family group. As already pointed out, the relative group gathers at various times such as at a funeral or a wedding. But as a rule the local group does the co-operative work—preparing for the funeral or for the wedding—while the relative group merely gathers together for the important event, to mourn or to celebrate.

A *buraku* comes together most quickly and strongly in an emergency such as a funeral; for housebuilding it is also brought together. These forms of co-operation may all be regarded as *buraku* integrative forces. Furthermore, these events bring relatives together and so may be considered as integrative forces bringing together the extended family. Bridge-fixing or other civic enterprise is a *buraku* integrative force but in no way affects the family as does the crisis of death or the lesser one of building a new house. *Kattari* (exchange labor) does not affect the *buraku* as a whole but serves to strengthen the bonds between members of a neighborhood group of four or five houses. Sometimes relatives also help in rice-transplanting. *Kumi*, while indirectly affecting the whole *buraku*, actively affect only the three or four families of each *kumi* who work together each time their turn comes around.

A tie that brings together men of several *buraku* is the *kō*. Unlike the other co-operative forms, *kō* membership is also connected with social classes. These groupings are discussed in the next chapter.

The effects of a money economy coming into the *mura* are seen in the increasing use of the contractor system in transplanting and in the breakdown of *kumi* and *kattari* in the business *buraku* of Kakui. The *kokumiai* system of transplanting in Nakashima is one of many ways in which the agricultural association is replacing older *buraku* structures.

EXCHANGE

In small peasant communities one very important method of maintaining social relationships is through gift exchange. A gift carries with it an obligation of a return of equal value and frequently involves a return visit. Most gift exchange between relatives occurs at a time of festival when a man is free to visit his kin; and so festivals serve as an occasion for renewing and strengthening family ties. The crises of life, such as birth, marriage, and death, all involving as they do an exchange of gifts, also serve to unite the family.

Connected with all the co-operative systems except the civic type is the obligation of a return of value for value. This is most clearly seen in exchange labor (*kattari*) but also appears in the other forms. *Kumi* members on duty at *dō* celebrations keep coppers contributed for tea, house-builders expect the man they help to help them later and are given food and drink for the present work, and the same applies to emergency and funeral aid. The only type of co-operation where this principle does not operate is in the civic co-operation of road- and bridge-fixing, and that is simply because there is no possible way of any return being given as each is helping the other simultaneously in performing the common task.

Besides the exchange of labor and goods involved in the helping forms of co-operation, there are many other strict forms of gift exchange in the community. What Professor Malinowski terms the principle of reciprocity is very marked. (However, most of the exchange systems are of a purely practical nature, and even in cases of ceremonial gift exchange no magical or supernatural sanctions are involved.) The most elaborate and formal manifestation of this principle is at marriage, where a long and involved series of exchanges of foods and goods takes place between the family of the groom and that of the bride. Helpers at funerals or housebuilding, besides the eventual return of labor, expect to be fed and given rice wine. People, when invited to naming ceremonies or any other kind of party, always bring a standard gift of rice and wine in exchange for the food and drink they will consume at the banquet.

Rice is the most common gift and is taken to all *kō* and *kumi* gatherings, to memorial services, to funerals, to all *buraku* parties—to all affairs when food is expected. It can be taken to a naming ceremony (in addition to the standard gift of cloth for baby *kimono*) or at Bon, or calling at New Year's, although usually on these two latter occasions *mochi* or cakes are taken. When calling on a sick person, one never takes rice, however, but rather some such edible as eggs, cakes, vegetables, or fruit. As soon as the person dies, these foods can no longer be taken, and rice is in order. Occasionally, an embarrassing situation arises when a woman starts out to call on some gravely sick person with a dozen eggs and discovers upon approaching the house that the person has just died.

Every gift must be acknowledged by a return gift. If it is a party or a memorial service where food is served, the uneaten food is taken home. Before the end of the party each guest asks for his box and proceeds to remove carefully all food from the tray into his box.

If it is a private call—to see a sick person, to discuss some business, or just a call on a friend to take over some fresh tomatoes or eggplants that have ripened—one gets a return called *outsuri*. A box must never be returned empty to a caller. If there are any new vegetables in the house or if eggs are kept, these will be put into the box. If not, a few *mochi* or wheat cakes will do—should this be just after a holiday when cakes are made. Two candles or a box of matches are acceptable return gifts. If there is absolutely nothing to give, or if this is an occasion when many callers come at once (as during sickness or during roof-fixing when *tōfu* is brought by all *buraku* neighbors), then two pieces of white paper (special return paper, *outsurigami*) are put into the box.

Usually after receiving a gift, one goes calling a few days later with an *orei*—a gratitude gift. This gift will depend on the *outsuri* one gave for the original gift. If that was very small, the *orei* gift must be good; if the *outsuri* was good, the *orei* gift does not have to be much of anything or might even be omitted. An *orei* gift is not taken if the original gift was brought as a payment for some favor, nor is it taken if a gift had been sent to one's house. In this case one merely takes the box back with *outsuri* in it.

SUMMARY OF FORMAL EXCHANGES

1. Labor
   Kattari–labor for labor
   Tetsudai (or *kasei*)—labor for some previous favor or labor to be later paid for with some gift (*orei*), as when a girl helps at a banquet
2. Money
   Regular *kō*—financial aid; interest on loan in return
   Farewell gift (*sembetsu*)—gift from place visited in return
3. Rice brought in *jūbako* to:
   a) Social *kō*, Goshoki *kuyō*, etc.; no return other than *shōchū* consumed at meeting
   b) Introductory (face-showing) party (*mishiri*), farewell party (*wakare*); banquet in return

    c) Funeral; *shōchū* and food in return. (Relatives who bring *shōchū* and banners and money receive in return more food than *buraku* helpers.)

4. Rice and *shōchū* brought to:
    a) Memorial service; *shōchū*, food, and cake in return
    b) Naming ceremony; *shōchū*, food, and cake in return
    c) *Chanomi* (after wedding); *shōchū*, food, and cake in return

5. Friendly call with a gift (*miyage*)—fresh cakes or some vegetable or fruit in season; anything in the house or two sheets of paper (*outsurigami*) in return

6. Gratitude gift for *miyage* (*orei*)—anything better than gift received and much better if return (*outsuri*) given at the time was small; paper in return

7. Gift taken as return for past favor or gift (*orei*)—rice or any other food; small *outsuri*, usually paper, in return

8. Calling on a sick person (*mimai*)—any edible except rice or *shōchū*; some food in the house or *outsuri* paper in return

9. Roof-fixing or housebuilding gift (*cha*)—two squares of *tōfu*, or tea, or some edible; paper in return

10. Drink exchanges (*sakazuki*)

11. Speech exchanges

Besides these common exchanges there is a special series involved at weddings between the two families concerned and between the go-between and the families. Also, in return for advice, a go-between for selling a horse or other property receives a gift from both parties to the deal in exchange for his troubles.

People are very exacting about these exchanges. A *buraku* will come to the aid of a family whose child has drowned but later will complain to one another that the family was not at all generous with the wine it furnished to helpers. Several neighboring women will give help in the kitchen at a wedding banquet and then belittle the gift which they receive later and say how small-minded the family is.

It is a system which on the surface appears easygoing and indefinite enough, but any helper is quick to resent too small a return for his "voluntary" aid. It is partly because of this that formerly on funeral and other occasions families in an effort to give a large and impressive ceremony and banquet often went seriously into debt. Today, for funerals, each *buraku* has a *bancho* on which is written the exact amount of food and drink a family is expected to give helpers.

When a man becomes so poor as to be unable to make adequate return for aid he receives, he usually does one of two things: (1) sells a daughter into prostitution or (2) leaves the *mura* and goes to work in the mines. In selling his daughter, a man seldom cures his ills and frequently leaves later for the mines anyway.

The system of exchanges tends to become more rigid and less personal in the business *buraku*. Money frequently replaces rice and goods among village officials and shopkeepers. Whereas, formerly on the festival of Bon, held in memory of all the dead, all members of a *buraku* called on each family who had suffered a loss during that year with gifts of cake and lanterns, today many *buraku* have a new custom whereby each member contributes ten sen and one representative calls to present the money to the afflicted families. Rich landowners are beginning to use contract labor at rice-transplanting. Shopkeepers also tend to hire people directly and pay cash for goods or labor received, thus dispensing with the troubles and incidentally the social relationships involved in conventional exchange obligations. The most extreme case of this is a man who runs a pear orchard for money. He never associates with his *buraku*. When he built a new house recently, it was with cash-paid labor; and the *buraku* neighbors say that, if a death occurs in his house, he will have to hire helpers to come in. Such cases are still exceptional in the *mura*, however, as most people observe the older customs of co-operation and exchange.

CHAPTER V

SOCIAL CLASSES AND ASSOCIATIONS

SOCIAL CLASSES

BEFORE Meiji there were the fixed and rigid class lines of feudal lord, *samurai*, farmer, artisan, and merchant. In Suye Mura this meant a large level class of farmers in most of the *buraku* with a few artisans and one or more *samurai*. In addition to the *samurai*, it seems there were also a certain number of foot soldiers (*ashigaru*) located in Nakashima. Some of the upper-class farmers today are descendants of these *ashigaru*.

Today class lines are not so arbitrary, nor are they so easily defined. New class groupings, based on wealth, and "old" native families have grown up. Occupation is still a factor inasmuch as being a landed farmer is considered to be good socially as well as economically. Certain new occupational classes such as village officials and schoolteachers have also grown up, who tend to speak condescendingly of the farmers.

As seen today, the inhabitants of Suye Mura fall into a wide range of social classes though not so wide and varied as in the towns. It is convenient to divide them into six groups, though, of course, it is realized that such sorting is to a degree arbitrary. The class nomenclature I have employed is that of Professor Lloyd Warner.

1. *The upper upper.*—This class includes not more than three people in any one *buraku*. There is no select social function to which they are not invited. They are given seats of honor at school affairs and as guests in anyone's

house. The village headman and village schoolmaster are included in this group. All members are old families, natives of the *mura*. They are all landed farmers except one. He is the son of a *samurai* and rather poor, but, because of his ancestry, he belongs in this group without question. A majority of the twelve village councilors belongs to this class. These households grow silk, employ up to three servants, and keep livestock, usually two or more horses. Members of this group are leaders in *mura* affairs as well as leaders in their own *buraku*.

The children of upper-upper parents are usually sent to high schools outside the *mura*, and the few families from which men have gone to college from Suye are all of this class.

While the upper upper is at the top in the *mura*, it is about upper middle in the near-by towns. People of this class have social status in the towns for any one or more of four reasons: (*a*) as parents of children in the agricultural school for boys or the girls' high school; (*b*) as members of the Taragi co-operative hospital; (*c*) as rich men with economic interests in the town; and (*d*) through relatives which they may have there.

2. *The lower upper.*—This class includes as many as five or six in such rich *buraku* as Kawaze. Members of this class are not always included at select social functions or necessarily given the seat of honor at school functions but are always welcomed at them. It includes lesser officials such as *kuchō* and some village councilors. Members are all landed farmers. It includes people who are leaders in their *buraku* but not of the *mura* as a whole. Sometimes they send children to higher schools. Silk is grown by members of this class. They employ up to two servants and have livestock—one or two cattle and a horse.

3. *The upper middle.*—This class includes some of the more well-to-do shopkeepers, though through their occupation they are often included among the upper groups; this is especially true of the schoolmaster. Some *kuchō* are of this class, but no village councilors, as they are all in the two upper classes. Schoolteachers come from this class. Wives of the members grow silk or have a trade. Small landowners belonging to this class also often tenant some land. If they need a servant, they employ one.

4. *The lower middle.*—The small shopkeepers and *tōfu*-makers belong to this class. The farmers in this class are less well to do but do grow silk (except in mountain *buraku*). It includes farmers who are both landowners and tenants. No servants are employed. Children sometimes work out as servants.

5. *The upper lower.*—People of this class are included in *buraku* co-operative affairs but are not included in lesser social affairs, such as women's *kō*. They are not members of either big silk *kumiai*. Children often work out as servants. They own little or no land. They are often not native.

6. *The lower lower.*—Members of this class are not included in any *buraku* affairs. They often work out at odd jobs. Children often work out as servants. They own no land and are not natives of Suye.

The class groups are closely related with economic groups. Only one upper upper is not rich, but, because the son of a *samurai*, he still rates highly in the *mura* on formal occasions though in daily life he lives more like his middle-class neighbors in Kakui. Formerly he was very rich but wasted away his fortune. As he has no son of his own, it is possible that the man who is adopted to marry his granddaughter will not be included in the upper-upper group. The lower groups are invariably poor.

The upper groups are old native families, and the lower groups are nonnatives. It is the stable upper groups who form the ruling class of the *mura*. From them come the headmen and village councilors.

Shopkeepers and brokers tend to fall in the middle classes and to come from other *mura*. (Middle-class farmers are usually native.) In the near-by towns, on the other hand, the shopkeepers are often natives. Shopkeepers are a more mobile group than farmers; they are not strongly attached to the soil. It is notable that all men from Suye who became schoolteachers are from the middle shopkeeper classes.

There is never any question by lower groups of the superior position of the upper upper in the *mura*.

Shopkeepers are not regarded as highly as rich landed farmers of old families. This is partly because of their trade and partly because most of them were born outside the *mura*. That farming is considered a higher occupation than shopkeeping is illustrated by the fact that the brother-in-law of the *shōchū*-factory owner, whose exclusive occupation is running the shop, refers to himself officially as a farmer because his in-laws are farmers.

Marriage is arranged within the social groups, i.e., upper groups taking brides from upper families, middle groups from middle families, etc. There is, however, a slight tendency for girls to marry up. If a girl is a good worker, she is likely to be chosen by a family socially higher than her own.

Adoption follows the same general rule. Brothers occasionally belong to two different classes because one of them was adopted into a better family. A younger brother who forms a branch family, on the other hand, is usually one class below that of the firstborn son.

Besides these horizontal class stratifications of the society, none of them very sharp, there are occupational class groupings.

A landed farmer, as already indicated, is in the upper-upper level. Even a poor and landless farmer is superior to a poor nonfarmer. Shopkeepers, what few there are, tend to identify themselves with farmers socially though economically attempting to become independent of agriculture. No broker openly gives his occupation as a broker; he is always a "farmer." But these *petits bourgeois* in embryo have many distinguishing traits. They use money instead of rice in their dealings; they do not co-operate so well; they do not observe the local customs of making special foods on local holidays; and they frequently speak in a superior, condescending manner of some rustic. Shopkeepers and brokers tend to obtain wives from the towns. Their sons often become schoolteachers, and, in turn, retired schoolteachers frequently open a small shop. Further, as they are to an extent independent of their neighbors, they are not subject to the sanctions of non-co-operation which may be used against an ordinary farmer who does not do his share of community work.

A separate occupational class is that of the schoolteachers. These men, like the shopkeepers, are not natives. But, whereas the shopkeepers stay indefinitely in the *buraku* and are dependent on it for a living, the schoolteacher is seldom in a *mura* more than five years. They are appointed by the prefecture and so are independent of the *mura*. Some are married, some single. Only three of the ten are women. They are busy all day at school teaching what the department of education bids them teach. Most of them know little of, and care less for, local customs. Their recreations and associations are mostly among themselves, and they meet with farmers socially only at drinking parties a few times a year. Being constantly changed from place to place by the government, their loyalties are chiefly to Japan as a nation rather than to any particular region.

Teachers' wives are still more isolated from farmers' wives than are teachers from farmers. These women are mostly graduates of high schools and come from the towns. They neither drink nor smoke in contrast to farmers' wives, who do both constantly. With their superior education and social refinement they have little in common with a farming woman. The peasant woman considers the average teacher's wife a snob; the teacher's wife considers the average farmer's wife a crude and uncouth, if kind-hearted, rustic.

A widow possesses a peculiar social status. Her husband having died, she no longer really possesses his status so that, unless and until she remarries, her exact social position is rather uncertain. Since she is no longer a young unmarried woman, she may be free concerning sex matters, and, owing to her peculiar position, she is the constant subject of jokes and is herself on a joking relationship with the people, especially the men, of her neighborhood. Any widow is considered to be more or less easy of access for the consideration of some small gift. In this village not many men can afford a real mistress or many trips to the *geisha* of Menda. The local widow of a *buraku* is one solution of this problem.[1]

ASSOCIATIONS

An association group is a group of people united by some common interest. Among the most important associations in Suye are those formed by the same-age (*dōnen*)

---

[1] Among the upper classes of Japan, before the Meiji era, a widow was supposed never to remarry and to be always faithful to her dead husband, that she might join him in afterlife. This strict rule, like much of the *samurai* moral code, did not apply to the peasant.

groups. Usually such a group of men forms a small *kō* as already described. The various economic *kō* also constitute important association groups. Richer men join expensive *kō*, while a group based more on friendship forms a less expensive one.

Temple membership in itself is scarcely an association as nearly the whole *mura* is Shinshū. If an out-of-*mura* lecturer comes to the Zen temple in Suye, both Shinshū and Zen followers attend his lectures.

The women all belong to one of two Buddhist women's societies, based on membership in either the Zen or the Shinshū temple. At least one woman belongs to both groups. A Buddhist women's society meets twice a year at the temple, makes some contribution to it, listens to a lecture by the priest, and then has a drinking party. Occasionally, money is sent to a main temple in Kyoto. When one of the members dies, a delegate of the group calls on the family of the deceased with a gift. This is comparable to the same custom among *dōnen* groups.

Associations based more solidly on common interests are the women's *kō*. The ten or twelve women who form a sociability *kō* are mostly of the same *buraku*—all farmers' wives and of the same social class. The group is a very friendly one.

A group of older men from several different *buraku* have formed an archery club which meets every week or so in slack working seasons. Under large trees or by some clear natural spring they shoot their arrows and drink *shōchū* for many hours. As in sociability *kō*, everyone contributes ten sen or so for food, and members take turns as host to supply the *shōchū*. If a member dies, the club members attend his funeral. Only more well-to-do men belong to this club, and not many of them are farmers. Like the

MEETING OF HEADS OF VILLAGE AGRICULTURAL
ASSOCIATIONS OF KUMA COUNTY

THE WOMEN'S PATRIOTIC SOCIETY

These women of Yunoharu Buraku are dressed in the aprons of the Women's
Patriotic Society on the occasion of the annual military review (*tenko*).

fencing and wrestling (*judō*) taught at the school, archery is regarded as a form of mental discipline.

A flower-arrangement class meets at the school every week under the guidance of a flower-arrangement teacher who comes from Hitoyoshi by bus. Only schoolteachers' wives and one village official's wife belong. It is a very gossipy group, but very little of the gossip deals with the local women. Schoolteachers and common acquaintances in neighboring towns are discussed. Of local customs they speak as of curious events, and women's drinking parties are mentioned with a smile. One of the rich farmer's daughters with a high-school education started attending the class, but "became too busy" and dropped out. Actually she felt very shy and out of place. The *mura* women are all a bit scornful of the flower class, and their remarks make it hard for any woman not strictly of the teachers' group to join.

On Sundays a music club meets. The teacher comes from Hitoyoshi. The group meets at the house of one of the members to play and receive lessons in playing the classical Japanese instruments of *koto*, *samisen*, and *shakuhachi*. The group consists of two men and six or seven women, including young girls. One of the men is a schoolteacher, and one the sole college-educated man in Suye. The women are mostly sisters or cousins of this college-educated man and daughters of richer farmers. The membership is all lower-upper or upper-upper class. Twice a year they give a free concert at school in conjunction with some players from Hitoyoshi. This serves to spread "culture" in the *mura* and incidentally to create good will for the *shōchū* manufactured by one of the players.

Practically all farmers' daughters learn to play the

samisen, but they either learn from some older woman in the *mura* or from a blind player from a neighboring *mura*. This player comes to Suye for a week or ten days a month. A group of girls pay a little money each and take lessons together. All of them stay in the same house for several days in succession, devoting all their time to playing. They rotate, moving from house to house, for lessons. The teacher gets her food and a bit of money out of it.

Recently some of the upper-class young men have formed a horse-riding club.

Such clubs as those described are mostly new in the *mura* and are similar to many music, riding, and other clubs to be found in towns and cities. It is notable that only the upper groups and schoolteacher groups—groups which have had many contacts with town life—are members of these clubs. In two cases (flower arrangement and music) a teacher comes in from the county capital of Hitoyoshi as instructor to the group. These clubs are an evidence of new inter-*buraku* class groupings growing up and replacing the older geographical groupings in the *mura*.

In addition to these authentic associations, there are several government- and school-sponsored "societies."

1. *Reservists' Association.*—All men who have been to the barracks are automatically members of the Reservists' Association on their return. This association turns out in force to welcome returned soldiers from the barracks, meets once a year at the *mura* shrine for the memorial service for dead soldiers and, most important of all, functions at the annual reservists' examination (*tenko*) by army officers from Kumamoto barracks. Frequently they assist at big school affairs by putting on, for instance, a mimic battle at the annual athletic meet. A man retires from this association at the age of forty. It has a *mura*

head and *buraku* subheads. The *mura* association is a branch of a national organization.

2. *Women's Patriotic Association.*—All women of the *mura* nominally belong to the Women's Patriotic Association. This is also a government-sponsored organization with a *mura* head and *buraku* subheads. It welcomes men upon their return from the barracks or the army. The women serve food at the annual reservists' meetings, at the firemen's competition meetings, and at any other village affairs when high officials from towns are present. Recently it has been ruled that all women on such occasions should wear a white apron and shoulder band with the name of the association written on it. (Large towns have been doing this for a long time.) Once in a while *buraku* divisions of the association meet, contribute money, and prepare consolation bags (*imombukuro*) which they send to soldiers in Manchukuo. They actually give them to the village office, which sends them to the prefectural office in Kumamoto, whence they go to Manchukuo. They send similar bags to afflicted regions of Japan in case of some big calamity, such as an earthquake or fire. When certain parts of the *mura* suffer from floods, the women's association of each *buraku* gathers to prepare food which is sent to unfortunate *buraku*. Now and again the women are summoned to school where a talk is given by some visiting lecturer or a local schoolteacher on the duties of the Women's Patriotic Association. In most of the activities listed, however, it is difficult to distinguish between the woman as a member of her *buraku* and the woman as member of the Women's Patriotic Association.

The men's societies, such as the Reservists' Association, while originating from outside, are at least actively functioning groups after they have begun, but to try to unite *mura* women into an active group showing initiative and uplift spirit in civic affairs is rather a hopeless job. At the head of each is a man, either the priest (in the older Buddhist society) or the schoolmaster (in the newer Patriotic Society). Both have nominal women subheads, but, not used to leading, women are very reluctant to accept the nomination. They never meet on their own initiative, but only when told to do so by the school or the village office. Even when such matters as improving kitchens or economizing on food or preparing pickles in some special way are discussed by the schoolmaster, women listen passively, never raising any questions, and then go home and soon forget about it. (In some progressive *mura* much influenced by the government economic reconstruction movement, men have taken matters in their hands and have actually made women co-operate in various moves of economy and in improving the kitchens for their own benefit). Meetings of the association are characterized by one of the men schoolteachers getting up and leading the meeting through a long program he has made out ahead of time. After a lecture he says "we resolve" and lo, the whole program is resolved without a murmur. The schoolteacher is earnest in his efforts to make the patriotic society exist in more than name.

3. *Young People's Association.*—Young men and young women after graduation from grammar school form a Young People's Association (*seinendan* for men, *shojokai* for girls) which meets occasionally at school. The young men learn drill; the young ladies, sewing and cooking with a bit of accounting and physiology thrown in. They are expected to turn out in uniforms on all big school occasions. The boys' uniform consists of dull khaki leggings, pants, and jacket; the girls of a plain gray smock which is worn

over the *kimono*. These young people's societies have each
a *mura* head and *buraku* subheads and are branches of a
national organization. The difference between *seinendan*
and *seinen-gakkō*[2] is purely technical. Twice a year the
young people have a less formal meeting, rather a party
where boys and girls mix. They buy refreshments with
their pocket money, sit around, giggle, and flirt mildly.
Each age group holds the party separately. Older girls of
marriageable age do not come to these parties because they
feel too bashful.

4. *Firemen's Association.*—Most *buraku* have a firemen's
association and a fire pump run by hand. One man between twenty-five and forty from each house is a member.
Their duty is to extinguish fires and to help in time of flood
or crime. They are united into a village organization and,
when on duty, all wear special caps and coats. They are
organized into *buraku* groups each with its own head, and
these groups in turn are organized into a village division
with head, vice-head, and treasurer, quite unlike the native
kumi system, which has no chiefs. The village organizations are united into a national one, headed by some prince
as honorary president. This official organization of firemen is a new thing. Formerly the young men from twenty-
five to forty of the *mura* were all volunteer firemen, and
there was no separate firemen's organization. Mountain
buraku like Hirayama still do without official "firemen." In
case of a fire there, everyone turns out to extinguish it.

All these societies, introduced from the outside, are
much in evidence at school ceremonies such as Meiji Day,
reservists' examination, school graduation days, and athletic meets. They are all characterized by having a *mura*
head and *buraku* subhead, whereas any merely local asso-

[2] See p. 65.

ciation is notable for its lack of any such hierarchical organization. All are branches of national organizations. The village headman is honorary head of most of these organizations, and, like the agricultural association, they tend to unify the *mura* at the expense of the *buraku*. In daily life and informal associations the societies as such play practically no part at all. These national organizations cover all social classes and all occupational classes. In fact, their only possible common ground is nationalism —and there lies the key to their existence. As a means of increasing national unity, they form part of the national policy, and, if the government and school should cease to encourage them, they would die a natural death.

SOCIAL SANCTIONS

Most matters of law are looked after by the policemen in the next *mura*. The nearest police station is in Taragi. Here are stationed ten or so police, including one plain-clothes man. The latter looks after publications and foreigners—mostly Chinese in the Kuma region.

The Taragi police visit Suye on such occasions as the firemen's exhibition in January and the reservists' examination in August. Occasionally they call at the village office to see how things are going. To enforce the law, they visited Suye only once during the year to take a Korean mountain worker in Hirayama to jail to prevent him from beating his wife to death. The constable in the next *mura* visits the village office about once a week as he is technically policeman for both Fukada and Suye. He also attends the firemen's exhibition and reservists' examination. He is present at any political speeches at election time. In Japan the police may stop a speaker any time he says anything they deem to be lèse majesté. Only twice did he have to come to Suye to enforce the law. Once was one winter morning when three transient beggars robbed both Inari shrines in Kakui of rice that had been offered to the god. The priests of both shrines acted as prosecutors and gave harsh words to the culprits after they had been caught by the young men of the *buraku*. The other time the police-man came was on the occasion of a drowning. Again there was little for him to do as the *buraku* had already begun helping the bereaved family, had begun searching the river-banks, and had gone to the praying priest for a charm to help find the body. The policeman's contribution was to have the firemen of the *buraku* ordered to the rescue. Since most of these men were already assisting as *buraku* neighbors, to have them out as firemen was making official out of unofficial aid. This is similar to the way the Women's Society is making an official out of an unofficial system. For the most part the *mura* can get along pretty well without a prefectural policeman.

The most powerful local sanction against a *buraku* mem-ber who does wrong is to refuse him co-operation. This means that he receives no help at housebuilding or roof-fixing or at transplanting. Neither can he belong to *kō*, and no one will help him bury his dead. For a successful farmer such aid is an absolute necessity, and in a farming *buraku* there is seldom need to invoke such a sanction. In a *buraku* with several small shops, such as Kakui, the economic in-terests of the farmer and shopkeeper are different, thus opening the way to misunderstandings and trouble. Fur-thermore, the sanction of non-co-operation breaks down against a shopkeeper, who is not so dependent on voluntary aid in his affairs. He deals in money and so can hire assist-ance. Often the shopkeeper pays a fine instead of joining in *buraku* community work. Thus affairs do not run so smoothly in the shopkeeper *buraku* as in the others. In the towns this trend is more marked; here the *buraku* has almost no sanctional power at all, and it is in the towns that the police have the most work to do.

Besides the sanction of non-co-operation, there is one of ridicule. This applies more to younger people. A young man or woman is always careful to do the traditional thing for fear someone will laugh. This also is the chief sanction to keep love affairs clandestine. As soon as *buraku* people get wind of an affair, they laugh at the principals. Older people are not subject to this sanction, for after a man or woman reaches sixty-one, he or she does and says pretty well what he or she likes. This is especially true of old women who have been repressed as young women and wives for decades. The older a woman becomes, the more she takes the liberties so long withheld from her of talking back to a man, of doing less work, and of ordering young people to do it. With the years she becomes as bold and ribald in her talk as any man.

In case of adultery an aggrieved husband may fight his wife's lover, and society assumes no rights of punishment in such cases. A woman has no means of punishing an unfaithful husband, but she might leave him, and she will most certainly show her hatred for the woman who has won his favor. An injured wife may become very jealous, and there are several cases in Suye where such a wife refuses to stay in the same room with or attend the same party as the woman with whom her husband has had an affair.

There may have been other sanctions in *buraku* society before the advent of police. What would happen in case of murder, for instance? It is probable that this would also be considered a personal matter, not to be dealt with by social sanctions.

AVOIDANCE

People in Suye will go a long way to avoid open face-to-face trouble. Thus when in a group of people anyone says anything, the others will all nod and say, "Yes, yes." What the next person says may be quite different, but again the chorus answers "Aye."

The principle of the go-between is to avoid direct and embarrassing situations.[3] Thus in the all-important social contract of marriage the principle reaches its height with not one but two different go-betweens. It is this need for a go-between that has created the broker. Like the go-between in marriage, he is rewarded for his services by both parties. It is because he has abused his function and gone into the business for profit that he is so heartily disliked and despised by farmers.

Another mode of avoiding an embarrassing situation is not to see it if it occurs. When a young man wraps a towel around his face at night and goes visiting some girl, he is not recognized. The girl to whom he makes advances will probably recognize him soon enough; however, if she repulses him, it is in the best interests of both that she "not know" who it was that came into her bedroom. Thus, the next day as they pass each other on the path any embarrassment is avoided.

When a caller comes to a house, the host, if not properly dressed, will not speak to his guest but will leave the room as if he had not seen him. After dressing, he reappears and bows a formal welcome to the guest, and the conversation begins.

At funeral parties the relatives have a banquet in one room, and the helpers a simple supper in another room or

---

[3] Similar avoidance patterns exist in rural China. See Daniel H. Kulp, *Country Life in South China* [New York, 1925], p. 99.

are even served on the ground in the yard. Each group acts as if the other were not there.

It is this mortal fear of being caught in an embarrassing situation that gives the sanction of laughter and ridicule such force. A girl will not even cook beans for a *dō* celebration if she thinks that she is not a good enough cook and that some *dō* visitors might remark on it. A man or woman, especially if young, is always reluctant to do this or that because he or she is *hazukashi*, "bashful."

MISFITS

Physical malformation does not necessarily disqualify one from a normal life in Suye. There are only a few cripples and feeble minds in the *mura*. One deaf and dumb woman, now a widow, runs her household remarkably well. She has had two successive husbands, attends all *buraku* functions, and talks to her friends by means of graphic hand signs. She even dances at the drinking parties. A feeble-minded boy, more handicapped by blindness than a weak mind, has been given the job of permanent nursemaid in his household.

With such an emphasis on co-operation the most striking type of misfit is an individualist. The commonest solution for such a man is to emigrate. Today most of the cases of men who "did not get along" have gone to Manchukuo, the land of opportunity. The same is doubtless true of many Japanese who have emigrated to America from other regions.

A man with a university education does not fit into the *mura* patterns. Of the seven who have gone to universities, only one has come back to live there. He is not at all satisfied with his lot, and, while making a virtue of being in the country and being a farmer, his head is always buzzing with ideas to change the folkways of Suye.[4] His exceptional position made it very hard for him to select a suitable bride. As a farmer he could not get a city girl with good education, for such girls do not marry into the country; because of his education, he did not feel he would be satisfied with just a farmer's daughter. The final compromise was a small shopkeeper's daughter from Hitoyoshi who combined education with not too high a social standing.

A woman's freedom of movement is not that of a man. By Japanese custom a woman is expected to be a dutiful wife and true at all times to her husband. She must live and work where her husband lives and works, and so a non-co-operative woman is rare. When she does occur, she is called *yakamashii* ("hard to get along with") and is usually disliked and feared as a sorceress. Sometimes a girl who has been to work in a factory for a couple of years is dissatisfied with *mura* life on her return.

The most frequent difficulty of women involves not their social but their sexual lives. Many cases of insanity and most of *hysteri* are clearly due to sexual maladjustments. The term *hysteri* is applied to all women who are known for their instability, nervousness, or promiscuity. Occasionally, talking of a man famous for his sexual freedom, a woman will say that "he has *hysteri*."

The society is one where a girl has no say in the matter of her marriage and must take whatever her husband may give her of sexual satisfaction. A man may have as many affairs as he pleases, and his wife cannot object. He may visit the *geisha* restaurants of Menda and not come home

[4] It is he who organized the music and riding clubs and who introduced several new green vegetables such as cabbage and spinach into the *mura*. Recently he was making plans to introduce a horse-powered flour mill in the mountain *buraku* of Hirayama where there is no electricity.

until all hours, and she has no recourse but to submit. Furthermore, she has no similar rights. One result of this situation is the very sexual nature of the women's dances at drinking parties. Men for the most part sing and clap their hands or do some rather innocent dance, but the married women, once the party is well along, indulge in all kinds of imitations and exaggerations of copulation to the accompaniment of a vigorous female chorus which invariably ends up in roars of laughter. Such is the normal and accepted expression of a woman's sexual feelings. The "abnormal" is *hysteri*, when women, not drunk, have a tendency to indulge in similar antics and attempt more actively to seduce men.

Usually a woman suffering from *hysteri* is confined to her house, and she never appears at parties. One woman, who seemed normal enough in everyday life despite a slight preoccupation with sex in her conversation, never appeared at *buraku* parties. The only explanation ever offered was that she suffered from *hysteri*. It is probable that on some previous occasions she had tried too seriously to rape a man, for it is said that she used to attend parties. Most women's mental diseases are said to "begin in the womb" and then go to the head.

"GEISHA"

In Suye about eight men have sold their daughters as *geisha*. One man had a *kō* debt so he sold a daughter as a *jorō* (prostitute) to a Kumamoto brothel-keeper. Then, having still a bit of debt left, he sold a second daughter. Another man's wife died, and, being poor and addicted to drink, he sold a daughter as a *geisha* in Taragi.[5] Men who thus sell their daughters are always poor, but a second fact is interesting—they are not natives of the village, not old families.

[5] Country *geisha* also function as prostitutes.

THE ARCHERY CLUB

GEISHA FROM MENDA VISITING INARI
SHRINE ON OCCASION OF A FESTIVAL

A man is not looked down upon for selling his daughter, for only a man of not very high social standing to begin with ever sells his daughter. A poor man attempting to set his family on a firm social and economic foundation in farming never does so.

Schoolmates of a young girl thus sold might stop to talk to her on a visit to Menda or Taragi, and if she ever comes home on a visit, old friends will come for a chat. However, once a girl has been sold, though the original period is usually only three years, she never comes back to live in the village but moves from town to town and from restaurant to restaurant. Then, if she does not die first, she may set up a small noodle restaurant in some town far from her native place. Really intelligent *geisha* sometimes run *geisha* houses themselves in their old age.

A *geisha* is very seldom taken in marriage. More frequently she is bought out by some admirer and kept as a concubine. In the event of a marriage the restaurant owner acts as her father. The girls are addressed as *nēsan* (elder sister), and they address the older women in the house as *obasan* (aunt).[6]

[6] *Geisha* have an important function in Japanese social organization. A wife is married for family reasons: to bear children, mend clothes, and cook food. Her duty is to love her husband and to work for him. She is not like a servant because a servant does her work without love; she is better than a servant. However satisfactory and desirable this loving slave in the home is, the eternal submissiveness of a wife leaves a need to be satisfied. That need is for some clever or seemingly clever female conversation, someone to laugh at one, someone to hold out love and then pretend to snatch it away. This the small businessman, village official, middle class Japanese misses in his wife, and hence the need for and existence of the *geisha* girl in Japanese society. To love one's wife as a woman is very rare. There is a special term for such a loved wife.

The farmer does not need this. For one thing, women are much freer in peasant life; they say and do things no well-bred Japanese woman would think of saying or doing. So, while the farmer's wife cannot dress as a *geisha* does, she may laugh and joke and dance at a party as freely as ever any *geisha* laughs or jokes or dances. There is ample opportunity at these parties for both men and women to express themselves.

CHAPTER VI

THE LIFE-HISTORY OF THE INDIVIDUAL

IN THE life of each individual in Suye there is a series of important events marking his various changes of status in the community. After birth, the chief events of a man's life are entering school, entering the barracks, entering married life, becoming a house head, reaching old age, and dying. For a woman the list varies somewhat from this: she does not go to the barracks nor does she usually become a house head, and she has one experience not shared by her husband, that of giving birth to a child. Practically all these events call for a gathering of the *buraku* and also of the relatives to drink and to celebrate, thus recognizing the individual's change of status in his *buraku* and in his kin group. The parties follow the pattern already outlined, and the different occasions call for various types of gift exchange as described below.

BIRTH

When delivery is easy,
Childbearing is easy too.[1]
—*Rokuchōshi hayashi*

Two things are always done as secretly as possible in Suye—sexual intercourse and its consequence, child delivery. Sexual intercourse, leading as it usually does to conception, is called "making a baby" (*kodomo tsukuru*). Childbirth being so secret, a woman never cries out, for,

[1] San ga yasuka tokya
Komochi yasuka bai.

178

if she did, the neighbors would know what she was doing, and she would be ashamed.[2]

Births follow one another pretty regularly. Farmers have heard of birth control but do not know how to obtain it or are afraid of the police. It is believed in the *mura* that schoolteachers use birth control, proof of which might be the fact that most of them have few or no children. However, one amusing incident occurred in the *mura* when a girl who had gone away to work in a factory sent home to her mother a condom, telling her to give it to father. This incident caused considerable laughter and broad humor among the neighbors.

There is practically no infanticide in the *mura*. The only known case in recent years occurred in a family, both poor and nonnative, in which the mother was regarded by the villagers as insane.[3]

A baby boy just born is often called *taiho* (cannon) or *rikugun* (army); a baby girl *gunkan* (warship) or *kaigun* (navy).[4] These terms are used among friends in a jocular sense.

Soon after the neighbors have heard that a woman has had a baby, they call on her with a gift of *ame*[5] candy, which is considered to be good for her. There are no real

[2] This cultural pattern of not crying in childbirth, found also among various Siberian tribes, e.g., the Chukchee, has been of late years noticed by Japanese publicists as a symbol of the peculiar superiority of the Japanese to all other peoples.

[3] For the seven *buraku* in which records were made, there were, in 1936, 72 boys and 69 girls in the age group 0–5, which is in contrast to the marked minority of girls in this age group in Chinese villages as reported by Kulp and by Fei.

[4] It is worth noting in this connection that Freud identifies weapons as male dream symbols and ships as female ones (see Sigmund Freud, *A General Introduction to Psycho-analysis* [New York, 1935]).

[5] *Ame* is a molasses-like candy made from the bran and shoots of various grains.

food taboos after childbirth, but certain foods are recommended such as soft rice, *tai* fish, *iwashi* fish, tuna fish, soups, and a few vegetables, while others such as pumpkin, meat, certain kinds of fish, and sweets except *ame* are avoided. The reasons given for these preferences and avoidances are that they are good or bad for the health of the new mother.

For two or three days after birth the child eats nothing. On the third day[6] the midwife, a few relatives, and close friends are invited to a naming ceremony (*kamitate* or *natsuke*). Among those invited is usually the man who was go-between for the wedding of the baby's parents. The midwife usually arrives first and bathes the baby. When most of the guests have arrived and had tea in the *daidokoro*, they are invited into the *zashiki* where the midwife is seated in the place of honor next the *tokonoma*. A tray of food, chiefly fish soups, and a tray of formal congratulatory cake are served. The cake has been purchased from the local cakemaker if the family is poor, from a caterer in a near-by town if more well to do. It is made of dry rice flour pressed into shapes of *tai* fish, pine, plum, and bushy-tailed tortoise, the traditional Japanese symbols of good fortune and long life, and into the shape of Momotaro coming out of a peach. The peach is a female sex symbol in Japan,[7] and Momotaro is a legendary hero in a famous Japanese fairy tale where he brings wealth and happiness to his foster-parents. A *shōchū* cup is on each person's tray, and he is expected to begin drinking immediately. The father exchanges drinks with the midwife, then with other guests.

When everyone is served, the selection of the name is

[6] In many regions of Japan on the seventh day.

[7] Cf. Freud, *op. cit.*

performed. Sometimes the father selects a name. The customary way, however, is for all present to suggest names and write them on paper. These papers are rolled up into small wads and put in a paper basket made from a square piece of writing paper. Then the midwife takes a Buddhist rosary from the *butsudan* and dips the tassel in *omiki*[8] that has been offered at the *tokonoma*, then into the paper basket. After a few attempts one of the wads clings to the tassel. It is opened, and the name on it read by the midwife. The name is discussed, and, if everyone seems to approve, it is accepted; but if for some reason it is not liked, the midwife may try for another. Even so, if the father has his heart set on some name, he is likely to insist on it regardless of wads and rosaries.

To such a naming party, as with almost every ceremony and party except weddings and funerals, only one person from each house invited is expected to come—either the head or his wife, son or daughter, but not a servant.

The exchanges of goods at a birth are: (1) a relative or close friend sends some material for baby *kimono* and, if he attends the naming-ceremony, brings rice and *shōchū;* (2) the guests receive feast food and *shōchū* in return.

The midwife, having given her services for which she is paid, does not send any *kimono* material but does bring rice and *shōchū* in exchange for the feast food. The parents feel themselves under an obligation to the midwife, and it is considered proper, although not always done, to call on her a month later, at *hiaki* (see below) with *sekihan* (festive rice mixed with red beans).

This naming ceremony and party is the first introduction of a child into society. The local group now recognizes the child as a new member, with a name and a real, if

---

[8] Wine that has been offered to some deity is called *omiki*.

limited, personality. This celebration is the first party of
one's life and one of the lesser ones. As with subsequent
rites de passage it is not the individual concerned who
counts but the event. The parents gain status through
adding another member of their family to the community,
the community takes the opportunity to welcome a new
individual into their society and, incidentally, to get together for good fellowship cemented by plenty to drink and
by indulging in the old familiar folk songs and folk dances.

The birth of a child is a much more certain sign of a
permanent marriage than is a wedding ceremony. Indeed,
a marriage is often not put in the village office records until
after a child is on its way. The birth of a child also gives
the new wife a definite standing among her new neighbors.
She is now truly a married woman and may indulge in the
privileges of smoking, drinking, and sexual jokes. An unmarried woman may laugh at a broad joke, but it is unseemly for her to make one herself.

A few days after the naming ceremony the father goes
to the village office and records the birth of the child,
giving sex, name, and parents' names. If the child is a
bastard, the birth is recorded, but there is no naming
party. The child in this case takes the family name of the
mother and is brought up in her house.

At thirty-one days if a boy, thirty-three if a girl, a child
is taken to visit the shrine of the village patron god
(*ujigami*). On this day the mother with the child and often
one or two other female relatives, such as an aunt, dress in
their finest and also dress the child in his best silk. At the
shrine a candle is lit, the mother claps her hands for the god's
attention, and a copper and some *shōchū* are offered. The
child, by this ceremony, is introduced to the deity whose
good will allowed him to be born and to survive his first
thirty-odd most dangerous days. Then the party walks

back home. If not taken to the *ujigami*, the child is taken to some local *buraku* Shinto shrine and is also sometimes taken to the Kwannon *dō*. Kwannon is regarded as a deity of mothers and so is often prayed to for children or to make child delivery easy. Sometimes a man on his way to call the midwife will stop at a Kwannon *dō* to light a candle. The mother sometimes takes the child to her native home to visit the *ujigami* there. *Sekihan* is cooked to be distributed to all those who came to the naming ceremony and who gave gifts. This is often replaced by some wheat or rice cakes (*dango*) and completes the reciprocal obligations incurred by the family at the time of the child's birth.

This day and event are called *hiaki*. Before this time the child has not been carried across rivers or on the back, and the mother, theoretically, has had no sexual intercourse with her husband. During the first thirty days or so of a child's life his soul is not very well fixed in his body —it is a period of danger and uncertainty. *Hiaki*, therefore, represents the end of the birth period and is, significantly, the same term as that used for the end of the forty-nine-day period of mourning for the dead.

The child has now passed another stage. From now on he may be carried on the back and may cross water safely, for he is now recognized by the gods as well as by the people of his world.

The child is nursed for several years by the mother, or until the next child is born. Many people can remember when they suckled their mothers. Then comes a critical period of weaning at which stage children frequently die. If a mother's milk goes dry and a child must be weaned early, he is fed on rice water, i.e., water in which raw rice has been cooked.

EDUCATION AND SCHOOL

During the first year a child is the favored one in the family. At any time he may drink milk from his mother's breast, and whatever he cries for will be given to him. He is cuddled and fondled and rocked to sleep. He learns by imitation as his mother repeats unendingly baby talk for this and that.

But almost inevitably his mother bears another baby, and the child faces his first hard knocks. While the mother devotes her attention to the newcomer, the child is turned over to an older sibling or nursemaid who carries him about on her back or sits him down somewhere to play. When he cries, he may not be listened to, for his mother no longer gives him first attention. This rapid weaning from milk and maternal attention results in several weeks of temper tantrums. Occasionally, the tantrums are effective, especially if they last long enough, but eventually the child readjusts himself; he gets acquainted with other children also put out to play, and he is soon a member of a new age group of the two- and three-year-olds of the neighborhood. He learns to get along with his contemporaries.

Even in these early years a boy receives a few special educational influences different from those of his sister. On a walk to some shrine festival the mother may tell the sister to walk behind because she is the lady and he the gentleman. And, if a first son, the boy will always have preferred treatment over his younger brothers.

He learns about sex early because older children frequently engage in sex play, his mother often draws attention to his genitals when playing with him, and he sleeps in the same room as his parents.

In general, children are very much spoiled. They can and do strike their mothers in a rage and call them the favorite Japanese epithet of *baka!* (fool). Anything a child asks for or cries for long enough he gets. He learns the ways of society not through discipline but through example and instruction patiently and endlessly repeated by his mother. The father, softhearted to the younger children, becomes more strict as they grow older. As a child grows older and finds other people not so inclined to do his bidding, he develops a strong sentimental love for his mother.

At full six years the child goes with all the other little six-year-olds and their fathers or mothers in April to the village shrine of Suwa-san. Here, with teachers and other older school children, a short Shinto ritual is performed. The priest gives the young a little talk on the virtues and greatness of Japan, the Emperor, and the gods and then hands to each of the neophytes a copy of the first-year book of ethics[9] published by the department of education. This is a child's first introduction to a world beyond his *buraku* and *mura*. After the shrine service he attends school for the first time as a student, dressed up in a new black uniform and cap. (He has been here often before with his mother when she came to some meeting or party held in the school auditorium, or with his nurse to play in the schoolyard.) The trip to the shrine did not mean much to him, but it was significant of the close association of official Shinto and the public-school system.

At school he meets for the first time children from all over the village. His constant association with them for the next six years is an important one both for him and for the unity of the village. The ties of men who were classmates in school are very close.

[9] As generally translated. Actually these books, one for each grade, are more concerned with national civics, the virtue of being a soldier, of revering the Emperor, etc.

The school building, a long one- or two-storied wooden structure, is partly paid for by village taxes, partly by prefectural and central government funds. As there are no heating facilities, children shiver and sniffle their way through the winter months. There is a confirmed belief that cold and discomfort are good for learning and mental discipline. If any child complains of the cold, the teacher tells him to think of the brave soldiers in Manchukuo, where it is *really* cold. Every day after school hours pupils clean up the yard with straw brooms, while girls get on their hands and knees to wipe up the floors. A school servant exists but chiefly for the purpose of running errands and making tea for the teachers to drink between classes.

Every morning now the child gets up about five and washes; he need not dress as he probably slept in his school uniform. After bowing to the household gods, he has a breakfast of bean soup and rice and runs out of the house and off to school. If he lives far from school, this trip by foot may be as long as two or three miles; if close by, it may be only a few yards. On the way he plays games, chiefly a kind of cops and robbers. These games are played with boys and girls alike amid shouts and shrieks as someone is captured. On entering the school grounds, he bows toward the closet in the main auditorium where the Emperor's portrait is housed. (More well-to-do schools have a special concrete house costing a thousand yen or more to house the sacred photograph.)

At school shortly before eight all the children from first grade to sixth line up in the schoolyard for radio exercises. From 7:50 to 8:00 the entire youth of the nation under the leadership of hundreds of teachers goes through the same daily dozen to the shrill directions of the same government radio announcer.

After this, the school children break ranks and file into

RADIO EXERCISES IN SCHOOLYARD

VILLAGERS AT A SCHOOL PLAY

The same audience sits listening to such speeches as given in Appendix III

their various classrooms. Here the boys or girls find their
places, small fixed cramped wooden benches and desks,
each sex on a different side of the room. The teacher in
black uniform comes in—all children rise and bow to him,
receiving a slight bow in return—and class begins, with
singing perhaps. Many of the songs are simple little nurs-
ery rhymes about birds and insects, but the first one the
children learn describes the "beautiful national flag with
the red sun on it" and the next one is called "The Soldier"
("With the gun over his shoulder the soldier marches, to
the sound of the bugle he marches; the beautiful soldier,
I love the soldier"). Then they learn to read and write.
In their first-year reader they again read of the soldier
and the flag.

The older children are expected to help the newcomers
find their way around school. From now on for six years
the child goes to school from April to July and from August
to April again. School is from nine to twelve noon for first-
year children, eight-thirty to three-thirty after that. Most
of the time is taken up with singing, reading, and athletics
—all three with a leaven of nationalism. No attempt is
made to teach children to think critically either in primary
school or in high school. The schoolmaster of the primary
school sets as his aim the rules for primary-school education of the department of education in Tokyo, the schoolmaster of the middle school sets as his aim the rules of
middle-school education of the department of education,
and so also for the agricultural school, girls' high school,
etc. The schoolmasters vary from the sacred word of the
department only on the side of greater nationalism. In the
agricultural school in Menda, for instance, boys are given
many lectures on Japanese spirit, and second sons are encouraged to emigrate to Manchukuo.

The great difficulty of learning two or three thousand

characters in the first six years, in addition to two sets of fifty-syllable characters, gives but little chance for a student to do much original composition. Geography, arithmetic, and drawing are taught. The drawing is European style, but in arithmetic emphasis is on the use of the *soroban* (abacus)—so much so that many a man can scarcely add two and three without the aid of this device. In Suye boys and girls are also given some practical lessons in farming on a few *chō* of paddy and upland fields belonging to the school.

In higher grades some geography, history, and general science find their way into the curriculum, but the major part of the child's time is still taken up with reading and writing, singing, and ethics. The reading lessons are performed by the deafening method of the whole class reading aloud at once.

In rural schools practically all children are promoted every year, the emphasis in teaching being more moral than intellectual. Teachers feel that, if they left some child behind his class, he would feel very badly about it and that the resulting psychological effect and family chagrin would not be compensated for by any good the child might receive mentally by repeating a school grade. Similarly, at school athletic contests all entrants, not only first, second, and third, receive prizes. By giving prizes thus generously, no one feels unduly slighted. While occasionally people are shown the virtues of initiative and leadership, they are more often shown the virtues of co-operation, and the good but mediocre child is held out to be superior to the bad but brilliant one.

Unquestioning acceptance of everything the teacher says at school is the rule. Occasionally, this causes trouble at home when the father says something to the boy and he replies that the teacher did not say so. The more a child is educated, the wider becomes the gap between the old people's folkways and the young people's ideas. By the time they reach university the gap is too wide to bridge, hence college graduates from villages almost never return to their homes.

To solve this and other behavior problems that arise, there is an annual parents' day on which old people, many of whom went to no school at all or to only a four-year elementary course, come to the school, see classes in action, and later have discussions with the teachers. With a touching faith in the rightness of their children's teachers, the parents discuss their parental troubles.

At frequent intervals during the school year there are other special days. Some are national holidays, such as the Emperor Meiji's death day, when there is a general assembly with a solemn reading of the Imperial rescript on education while all present bow their heads, followed by an uplifting lecture by the schoolmaster and by the singing of the national anthem. On other occasions the students have more fun; for instance, at the annual athletic meet, for which they train for weeks ahead. This is attended by practically everyone in the village, the families coming with lunch baskets to stay all day. People of a *buraku* sit together. Another big day is the old students' day, when the graduates come to watch the present students perform skits and dances.

After six years a boy or girl has learned enough to read simple things. He has also imbibed a good deal of nationalism and martial Japanese spirit by means of games of war and the watching of young men drilling in the schoolyard four times a month. If he leaves school at this point, he will probably forget much of his reading ability and his nationalism will lie dormant in a life whose primary object is to raise good rice and get along amicably with his neighbors.

At school the children, especially boys, form close friendships with their own classmates, children mostly of the same age. Classmates are called *dōkyosei;* people of the same age, *dōnen.* It is the *dōnen* tie which is more important. All through life male *dōnen* remain close. When two men meet for the first time, if they turn out to be of the same age, they are well on the way toward being friends. The ties of *dōnen* increase with age. As a man grows old and the sexual desires die down, parties of *dōnen* are the only true pleasures left in life, and the farmers of Suye say that a *dōnen* then becomes closer than a wife.

The primary school came to Suye about sixty years ago. It was then a four-year course. Most of the older generation have attended this. Thirty years later a six-year course was begun, and more recently have come the continuation classes called *seinen gakkō* and *kōtō shōgakkō.* The *seinen gakkō* is a young people's school that meets at night and on *mura* rest days. The *kōtō shōgakkō* is full-time regular school for two or three years after the sixth grade. The *seinen gakkō* instructs girls in sewing and cooking and boys in fencing, wrestling, some general knowledge, and a lot of military drill.

All young men in the *mura,* including young servants from outside, are expected to attend *seinen gakkō.* The women's participation is much more limited; some do not go at all, and those who do go, go only on *mura* holidays, there being no night school for them.

Before leaving the classroom all pupils stand and bow to the teacher, and before leaving the schoolyard at the end of the school day all classes line up for dismissal by the schoolmaster, and every child bows in the direction of the Emperor's portrait. If not going home right away, a boy may while away the afternoon with other little boys playing war games. The girls will play at juggling beanbags or bouncing a ball, as often as not with a baby sibling bouncing in rhythm on their backs. Parents like to have their children come home first, say, "I have returned," and then go off to play.

There are many songs to go with ball-bouncing and other games, also many lullabies sung by older children to soothe a baby carried on the back. An example of each is given below.

HAND-CLAPPING GAME SONG

Arutoki Hanako no	At one time Hanako's
Namida ga hori hori	Tears poured down
Hori hori	Poured down.
Ammari deta no de	Too many tears
Tamoto de nugūimasho	With the sleeve let us wipe
Nugūimasho	Let us wipe
Nugūta kimono wa	The wet *kimono*
Araimasho	Let us wash
Araimasho	Let us wash.
Aratta kimono wa	The washed *kimono*
Shiburimasho	Let us wring
Shiburimasho	Let us wring.
Shibutta kimono wa	The wrung *kimono*
Hoshimasho	Let us hang out
Hoshimasho	Let us hang out.
Hosh'ta kimono wa	The hung *kimono*
Tatamimasho	Let us fold
Tatamimasho	Let us fold.
Tatanda kimono wa	The folded *kimono*
Naoshimasho	Let us put away
Naoshimasho	Let us put away.
Naoshita kimono wa	The put-away *kimono*
Nezumi ga poki poki	The mice (ate), *poki poki*
Poki poki	*Poki poki*
On puku pon—na—pon	*On puku pon na pon.*

LULLABY (*KOMORI-UTA*)

Nenne ko Torahachi baba no mago
Baba oraren jī no mago
Jī wa doke ikaita
Jī wa machi fune kai ni
Fune wa naka tokya uma kōte
Uma wa doke tsunagaita
Uma wa sendan no ki tsunagaita
Nan kwasete tsunagaita
Hami kwasete tsunagaita

Go to sleep Torahachi, granma's grandchild.
Granma is not here, granpa's grandchild.
Granpa, where did he go?
Granpa went to town to buy a boat;
There was no boat, he bought a horse.
The horse, where did he tie (it)?
The horse he tied to a *sendan* tree.
What did he feed (it) tethered?
The bit he fed (it), tethered.

If a child's family is rich, he will probably be sent to high school. A girl will go to the girls' high school (*jogakkō*) in Taragi or, more exceptionally, in Hitoyoshi. A boy will be sent to the agricultural school (*nōgakkō*) in Menda or, more exceptionally, to the middle school in Hitoyoshi. A high-school education helps a girl's family to make a good marriage for her.[10]

More boys than girls receive education outside Suye. In the last ten years nine boys and no girls went from Suye families to some college or university. Of these, one became a government official in Tokyo; two, doctors in Hitoyoshi; one, an army doctor; one, a newspaper man in Tokyo; three are still in college. Only one has come back

---

[10] Today all social classes except the nobility are said to be equal, but on every boy's file is recorded whether or not he is descended from a *samurai*, and whether or not he is from the *eta* class.

to Suye. He came back because of illness while working at an office job in Kumamoto and because his father died, forcing him to come home and take care of his household consisting of his mother and three unmarried younger sisters. He has made a virtue of his necessity by deploring the fact that educated citizens of Suye leave the place and saying he must now stay here as a duty to his native village.

At fourteen or fifteen a young person begins taking his full share of farm work. At twenty about one boy in four goes off to the barracks; girls continue helping their mothers or perhaps work as maids for some richer families. Young men of poor families also work out as menservants.

ADOLESCENCE

Young men and women work together a great deal, often a son of the house and a maidservant or a daughter of the house and a manservant. As they work side by side in the mud of a paddy field or go to the forest to cut firewood in February, there is little chance for romance as each is too busy. Work clothes are always ragged, and no self-respecting farmer tries to look pretty at work; but there is opportunity for talk and jokes. In the evening, sitting by the fire pit, there is leisure for romantic thoughts.

In the old days when there was no electricity it was easy for a young man to enter a maid's room unobserved by the family and unseen by the girl until he actually lay down beside her. In such a case she could accept or refuse him as she pleased. Since his face was covered with a towel, he could not be recognized unless the girl happened to know him well already. Even so, if refused, the towel saved his face. The next day as they saw each other they could appear to know nothing of the night's attempt.

Today every house with electricity leaves its lights on all night,[11] and this makes clandestine affairs much more difficult. They still go on, however, though not so frequently as formerly. It is said that girls have become more "moral" now. One reason for this is school education. All young girls are encouraged to attend *shojokai* (Young Ladies' Society, which is part-time school for girls who have not gone beyond the sixth grade). These school meetings occurring on *mura* rest days take up most of the girls' leisure time, and it gives them something to do at home in the evening, for there is always some sewing assignment. They are told by the teacher about the value of virtue, so, as one man put it, "even a servant girl now has enough education to know that she must keep her virginity."

A girl never admits publicly that she likes a certain young man, but of an evening girls still go out for a walk occasionally. This is especially true of maidservants who, not living at home, have less strict parental supervision.

In the village there is little dressing up among older women with a view toward attracting male attention. Young unmarried women, however, dress up in their finest on big festival days, often with some young man in mind.

Love letters are much written and much denied. About the only use a young farm girl ever gets out of her grammar-school education is the ability to write a misspelled love letter. This letter-writing is a "fling" that all young girls must take before they are married. Nothing ever comes of it. It is mostly an innocent occupation which furnishes much excitement and gives the girls something to talk about when they meet and tease one another. There is a poem:

[11] Electricity is paid for by the number and wattage of bulbs, not by the kilowatt hour.

Hana tsubomi no jogakusei
Eigo de fumi kaku oya no mae
Fumi to wa futaoya shirazu shite
Erai benkyō to homete aru

High-school girl, beautiful as a flower bud,
Before her parents writes a love letter in English.
The two parents, not knowing it to be a love letter,
Praise her for studying so much.

Even though a young woman is made pregnant by some secret lover, she rarely marries him. The love affairs are secret and individual, but marriages are arranged by the families and, after secret preliminaries, public. Usually an affair does not get beyond the love-letter and joking stage.

If a girl becomes pregnant, the parents try to arrange a marriage for her before the child is born. This usually results in her marrying into a class below her as it is difficult to arrange a quick marriage for a pregnant daughter in one's own social class, especially among the lower upper and upper upper. Such girls often marry widowers.

While the actual sex act is very private, jokes about it and imitations of it in dances are both free and frequent. Young children, especially boys, often play at sex games, jokingly chasing girls and exposing themselves.

When puberty is reached, boys and girls, especially girls, become shy and reserved in their relations with one another. Girls tend to go in groups together and boys to do the same. With this separation begins the sharp social division of the sexes that lasts until old age. From now on a couple, married or single, is a rare sight on the public streets. Even when going to the same place a man and wife will go separately.

CONSCRIPTION

Every year the army holds physical and mental examinations for men twenty years old. The so-called mental test is largely a civics and patriotic attitude test. In Kuma the examinations are held in Hitoyoshi about June. Fifteen or twenty young men of Suye are called each year for this. As one must report from the village in which one's *koseki* is kept, this often means a return home from some other region where one is working as a servant at the time examination comes up. From Suye in 1936 about half the boys examined were working in other villages as menservants.

The examination is a routine medical one accompanied by a long talk on patriotism and the duties of a soldier. That some boys do not care to be conscripted can be seen from the warning given by the colonel in charge not to tell lies.

Even before this official medical examination all men to come up in a given year are first examined in the village by a doctor hired by the village office. This preliminary examination is chiefly concerned with trachoma and venereal diseases.[12]

About a third of the young men pass the examination. Families of boys who do not pass, while somewhat sorry to miss the honor and glory of sending a son to serve the country, actually are rather glad to keep him at home. When an able-bodied young man is suddenly taken away from a farming family, its productivity is reduced. Often a family must hire a manservant to replace the conscripted son, and farmers always complain that such a hired man is not so good as their own son. For a poor family there is nothing to be done but grin and bear it.

Though it is actually only to the training barracks that a young man goes, the whole attitude on his departure and

---

[12] In this preliminary examination in Suye in 1936 there were no cases of venereal disease.

return is as if he had been in active service in defense of the country. It is probable that much of this attitude has been instilled into the people by the authorities. The conscript army only began under Meiji with the dissolving of the old hereditary soldier class (*samurai*). The very allowing of a common man to be a defender of the godly Emperor and his country is made to appear a great honor. When the time comes for the soldier to leave, usually in January, preparations are made by the family for a big send-off party.

When a boy has been chosen to serve in the barracks, someone from his household goes to the woods and cuts a tall bamboo, trimming off all but a topknot of branches. Just below the top spray of leaves a national flag is fastened, and this flag pole is erected in the house yard. The front entrance of the house is decorated with an ever-green arch, two national flags crossed, and a sign reading: "Congratulations on Entering the Service" (*Shuku nyu dan*).

Whenever anyone goes on a long journey to be away from home a long time, he holds a going-away (*wakare*, "separation") party for the *buraku* a few days before leaving; then the *buraku* in return sees him off to the edge of the village and returns to his house to sing, drink, and dance for several hours to "lighten the feet of the traveler."

For a departing soldier this going-away party is a tremendous one—one of the largest parties his family will give for years. All the *buraku* is invited, as well as the village headman and all village officials, schoolmaster, and all schoolteachers, and the head of the village Reservists' Association. Besides these, several of the boy's paternal relatives may come, or, if not, they will send gifts for the occasion.

To these soldier send-off affairs only male guests come, usually house heads. They come dressed in silk *montsuki* (formal *kimono*), the first ones arriving about the middle of the afternoon. Each guest brings an envelope with fifty sen or one yen in it as *sembetsu* (farewell gift money). While having tea in the *daidokoro*, one puts this envelope on the tray and gives it to the master or mistress of the house.

By the *tokonoma* is a small cut willow tree. Guests are given paper on which to write poems for the soldier, and these poems, after having been read aloud, are tied to the willow tree.

When everyone is present, the master of the house makes a speech thanking the guests for coming, apologizing for the poor food served. Then the headman responds for the company. He gives words of praise to the house head that his son is thus honored and words of advice to the son to be patriotic. Then perhaps the head of the Reservists will say a few words. The son who is to leave answers the speeches of the guests. During the speeches everyone kneels in formal manner, with eyes downcast out of respect for the speakers.

Meanwhile the serving girls have brought out trays of food to each guest. The food served includes *kazunoko* (fish eggs), a dish also characterizing wedding and other banquets on happy occasions. At present the feast food of soldier parties is rather meager. Formerly it was quite lavish, with the result that families sending off soldier sons would be fifty or a hundred yen the poorer after a party; but now, by advice of the village office and agreement among themselves, villagers limit the amount spent on fish to twenty-five sen a head. There is no limit on *shōchū*, however.

By the time of the last speech, several drinks have already been consumed between readings of poems. The host and his son now go around the room and exchange cups with each guest. Then guests also make the rounds, and it is not long before everyone is feeling gay. This follows a pattern often met in village functions. At first all is very stiff and formal, then an hour later, after the drinks have circulated, all is easy and informal, often verging on the hilarious. In fact, the more formal the beginning of such a function, the more riotous the end.

Guests stay until after dark. A few days later the hero of all this leaves on the 10:21 A.M. train from Menda to go to the barracks in Kumamoto. Early in the morning all the *buraku* people, women as well as men, come to his house with *shōchū*-filled *gara* to exchange drinks with him. Someone will bring a *samisen*, and songs will be sung. Soldiers of several *buraku* often leave the same day. All the school children gather at school to march with the soldiers to the bridge across the river in the next *mura* of Fukada. After the early-morning party of *buraku* neighbors in each soldier's home has given everyone lively spirits, they start off. Both men and women join in this party and procession. Someone carries the willow poem tree. Some young woman plays the *samisen*, while others carry *gara* and give drinks to anyone they pass. One woman makes a point of pouring drinks for exchanges with the departing soldier. As the procession goes by, people come out of their houses with *gara* and exchange drinks with the soldiers.

It is cold weather, and everyone wears heavy clothes and felt hats. The *shōchū* warms their vitals. All the soldiers, their accompanying *buraku*, and the school children merge in Kakui, and from here a long procession winds to the end of the *mura*, where the party halts. The schoolmaster

makes a parting speech to the soldiers, and they make replies. Then three *banzai* are given for them, and most of
the people return home. Only close friends, relatives, and
village officials go on. At the station the soldiers take a
branch from the willow tree, and more *banzai* are given as
the train pulls out.

The event rather than the individual person concerned
is what counts in this send-off. There is no crowding
about a soldier to give him a last-minute message. Rather
one shouts *Banzai!* for the departure of a soldier.

After the train pulls out, the party slowly returns home.
Most people—men, women, and their suckling babes—go
back to the soldiers' homes. Here everybody has more
shōchū—this "lightening of the footsteps of the traveler"
may last all through the afternoon. Only the people of the
buraku attend these post-departure parties, each soldier's
home holding a separate one.

The ceremonial evergreen gate by the soldier's house
comes down a few weeks after he leaves, but the flag is
left up rain or shine the whole time the son is away. By
looking around in a *buraku* one can tell just which houses
have soldiers in training or overseas by the location of
these flags.

The willow tree on which the poems are hung is planted
as soon as the party returns from the station. If it takes
root, the omen is good, and the parents may expect their
son to return home safely. The willow has symbolic meaning, it being said that, as the branches of this tree grow
toward its roots, so the wanderer will come back to the
place of his birth. In towns this planting of the willow is
not observed, and it is merely thrown away after the boy
leaves on the train.

A year or more is spent in the barracks. Here are hundreds of similar boys living under the same conditions of military training. Fathers sometimes visit sons in the barracks, and sons occasionally come home on leave but in such an event there is no special party.

At the end of the barracks term the young man makes a triumphal return. He is met at the train by his father and friends. School children, the Young Men's Association, and Reservists all come to meet him at the train. His father and his age group will often go to Hitoyoshi to meet him. The women of his *buraku* dress up in outlandish costumes, often as soldiers or tramps, and meet the returning procession by the bridge in the next *mura*. The women make obscene jokes as if they were men, try to rape the young school girls, and in general cause bursts of laughter and gaiety. They are always well disguised, and it is not always possible to tell the identity of a given masquerader.

At the soldier's home the front gate now, as at his departure, is specially decorated with branches of evergreen and flags. A welcome party is held there. Again the guests are all men; but, after the party is begun, older *buraku* women come to drink and to dance, one or two younger ones to play the *samisen*. The party ends in song and dance many hours later.

The soldier, like any returned traveler, brings back with him some small gift for everyone who attended his farewell party and brought him money as *sembetsu*.

When a young man comes back from the barracks, he is no longer a rustic farmer but a chauvinistic Japanese subject. He finds it difficult to readjust himself to the unexciting routine of farm work and local custom. The occasional soldier who has been sent to Tokyo as an Imperial guard or to Manchukuo to fight what he really believes to be bandits feels the ennui more strongly than others.

After a few months, however, he drops back into village patterns, and it is not long before he is married to some girl selected by his parents.

Sometime before going to the barracks, or on any long and important first trip from Suye, and upon his return, a man makes a trip to Mount Ichifusa. Mount Ichifusa is a great imposing mountain standing out above the rest of the range surrounding Kuma County. It is at the head of the valley, i.e., the eastern end (see Map I). This mountain has a shrine on it and is considered sacred, its celebration being on the sixteenth of the third month (lunar). People from all over the region make pilgrimages to it on that day.

On this day or some other, the traveler makes a trip to the mountain shrine, pays respects to the god, offers some *shōchū*, and takes some earth of Ichifusa done up in a paper to act as a charm or talisman (*omamori*). The trip is made on foot; the scenery is impressive with immense cryptomeria, the largest trees to be seen anywhere in the region. If one goes in the spring, the mountain is a profusion of beautiful azalea; if in autumn, of brilliant maple leaves. To approach this mountain, visible from all Kuma east of Hitoyoshi, and find it as impressive as it seems from a distance, to gain from it a perfect view of all Kuma Valley below one—these are soul-satisfying things. Taking some earth from this mountain gives a man a feeling of security when away from home. One young man who had served in Manchukuo and who was wounded there said that in the morning of the unlucky day he had had to leave camp in a hurry and thus forgot his *omamori* of Ichifusa earth. As soon as he realized it—on a sledge miles from camp—he felt uneasy. Before the day was over he was wounded in the leg by a "bandit." Some time after returning home, often on the next Ichifusa Day, the returned soldier takes the earth back to the sacred mountain.

MARRIAGE

A year or two after returning from the barracks, i.e., at twenty-three or twenty-four, a young man marries. His wife will be seventeen or eighteen years old. Long before the village as a whole realizes that any marriage is afoot, secret negotiations have begun. Of the three big events—birth, marriage, and death—only marriage can be controlled by a villager, and it is controlled to the greatest possible degree.

Marriage is primarily a social and economic arrangement between two families. When a boy's family feels that it is time he was married, they tell some close friend of the family to keep a look out for a likely girl. Sometime later this friend reports that he has found someone who might be suitable. This friend is called *naishōkiki* (secret finder-out) and is often a woman. A semisecret meeting of the two people concerned is arranged. Perhaps the boy and one of his parents go over to see how so-and-so's silk worms are getting along, so-and-so's daughter who is tending them being the girl in question. Or perhaps by seeming chance they may both appear at a healing spring the same afternoon, the girl being with the *naishōkiki*. This preliminary meeting is supposed to be by sheer chance and to have no significance, but actually it is prearranged in a round-about noncommittal way. Afterward the opinions of the boy and girl are sounded, and, if either voices violent disapproval, the matter is likely to be dropped—with no embarrassment to anyone, since nothing has been openly or admittedly started. If, however, this first meeting is satisfactory, matters will proceed. If the girl's family is of another *mura*, they will secretly investigate the boy's family to see that there is nothing wrong with it such as madness or leprosy, and to determine its social and economic condition as far as possible. The boy's family also does this of the girl's family. If both families are of the same *mura* and are well known to each other, such investigation is unnecessary as it is impossible to keep family skeletons hidden from fellow-villagers. Similarly, one need not do this if the boy and girl concerned are first cousins. Some people prefer cousin marriages as they reduce the cost of a marriage, it being all within the family; also, probably because each family feels sure of the other family, and has no fear of acquiring some unexpected disease to affect descendants, or some queer family as relatives.

When all these preliminary and secret moves have been made, an official go-between (*nakaudo*) is selected. The selection of a *nakaudo* is important as he performs the marriage ceremony and is responsible for the future welfare of the marriage. Usually some outstanding person in the community is chosen as *nakaudo* such as a headman, village councilor, or a rich landowner. The groom's family usually selects him.

If the man chosen as *nakaudo* accepts, he will take charge of the negotiations between the two families. From the time the two families have decided on a marriage between their children, they begin to keep at a distance. This is so that, if anything goes wrong from now on, or a divorce takes place after the marriage, it will not be so embarrassing as if they had been on very close personal terms.

Well-to-do families hold a formal betrothal or *yuinō*.

This is not true of the majority of families. At *yuinō* a banquet is given only for the members of the two families concerned, and the bride is presented with a formal *kimono* (*montsuki*) bearing the groom's crest which she will wear at the wedding.

From now on the bride and her family are busy working on wedding clothes and trousseau. The groom's family fix up their house, putting in new paper on the paper doors (*shōji*) and new mats (*tatami*) on the floor if they can afford it. Often a kitchen is renovated for the bride to work in. The groom's family prepare to receive the bride, and the bride's family prepare for her reception. A good day for the marriage is decided upon. Certain unlucky days are avoided. Nearly all the marriages in Suye occur in the tenth, eleventh, and twelfth months (lunar); a few in the third and fourth months.

On the day before the wedding the womenfolk of both houses are very busy with banquet preparations, and on the day of the wedding there is even more ado and excitement in the bride's house. A hairdresser comes early in the morning to arrange the hair of all the women of the family and of all women relatives present into a special formal hairdress. The bride's hair is done last as it needs most attention.

Relatives come in the morning, bringing their formal clothes to change into later and bringing gifts of various clothes, fish, and *sake*. The *sake* comes in special red-lacquer buckets. Those sent by the groom have attached to them conventionalized male and female butterflies of paper. Some bring money in lieu of goods. All gifts are wrapped in a special wedding manner and presented on trays with many bows.

While men relatives arrive later and act as guests, the

women help around the house and only come out to greet guests, not partaking of the banquet food. Preparation of the banquet food is done by the fishman, who also arrives early with beautifully decorated gift boxes (*orizume*) and much fish.

Her hair done up and decorated with a special set of pins, the bride has her bath and is finally dressed in her very formal wedding *kimono*, her elaborate coiffure covered with a white piece of silk (*tsunokakushi*, the "horn concealer"),[13] a traditional purse containing a mirror, pin, and crystal ball, and a fan tucked in her very wide and very tight belt.

All is now ready to receive the groom's party, usually consisting of the groom, one or both of his parents, and the go-between (*nakaudo*) and his wife (who more or less takes charge of the bride). They bring gifts of fish, *sake*, tea, and rice cakes (*mochi*) for the bride. After drinking the first cup of tea, they bring in the gifts done up in special wrappers. The gifts are received by the bride's mother, who puts them in the corner where the trousseau and other gifts are displayed. (The wrapper she will later return; the basket containing fish she will use to take back her return gift of fish.)

The bride's male relatives come, and the banquet is begun. The *nakaudo* sits in the place of honor; next comes the bride's father and male relatives. The bridegroom's relatives sit on the other side. Trays of food contain many fish soups of which the fish is always taken home. So little of the banquet food is supposed to be eaten that, both here and later at the groom's house, an ordinary meal of *miso* soup and rice with relish is served to the guests

[13] Woman, being evil, is supposed to have horns. These are concealed in the bride by the *tsunokakushi*.

at the end of the party. Only *sake* is drunk on wedding occasions, and it is poured with great ceremony by serving girls. The bride joins the banquet later. She hardly touches her food and takes her gift box with her, in return for which her mother will bring home the food served to the bride at the groom's house.

After the banquet and a few exchanges of drinks the trousseau and gifts are moved onto a wagon, and the party is ready to start out. Usually a bus is hired on such occasions, for there is a special arrangement whereby the party is taken to and from the wedding for fifteen yen. The procession walks toward the bus while neighbors stare and discuss the bride in whispers.

At the groom's house similar preparations have gone on all day, and the guests are received at the gate by the groom's relatives. The house is spick and span. The same pattern is followed—tea, presentation of bride's gifts, banquet.

However, before this begins, while guests are seated in the *zashiki*, the bride and groom are taken into a separate room (or behind a screen in the same room) and the *san-san-ku-do* ceremony is performed under the direction of the go-between. This is the marriage ceremony of the "three-three-nine times" drink. Two children pour out the *sake* in three small pours from a special container into a tier of three cups one on top of the other. First the groom has a drink out of the smallest cup, then the bride, then the same is done with the second and the third cup. Drinks are also exchanged between the bride and the groom's father; and there are also exchanges with the *nakaudo* and his wife.[14] A serving girl brings in some dried seaweed and

[14] The exact order of drinking of the *san-san-ku-do* varies in different regions of Japan and from wedding to wedding in the same region.

cuttlefish of which a small amount is handed to each to be wrapped up in a tiny piece of paper and put away.

After the *san-san-ku-do* the *noshi* is brought into the banquet hall on a tray. The *noshi* is a small strip of dried fish in a red and white paper folded in a special pattern. This *noshi* is a more elaborate form of a similar paper also called *noshi* which is attached to all formal gifts, including wedding gifts. It is presented to the groom's father, and the go-between announces that "the *noshi* has been received." No one seems to know just what this symbolizes, but apparently it indicates that the gift of the bride has been received. Like many other parts of the wedding ceremony, this is not indigenous to Kuma so that not only has the meaning disappeared but radical variations occur. For instance, according to some, *noshi* are exchanged between bride and groom, and sometimes the groom presents a *noshi* to the bride's family in which case the go-between announces that "the *noshi* has been presented." After this the bride's *tsunokakushi* is removed, and the formal ceremony is over.

The bride joins the company to sit demurely through the banquet; the groom remains in the back room and will come out toward the end of the banquet. Until his arrival everything is very formal, and, although drinks are poured out, no one makes the rounds, everyone sitting in a formal position on his heels. At a better wedding there is congratulatory wedding chanting during the *san-san-ku-do* and once during the banquet.

At the end of the banquet when fish, presented by the bride, has been taken around by a serving girl along with a special *sake* cup, out of which each guest drinks, it is announced by the groom's father that the ceremony is over, and everyone is asked to relax and sit at ease. Men change their position, cross their legs, and begin to make the rounds exchanging drinks. The bride goes out to change into one of her trousseau *kimono*, and other women might also change at this point into other dressy, but less formal, clothes. Men will play *ken*, and music and dancing will commence. Soon after the singing and dancing begins, a group of *buraku* young men, with faces covered by towels, bring in the nearest stone Jizō on which they have pasted an obscene verse or two and a request for some *shōchū*. After depositing their burden amid shouts and jokes, they retire to the kitchen where some of the serving girls give them the desired *shōchū*. The Jizō is said to be good to keep the bride from running home. A few days after the wedding, the Jizō is replaced in his niche by some pathway and adorned with a new bib sewn by the bride.[15]

During the singing and dancing stage of a wedding banquet, many rather broad jokes are made at the expense of the bride and groom. As the host supplies plenty of *sake* and *shōchū*, a great deal of liquor is drunk, and both men and women are soon dancing boisterously to the rhythm of two or three *samisen* and the handclaps of all who are not busy playing *ken* or exchanging drinks. The wedding is the extreme example of the pattern whereby a social gathering begins with stiff formality and ends with orgiastic abandon.

The party lasts until eleven or midnight. After the guests have been served supper and rice, they are ready to go home. Now the bride, as hostess, will serve tea made of the two measures brought to her by the groom and with the groom's family will come to the gate to see off her parents. Thus she assumes her role of daughter in the new household.

[15] For further discussion of the Jizō see chap. vii.

On the day following a wedding the girls who had been asked to assist come again to help clean up. The whole morning is spent putting the house in shape again. On this day there is a party given for the village officials, schoolteachers, and other people of consequence in the *mura*. The *buraku* as a whole (usually represented by the women) is invited the day after. These post-wedding parties are called *chanomi* and serve to introduce the bride to the community. Special formalized congratulatory wedding cakes are served at all three parties.

Three days (usually later but supposed to be the third day) after the wedding, bride and groom dress up in fine clothes for a visit to the *nakaudo*. They present him with a gift—a return gift for the one he gave at the wedding and one which must be better than his gift as it also serves as a return for his services as *nakaudo*.

From now on the *nakaudo* has close connections with the family. He will be invited to every child's naming ceremony and will probably attend as a mourner at funerals in the family. But, most important, he must continue to act as go-between for the two families related through the marriage. If there is trouble between bride and groom—if the bride goes home and stays too long—he must try to reconcile them. If this is impossible, he must arrange a separation as smoothly as possible.

Not all weddings are as elaborate as the foregoing description indicates. Some poorer families, and formerly nearly everyone in Suye, used *shōchū*, the local drink, in the *san-san-ku-do*, and much of the formality including the *noshi* and elaborate banquet food was lacking. As in dress, so in weddings: the ordinary farmer of today does many things only *samurai* were allowed to do in feudal times.

TRIAL MARRIAGE

A somewhat different type of marriage local to and much practiced in Kuma County is the *mikka kasei*[16] or three-day rent marriage. In this case, instead of a big wedding, the girl, her parents, and some female relative, or sometimes the go-between couple, go one day to the house of the groom. She stays there three days, then returns home.

If after this both families, especially the groom's, still favor the match, there will be a formal marriage later. Very often there will be no formal marriage at all, and a small party will be held to replace one. Even though bride and groom like the match, if the groom's family dislike the girl after her visit, she will not be asked to return.

Such is the supposed pattern of the Kuma type of marriage. Actually, however, she will stay longer than three days, often not returning home at all before the formal marriage. The first arrival at the groom's family is done very quietly, no formal hairdress is used and no special clothes worn. Gifts of *shōchū* and *mochi* are taken. Thus, if the marriage prove unsuccessful, there will be no great public loss of face on either side.

The most ritualistic form of exchange of gifts takes place at weddings. When the wedding is definitely settled, at the formal *yuinō* party the groom's parents present the bride with a formal *montsuki* and *haori* bearing his crest in which she is to be married, a dress *kimono*, a roll of silk, footgear, and hair apparel, also *sake* and fish. In exchange for *sake* and fish they receive a banquet. The other gifts are acknowledged when the bride brings her trousseau consisting of clothes, chests of drawers, and various household articles.

---

[16] *Kasei* is the word used for voluntary labor not requiring a return in labor but rather in some gift form, as when a relative helps at rice-transplanting.

At the wedding the groom's family when calling for the bride brings two buckets of *sake* and a certain number of *mochi*, depending on the size of the wedding. All things presented come in even numbers: two measures of tea, ten or twenty or thirty *mochi*, two *tai* fish, two pair of *geta*, two pair of toe thongs. These gifts are reciprocated exactly by the bride's family when they accompany the bride to the groom's house. The basket in which the groom's family brought the fish is used for fish taken back.

All the bride's relatives bring fish to the bride's house; this is served to the groom's family, and what is not eaten is taken home by them. At the wedding banquet the fish presented by the groom's relatives is served to the bride's relatives, and what is not finished is taken home by them. All relatives at the wedding bring gifts of *kimono* material, *sake*, or money, in exchange for which they receive banquet food and gift boxes of food which they take home.

While the bride, who is served banquet food in her own home before leaving, takes it with her, her mother brings home the food served to the bride at the groom's house.

The people who go to the most trouble in helping arrange a wedding—the two go-betweens—receive a special gift in gratitude for their trouble, while at the wedding they receive the banquet food in return for their gifts.

A man's bride is usually below him in education and experience. A man is more likely to have gone to the agricultural school while she stayed in her village sewing with the Young Women's Society. Even if he did not go outside the village to high school, he will have received some advanced lessons in geography and arithmetic in young men's classes at school and perhaps have gone to the barracks in Kumamoto or even overseas. While she may never have been away from home except for one or two school excursions to some city or historic spot, he has traveled far and lived away from the village for a year or so and thus gained a wider horizon. It is not meant for a dutiful wife to have too much learning; her job is to stay home, bear children, and work hard.

However, if a girl's parents have gone to the expense of sending her through a high school, they will usually see to it that this education is not wasted in an unequal match. She is more likely to be married to a teacher or into a richer family where she will not have to spend all her time doing hard farm labor.

Before marriage a boy is his father's son. After marriage, especially after becoming a father, he is a full-fledged member of the community and takes his fair share of all community farm labor. He is now regarded as mature.

If a man is an oldest son, he will continue to live after marriage with his parents in the same house in which he was born. A second or third son, on the other hand, is likely to be adopted out to some childless couple or to some family which has daughters but no sons. In the case of adoptive marriage everything is done as if the girl were the groom; her family goes to fetch him, the wedding is in her house, the man goes to live at his wife's home, and he assumes her name as do his children.

After marriage a man becomes adult, a part of the community, but it is not until the house head dies or retires that he becomes head of the house in which he lives. A bride also is not her own mistress so long as there is a mother-in-law to direct the affairs of the household.

The marriage itself is as likely as not to break up before a child is born. If bride and mother-in-law cannot get along together or if the husband is too exacting, the bride may return home. With the birth of a child things become more fixed, and it is usually not until this time that a marriage is recorded in the village office.

As a man becomes older, his voice carries more weight in *buraku* affairs. Younger men of twenty-five to forty do the public work acting as firemen, pallbearers, etc., while older men do the advising. When a man becomes very old, however, he is likely to find the responsibilities of being active head of a house irksome. At this point—around seventy— he is likely to retire, to go *inkyo*. He then lives in a separate room in the house and, while he may attend household festivities, need not bother his head about financial or other responsibilities.

SIXTY-FIRST BIRTHDAY

At sixty-one a man or a woman holds a party to cele- brate reaching the last and oldest age group. This party is usually a small one, restricted to close relatives and a few good friends. At this time a man enters second childhood and may again wear red—an old man will frequently wear a bright red *G*-string, and an old grandmother don a crim- son underskirt. As with children, the old people may do and say what they like without fear of criticism; and furthermore, if they demand something, it must be given them.

Both men and women tend to be more individualistic and free as they get older. This is seen in ribald conversa- tion, in which young men seldom and girls never partici- pate. Old people, not so busy with work, become more concerned with the Buddhist faith and the afterlife as age creeps on.

In case of illness friends make calls of sympathy (*mimai*). They bring as a gift not rice but something to be eaten uncooked such as fruit or eggs (eggs are often eaten raw).

If the illness is serious, someone from each house in the *buraku* will call at one time or another to express sympathy. After tea and relish in the *daidokoro* the gift is presented. Then the caller goes to the sickroom and talks a while with the sick person, then comes out and has more tea in the *daidokoro*. On departure his *furoshiki* and *jūbako* are returned to him.

DEATH

Then one day a man dies. His family gather about him to keep a deathwatch, and relatives are telegraphed to and come immediately to attend the funeral, which usually takes place the next day. (A telegram still means bad news in Suye.) Someone—often a child—is sent to inform the *nushidōri* of the event, and in turn he lets every house in the *buraku* know. A neighbor goes to tell the priest.

The morning of the funeral some *buraku* young men, chosen by the *nushidōri*, dig the grave in the *buraku* or family graveyard. As noted in the chapter on co-operation, the *nushidōri* consults with the deceased's family as to what is wanted for the funeral, i.e., a *tamaya* (soul house —a wooden structure placed over the actual coffin), bought from Menda or homemade by the neighbors, a priest or an amateur *kebōzu*.[17] Someone is sent, or rather volunteers to go, to Menda to buy the required things.

Meanwhile the bereaved family receives callers. The closest to the deceased, a spouse or child, is often much upset and sits beside the corpse and weeps. Relatives call, bringing gifts of rice, *shōchū*, and colored cloth for funeral banners. As they come to the house, they are served tea and beans by some *buraku* helper, after which they go in to inspect the corpse. They do not help in coffin and graveyard preparations.

[17] See chap. vii.

During the afternoon the male *buraku* helpers sit in the yard, make *tamaya*, coffin, paper flags to be inscribed with sutras and later thrown in the grave, poles for colored banners given by relatives, paper lanterns to be carried in the procession and discarded later, and a wooden candlestand called *rokujizō*. The women helpers are busy preparing food for the funeral feast to be given before the trip to the grave takes place. The pallbearers spend the afternoon digging the grave, which occupation they interrupt occasionally when the women bring them food and tea. Pallbearers and gravediggers are usually younger men appointed by the *nushidōri*.

When the coffin is ready, the body is undressed by close relatives behind an inverted screen. It is washed very thoroughly and dressed in a white pilgrim's outfit which has been prepared by a woman relative during the morning. A Buddhist rosary is put in its hand and a couple of coins in a bag hanging in front (for the ferryman in the next world). The deceased's fan is also inclosed, a fan being an indispensable part of a fully dressed individual. Often something the deceased liked very much is included. If the person died on *tomobiki* (an unlucky day for funerals), a straw doll is made and put in the coffin with the corpse; otherwise it would call some living person to the grave soon after. Often the dressers talk to the corpse, explaining what they are doing. Bunches of burning incense are held by all participants because the corpse kept in the house has a distinct odor. This is often remarked on bluntly during its washing and dressing. Those who help in this work all rush immediately to wash their hands in salt water when they have finished.

By now the priest has arrived. He waits in a neighbor's house until the family is ready for him. Soon the funeral feast begins, with the Buddhist priest placed in the seat of

WELL-TO-DO YOUNG MAN IN HOLIDAY ATTIRE
AT A SCHOOL ATHLETIC MEET

Man below him is Inari healing priest; women at right are all from one *buraku*

BURAKU HELPERS EATING AND DRINKING AFTER THE
WORK ON FUNERAL PARAPHERNALIA IS FINISHED

Note *geta* removed before stepping on the mats laid out on the ground

honor near the *tokonoma*. This funeral feast contains no fish. The formalized cakes served are dead white and are made of the same dry flour as is used in naming-ceremony and wedding cakes but lack the color. *Konnyaku*, *tōfu*, and seaweed are served instead of fish and are, during this meal, referred to as *sakana* (fish). Before starting the banquet all participants change into their most formal clothes and women have their hair arranged in a special funeral hairdress.

The members of the family exchange drinks with the priest. When the feast, a farewell meal with the dead, is over, the trays are removed and the funeral begins. The priest sits in front of the coffin with a bell and in some cases a gong and recites sutras.

Meanwhile the male *buraku* helpers have been eating and drinking in the yard or the barn and enjoying themselves. Usually they do not bother much with the funeral service, though a group of neighborhood children and the little nurses with their charges turn up outside to peer in.

As soon as the funeral service is over, however, the *buraku* men start work. They go into the house, bring out the coffin, and prepare to take it to the cemetery. Before leaving the house with the coffin they must each drink a teacup full of *shōchū* passed to them by one of the serving women. When the coffin is gone, one of the women throws a straw matting over the place where it was, to be kept there until the funeral procession is out of sight. The floor is swept with a bundle of straw.

The words of the priest are not understood by anyone present at the funeral; the meaning of most of the rituals is also unknown. However, the main purpose of the funeral ceremony is clear, namely, to send the dead man's soul safely to paradise.

Formerly funerals were very expensive as the afflicted

family was expected to give a sumptuous banquet, and relatives to give lavish gifts of colored cloth for the grave-yard. Of late, economy measures, partly inaugurated by the village office, have reduced the expense and also some of the color and importance of funerals in *buraku* life.

At a funeral many things are done in a way opposite to normal usage. The screen in the room by the corpse is inverted, and hanging scrolls are turned to face the wall. At the funeral banquet there is no fish; at drink exchange one is not supposed to repeat a drink before returning the cup, for that would indicate another death. Any clothes of the dead later put out to sun are hung inside out.

So ends a man's life. However, the ceremonies of which he is the ostensible cause are not yet finished. The next day is called *detsuki*. On this day relatives again come to the house of the dead. They did not stay overnight as that is considered a ritually bad thing to do. They visit the new grave, washing their hands before going into the ceme-tery. The priest also visits the house to receive money for his services and arrange with the relatives a program of seven memorial services (*kuyō*) for the deceased. These are supposed to be every seven days for forty-nine days by orthodox Buddhist rule, but in real life they come at inter-vals of six days or less. The villagers do not like them to extend into three months or over two years, which are two reasons for shortening the periods. The first and seventh of these *kuyō* take place at the house of the deceased, the other five at houses of various relatives as agreed upon at *detsuki*. Often an orthodox priest is present only for the first and seventh *kuyō*, a *kebōzu* officiating at the other five.

At the memorial service a priest comes and reads some sutras before the *butsudan* containing the deceased's *ihai* (wooden stick with posthumous name). Relatives come, visit the grave, then come back and sit in the *zashiki* while the priest reads. A small party is given by the host (no fish being served) with the priest in the place of honor. Relatives bring as a gift rice and *shōchū*. The last of the seven seven-day *kuyō* is called *hiaki* and represents the end of the mourning period just as the *hiaki* after birth ends the danger period of the infant; food taboos are now lifted.

Then come yearly ceremonies, also called *kuyō*, in memory of the dead man. They are held at the house of the dead. They are called one-, three-, seven-, thirteen-, seventeen-, twenty-five-, thirty-three-, and fifty-year ceremonies. They take place one, two, six, twelve, sixteen, twenty-four, thirty-two, and forty-nine full years after the death took place. The earlier ones are most fully observed. They are observed in much the same way as the seven-day *kuyō*. The purpose of these services is to insure the dead man a place in paradise. After the last of these, it may be said that a man ceases to influence the lives of his family.

There are several common features running through the three great events of a man's life (birth, marriage, and death). In the first place, an intermediary is present in all three: at birth the midwife to bring one into the world and give one a name; at marriage the *nakaudo* to bring two families together through their children; and at death the Buddhist priest to pave the way for one to enter paradise. At all three there is a party for relatives, and at this party the intermediary is always given the place of honor. All three are primarily family affairs. The appearance of the *buraku* at the funeral is the coming-together of people in time of calamity to aid the stricken family.

From the point of view of social value to the family the marriage is the most important. Through marriage come heirs and on heirs depend the future welfare of the family and through heirs one's *ihai* are properly taken care of. It is not surprising then to find the *nakaudo* who acts as intermediary for this event becoming thereafter something of a relative, being invited to naming ceremonies and often coming as a mourner to a funeral.

The birth of a child, though of potential value to both *buraku* and family, is not yet of proven value; furthermore, the child is very likely to die. If he does, another will probably be born. So the *buraku* is not concerned, and relatives from a distance are not called in. At the wedding, with its great importance to the family, relatives from far and near are called. There is a great banquet. The *buraku*'s interest in the event is recognized by the *chanomi*.

At death the family loses a member and comes together to mourn the event. The *buraku* also loses a member but, being larger than the family, is not so seriously affected. While they turn out to aid the unfortunate family at the funeral itself, they have no concern with the memorial services. The size of a funeral varies both with the age and with the social position. If a baby dies, only half the *buraku* need come and but few relatives. If a man or woman in the prime of life dies, the loss being greater, more relatives come and more *buraku* helpers. If an old man or woman dies, the loss is not so great—a man must die sometime—so the family is not particularly grief-stricken. But the relatives gather and the *buraku* comes to the rescue because of what the man was to society during his life, not what he was at the time he died.

CHAPTER VII

RELIGION

THE two traditional religions of Japan, Shinto and Buddhism, play a predominant part in the village life. However, Buddhism as a theological system and Shinto as a formal religion, while appreciated to some extent by the local Buddhist and Shinto priests, are little understood by the peasant; he looks to Buddhism as a means of soul salvation and to the pantheon of Shinto gods for protection in this life. The only religious system—and an important one in the local community life—is the festival calendar, marking as it does the phases of the moon and the seasons of the year.

Concerning Buddhism and Shinto, one man remarked: "Some people say one should not go to shrines but just worship Hotoke [Buddha]; others say one should visit shrines because Japan is the land of the *kami* [Shinto deities]. As for myself, since people have different opinions on the matter, it is not for me to condemn them or say they are wrong. I always visit the shrines as well as worship Hotoke."

There is no regular weekly or monthly attendance at either the shrines or the temples, nor is there any individual or congregational communion with the gods. For all this the priests represent the people, saying for them prayers and performing for them various rituals. The priest acts as intermediary between the people and the gods.

The beliefs and ritual observances of the people of Suye Mura may be roughly divided into seven classes and will be so described.

I. Shrine Shinto
II. Temple Buddhism
III. Gods and sacred objects of the household
    a) *Butsudan* and Hotoke (the Amida or Buddha in the Buddhist alcove)
    b) Kamidana and *taima* (talisman from Ise shrine, Shinto)
    c) Daikoku, Ebisu, Inari (Shinto)
    d) Nichirin (flowers to the sun, Shinto)
    e) Kitchen and well-gods (Shinto)
    f) Kojin or Jinushi (property-god, Shinto)
    g) Jizō (Buddhist)
    h) *Ofuda* and *omamori* (charms and talismans, Shinto and Buddhist)
    i) *Nanten* tree
    j) *Hoshimatsuri* (good-luck ceremonies for the household, Shinto and Buddhist)
IV. Gods of the wayside
    a) Deities in *dō*
    b) Wayside, stones, and images
    c) Deities of the water, mountain, etc.
V. Bewitchment and faith healing
    a) *Kitōshi*
    b) Sorcery
    c) Foxes
VI. Beliefs concerning the three crises of life
    a) Birth (Buddhist and Shinto)
    b) Marriage (not formally connected with either Buddhism or Shinto, though the *butsudan* is open for the occasion, and the *tokonoma* decorated)
    c) Death (Buddhist)
VII. Yearly festivals (Shinto and Buddhist)

SHINTO

There are two main bodies of belief concerning birth, death, afterlife, and the gods. These are the native beliefs termed Shinto and the beliefs, mostly imported hundreds of years ago from China, termed Buddhist. Much of the belief classified as Shinto is not originally Japanese, and many Shinto practices may be traced to China (e.g., house purification at New Year's, bewitchment by foxes, the moon festival). As far as the villager is concerned, however, all his beliefs, Buddhist or Shinto, are indigenous.

The word Shinto means "way of the gods" and was invented after the introduction of Buddhism to distinguish the native Japanese beliefs from those of Buddhism. Shinto includes a wide range of rather unsystematized ceremonies and beliefs. There are numerous gods, with the sun-goddess (Amaterasu-ō-mikami) as the most important. In the pantheon as given in the *Kojiki*, the sun-goddess is neither the first deity nor the deity who created the world. She is regarded today, however, as the most important first ancestor of the Japanese ruling family. All the people of Japan are regarded as being descended from the early gods and thus having a touch of the divine in their nature.

The two most reliable accounts of early Japanese history are the *Kojiki* and *Nihongi*. These volumes, forming the oldest extant Japanese literature, were written at court order in A.D. 712 and 720, respectively. One of their purposes was to establish the rulers of that period as the legitimate descendants of the gods. The early parts of these books describe the founding of the world (Japan) and the activities of the gods in those early days. This period is generally termed the Age of the Gods. Then in 660 B.C.[1] came Jimmu Tennō, regarded by Japanese as the first historical figure.

Shinto priests attempt to find the origin of all truly Japanese customs in these old texts. All wayside gods are identified with some deity or other who figured in the Age

---

[1] By Japanese chronology this is the year 1. This is the orthodox Japanese date, but most critical historians regard it as six hundred to a thousand years too early.

of the Gods. Native deities are called *kami* and Buddhist deities *butsu*, but in village parlance both are called mister or sir (*san* or *sama*).

The present-day emphasis on Shinto is a comparatively recent development begun by such patriotic native scholars as Motoori and his disciple Hirata in the nineteenth century. For many centuries before that time Buddhism had been uppermost both at the court in Kyoto and with the common people. Today Buddhism is weaker or absent from the court. It is still strong among the people, but the meaning has evaporated from many of its ceremonies.

Shinto includes three distinct series of beliefs.

I. Popular Shinto, which includes:
   a) The heterogeneous pantheon of household gods
   b) Local beliefs and ceremonies that vary from region to region such as the beliefs surrounding the sacred mountain Ichifusa in Kuma
   c) Beliefs surrounding certain popular gods such as Inari, god of crops and *geisha*
   d) Beliefs in bewitchment by foxes or possession by the evil-dog spirit
II. Shrine Shinto, which includes:
   a) The yearly series of rituals at the village Shinto shrine performed by the government-appointed Shinto priest
   b) Distribution of the sacred talisman (*taima*) from Ise shrine
   c) Teaching of school children by priest and teacher of official Shinto belief, divinity of the Emperor and purity of the Japanese race. Shrine Shinto is not regarded as a religion by the government in contrast to the Shinto sects.
III. Shinto sects:
   There are several popular sects of Shinto somewhat similar to sects of Buddhism. A member of one of these sects does not belong to any Buddhist sect and is buried according to Shinto rites, whereas ordinarily a person belongs to some Buddhist sect and at the same time recognizes the popular Shinto deities and shrine Shinto. Many of these sects have a belief in healing by faith similar to Christian Science. Because most popular sects of Shinto center about the sun-goddess, the ancestor of the royal family, and its priests often claim communion with the Shinto gods, they

often come close to lèse majesté. At least two Shinto sects have been suppressed and their shrines destroyed by the government.[2] The followers of these new Shinto sects are characterized by a pious fervor lacking among adherents of the older Buddhist sects. Indeed, the growth of these sects may be regarded as an "uncontrolled response" to the impact of Western culture of the same general type as certain nativistic movements in New Guinea and elsewhere.[3]

While Buddhism is more important to the individual, Shinto is more important to the *mura*. In every *mura* in Japan there is a Shinto shrine[4] and a Shinto priest. The shrine is sometimes partly subsidized by the prefecture, the rest of its support and the salary of its priest coming from village office funds and so ultimately from taxes on the villagers.

The village shrine (*sonsha*) is a residence for the patron god of the *mura* (*ujigami*). He protects and looks after the welfare of the *mura* as a whole.

The Shinto priest is a village man, usually a farmer, suggested by the village office, technically appointed by the prefectural office. For his priestly services he receives 254 yen a year from the village office plus about 270 yen in contributions from villagers. Whereas the headman goes to his office six days a week, the priest has only to look after the shrine and officiate at official Shinto ceremonies. He acts as caretaker of the shrine and representative of the *mura* in its relations with its patron god or *ujigami*.

[2] In Suye only one family, to my knowledge, belongs to a Shinto sect (Tenrikyō). Though they call in a Tenrikyō priest for burials, all other funeral arrangements are similar to their neighbors and are run on the idea of *buraku* cooperation. Instead of a *butsudan* in the house they have a little Tenrikyō shrine.

[3] See chap. viii. By far the best account in English of Shinto is W. G. Aston's *Shinto: The Way of the Gods* (London, 1905). Much of what he described a generation ago is still true of everyday rural life.

[4] In Japanese *tera* means Buddhist temple or shrine; *miya*, Shinto temple or shrine. By common usage however, *tera* is always translated as temple and *miya* as shrine.

The chief function of the Shinto priest is to perform the rituals necessary at official ceremonies. There are prescribed rituals the meaning of which is quite unknown to the ordinary villager. As a rule the ordinary villager never attends shrine ceremonies. Instead there are two men called *ujikosōdai* or representatives of the villagers who are expected, with village officials, to attend all such rituals. The schoolmaster often attends also.

The shrine is in Aso Buraku. It is old—the usual "three hundred years"—of plain wood and thatch roof. Before entering the shrine each person washes his hands and mouth at some near-by stream or from a receptacle for the purpose. Priest and officials usually come in ordinary *kimono*, then the priest changes to ceremonial garb, the others to formal dress (*hakama* and *montsuki*).

Descriptions of the rituals are given in Aston's *Shinto* and in Florenz' *Ancient Japanese Rituals*. As a rule they consist of purifying all present by the priest's waving a *sakaki* branch with *gohei* attached over each person's bowed head. Then each person presents in turn a smaller *sakaki* branch called *tamagushi* to the altar. This is to represent his sincerity of spirit during the ritual. The priest recites a prayer of purification, followed by one concerning the business on hand. This latter is often composed by the priest himself for the occasion and is the only original thing in the ceremony. At the close of the service the priest closes the shrine doors and brings down the offerings of food and wine, which are then eaten and drunk by those present. Sometimes at the beginning of the ceremony the priest calls down the god with a peculiar high-pitched siren-like call and "sends him back" at the end of the ceremony in a similar manner.

The festivals of the village shrine are, as noted, mostly

official affairs, attended by government officials but not bothered with by the average villager. One exception is the yearly festival of the god of the village shrine. This occurs now on November 27 by the new calendar.[5] Other villages of Kuma have their festivals at similar dates in the fall. The purpose of this festival is to thank the god of the village for all he has done, especially by way of good crops. At this time some outside priests are invited who, on the eve of the twenty-seventh perform sacred ritual dances (*okagura*) in order to please the god. Villagers say that of old these dances were representative of the sex life of the gods, but today nothing of this nature can be detected in the stiff formal posturings of the priests. The day of the twenty-seventh all officials and school children come for another ritual. In the afternoon a banquet is held at the priest's house for all schoolteachers, village officials, and other notables. Except for three female schoolteachers, this party of fifty or so consists entirely of men. Its expenses are partly paid by the village office.

The twenty-seventh of each month the priest visits the shrine and performs a brief ritual in behalf of the *mura*. Recently the prefecture decided that on this day school children should visit the shrine, pay respects to the *uji-gami*, and receive some words of wisdom from the priest. By an ironic combination of days the first of these visits and talks had to be held on the twenty-eighth because the twenty-seventh was a Sunday, and school was not in session.[6]

The particular priest in Suye is himself rather a nationalist, who considers everything foreign, including Buddhism,

[5] Formerly ninth or twenty-seventh of tenth month by lunar calendar; informants disagree. See also festival calendar below.

[6] A summary of the priest's speech on this day is given as Appen. V.

a corruption of the pristine purity of Japanese culture. He carries this belief to the extent of saying that silk originated in Japan and that the goddess of silk is a native Japanese deity. An interesting expression of his pride occurred at two parties held at the end of the last silkworm season of the year 1936 by the two sericultural associations. Formerly each *buraku* had its own party centering about a memorial service by a Buddhist priest for the souls of the dead silkworms. This year, for the first time, all members in the *mura* of one association held their party and celebration together at the school, inviting the Zen priest to read sutras. The other association, not to be outdone, had a similar big party at school a week or so later, but to be different they had a Shinto ceremony with the village Shinto priest in to perform a ritual of purification and thanks after the successful season. Whereas the head of the second association said the change was just to be different, the Shinto priest said the first association used a Buddhist priest because they did not know any better.

In case of severe drought the priest and other notable villagers including the schoolmaster go to a sacred waterfall in the mountain *buraku* of Hirayama to pray for rain. Often the women of a *buraku* will perform some dance to please the gods. These are the old *buraku* dances already described elsewhere, and it is not beyond belief that the obscene and mirth-provoking dances before the cave where the sun-goddess hid in the Age of the Gods were of a similar type.

Often, when a young man goes to the barracks or to work in some distant place, his mother or grandmother will make a pledge (*gwan*) to visit the shrine every twenty-seventh and offer *omiki* (i.e., cold *shōchū* which is offered at the shrine) in order that the traveler may return home in safety. Along with this might go a promise not to smoke or not to drink for a year. The priest's presence is not required on this occasion.

A characteristic of most local non-Buddhist ritual is to propitiate the unseen powers. The various village shrine celebrations are in honor of the patron deity of the *mura* in order that he continue to protect it. A ridgepole ceremony is to keep evil from befalling the owners of the new house, a bridge-building ceremony to beguile the river-god in order that he not harm users of the bridge.

The place of the Emperor in Shinto should be mentioned. He is considered to be descended from the sun-goddess, Amaterasu-ō-mikami. Some people connect Amaterasu with the sun; others say Nichirinsama and Amaterasu-ō-mikami are different gods. The bowing of farmers to the east on arising is by some ascribed to reverence for the sun, by others to reverence for the Emperor (whose palace is to the east of Suye). When school children or a group of people at school bow to the east before beginning work on hand, it is definitely toward the Emperor's palace. School children and teachers must bow to the Emperor's portrait on entering and leaving the auditorium containing it as well as on entering and leaving the school grounds. All important school meetings begin with elaborate bows to the Emperor and the reading of Imperial rescripts. The people are constantly told by schoolmasters, Shinto priests, and army officials that the Emperor is their godly head. Whenever he is mentioned, listeners must stand at attention; whenever his rescripts are read, listeners must bow.

BUDDHISM

Buddhism in Japan is a special form of the religion originally imported from China. There are many varieties, some of which originated in China, such as Zen with its emphasis on inner enlightenment, others of which originated in Japan, such as the militant Nichiren. The most popular sect in Kuma is the Shinshū sect. This should more properly be called Amidism than Buddhism as its central figure is not Shaka but Amida. Amidism developed in China. Its chief point of faith is that Amida has made it possible for mankind to reach heaven by faith alone. Sir Charles Eliot has a good account of Amidism in general and of the Shinshū sect in particular in his book *Japanese Buddhism*. The popular Jōdo form of Amidism was founded by the Japanese Saint Hōnen in the twelfth century. Eliot summarizes Jōdo thus: "If a man, no matter who, how wicked or unlettered, repeat these words [Namu Amida Butsu] with a believing heart, Amida will appear to him in the hour of death and conduct him to the happy land."[7] Shinran, a student of Hōnen, founded the branch of Jōdo known as Shinshū. In all essentials it is the same as Jōdo. The belief of Jōdo and Shinshū is called *tariki* or the reliance on a higher power as contrasted to *jiriki* or dependence on one's self (as in Zen) for salvation and enlightenment. The Shinshū sect is concerned mostly with personal salvation by faith in Amida. The Shinshū priest in Fukada maintains that, as Zen stresses the individual, it thus encourages self-centeredness and undermines the family system, a subtle bit of theological propaganda.

As it is now practiced in rural districts such as Suye, Buddhism is concerned chiefly with funerals and memorial services for the dead. Popular Buddhist beliefs and practices are not distinguishable in function from those of Shinto. The official priestly Shinto is full of rituals known only to the priests but watched by the people and considered

[7] *Japanese Buddhism* (London, 1935), p. 263.

beneficial by them. This is true also of the priestly Buddhism as it comes into play at funerals. The people depend on the priests as go-betweens between themselves and the deities. The priest is paid for performing his duty, and the worshiper merely adds "amen" to his prayers and incantations. There are no congregational responses made or hymns sung in Shinto or Japanese Buddhism.

In Suye itself there is only one regular Buddhist temple. It is called Ryōgenin and is of the Sōdō subsect of Zen Buddhism. The priest came from Nagasaki and had been in Suye twenty years.[8] The temple, in Kakui Buraku, has been established about four hundred years in Suye. It is rather a rundown place itself, and the priest's wife helps out the family income by raising silkworms, using half the temple as a worm-feeding-room, but the location is superb, being on a cliff by the Kuma River and overlooking the broad rice plain. In the foreground are the house clusters of Kawaze and Nakashima, in the background the mountains inclosing Kuma County. The village headman, after a trip to Tokyo and Kyoto, his first out of Kyushu, remarked that none of the famous beauty spots of Japan is more lovely than the view from Ryōgenin. The beauty of location is the chief asset of this temple; its membership is only fifty houses comprising Kakui and parts of Oade and Imamura. None of the very rich belongs to this temple. Practically all the rest of the *mura*, rich and poor alike, belong to the Shinshū temple in Fukada. One or two families in Nakashima belong to a Nichiren sect temple in Taragi, one family to a temple in Kurohiji, and one family to a popular Shinto sect.

In feudal days the Shinshū sect of Buddhism was pro-

---

[8] He died in November, 1936, just a week or so after the author left Suye. A priest from Menda replaced him.

hibited by the lords of Sagara, who favored Zen. Thus
many Zen temples were built, but Shinshū by no means
died out. Priests would make secret trips down from Kumamoto over the mountains of Itsuki and thus into Kuma
County by a back way. Secret meetings of Shinshū believers were held. There still are farmhouses in Suye where
such meetings were held. Believers would put a picture of
Amida inside the wall of the house and bow to it morning
and evening. So, while on the surface Shinshū disappeared
during the era of Sagara, as soon as the Meiji Restoration
took away this power, Shinshū came forth again, perhaps
stronger than ever. In the mountain *mura* of Itsuki, even
today, many houses, while professing Zen, have a Shinshū
butsudan. A leftover of this period are the *kebōzu* ("hairy
priests")[9] or unofficial Buddhist priests who can read
sutras but have no temple. Today they function only at
funerals of the poor, memorial services, etc.

In the old days there were several Shingon sect temples
in Kuma. Shaka *dō* in Aso Buraku, now only a *buraku
dō* celebrating on Buddha's birthday, was once such a
temple. In the grounds surrounding it are still many very
old graves of a type no longer made. There is a similar old
Shingon graveyard in Aramo Buraku of Fukada Mura.
The story goes that, when Buddhism was prohibited in
this region, a *samurai* killed the priest of the Aramo temple. So now, whenever wood is cut there, a Shinto priest
performs a special ceremony. Today there is no Shingon
temple either in or near Suye.

The Fukada temple was built over one hundred years
ago. It is of the Myōshijiha subsect of Shinshū Buddhism.

---

[9] Called "hairy" because, unlike regular priests, *kebōzu* do not shave their
heads. Shinshū Buddhism suffered similar difficulties in Kagoshima under the
lords of Satsuma. See H. B. Schwartz, *In Togo's Country* (Cincinnati, 1908),
pp. 56–57.

Most of the inhabitants of Fukada and Suye and many of
the mountain *mura* of Itsuki and Youra belong to it—in
all five hundred and fifty regular members, i.e., households.
The priests are kept very busy with funerals and memorial
services over this wide area.

The Zen and Shinshū priests aim at keeping and serving
their members through holding *kuyō* (memorial services),
attending funerals, and giving lectures. There is little attempt at moral uplift or proselyting. The priests of both
temples are liberal drinkers, and both are married. Neither
has any religious scruples concerning war. They also eat
chicken, the only meat ever seen in this region.

Followers of the temples visit them three or four times
a year, taking a gift of rice. Usually they go when a lecture is being given. Every so often a visiting priest gives a
series of lectures. Lord Redesdale in his *Tales of Old Japan*
gives some samples of priests' lectures. While they vary
somewhat from sect to sect, his samples are typical.

The first and fifteenth are important days of the month
to the local Zen temple. The priest reads special sutras for
"Oshaka" and for the Emperor's prosperity.[10] He reads
"ordinary" sutras daily. They are written in Chinese
characters and given a Japanese pronunciation. The priest
understands the sense of a given sutra but cannot translate it in detail.

On New Year's many *hoshimatsuri* are performed by
the Zen priest of Suye who goes to any house that asks
him regardless of sect and performs a purification of the
house for the whole family, giving them a special *hoshimatsuri ofuda*. For this he receives food and about five *gō*
(half a *shō*) of rice. Many people visit the temple at this

[10] The priest regards his chief duties as funerals, *kuyo*, *hoshimatsuri*, and
prayers to cure sickness.

time and pay respects to the Buddha and the Kwannon there. In the old days the Tenjin shrine[11] was also in the temple, but after Meiji this was separated and is now next door.

On the first and third of the first month, the priest reads a special sutra for the prosperity of the country. In the first or second month the main temple (Myōshinji) in Kyoto sends a priest who lectures. The purpose of the talks is to propagate the sect and educate its followers.

In the eleventh month is the big festival of the Zen temple, the *sengo kuyō*, or service for ancestors of the temple members. All members come and make generous gifts, some as much as a bushel of rice, to the temple. This is in gratitude to the priest for caring for the souls of their ancestors. At this time a visiting priest gives a three-day series of lectures on Buddhism. Many followers, of both Zen sect and Shinshū sect, listen. The night of the last of them the members have a big party, with plenty to eat and drink and many a dance.

There are certain other dates of importance to the local Zen temple, such as Buddha's birthday and Higan, which will be noted below in the festival calendar.

At the Shinshū temple in Fukada Mura New Year's is celebrated, as in the Zen temple, by visits to the temple with small gifts to the priest. The Shinshū priests perform no *hoshimatsuri*, and make no *ofuda*.

During spring Higan all worshipers visit the temple "because this is the time to reflect upon one's sins." Several followers of the temple hang up a *kakemono* representing the tortures of hell. Lectures are given at the temple. Certain *buraku* have Higan *gokuyō* (memorial services) given on a *kumi* system. A priest from the Shinshū temple

[11] See below, tenth month of festival calendar.

is invited to give a talk and is entertained at the house of one of the members of the *kumi* on duty. Each person contributes ten or fifteen sen to pay the priest and brings rice and *shōchū* for the meal.

Eitai kyō usually begins on April 10 (by new calendar) and lasts five days, but the date varies from temple to temple. An outside priest comes to lecture, reminding people of the mistakes of their ancestors in order to show the inconstancy of life and thus give an impetus toward enlightenment. The priest reads a sutra to express gratitude to Amida.

Uetsuke gokuyō, a transplanting memorial service, is held by *buraku* on the *kumi* system for the souls of all the insects killed during transplanting. The Shinshū priest gives a lecture. Some people visit the temple at this time. There are certain other religious occasions (*ottaya, nonori iwai*) observed by some *buraku* in this same manner.

Hōon kō, gratitude day for the founder, is held on the twenty-first to twenty-eighth of the eleventh month, but dates differ in different temples according to a time convenient for the farming community.

Goshoki kuyō service on the death day of Shinran, the founder of Shin, is held with *hōon kō* in Fukada, though in some temples it is separately celebrated. On this day most Shinshū followers visit the temple and take gifts, and sometimes a *buraku* as a whole sends a load of firewood or vegetables. A visiting lecturer comes and gives a series of lectures for six days. Certain *buraku* make a large dumpling of rice and red beans contributed by each member which is taken to the temple to be purified, then brought back and distributed to all the members.

The Women's Buddhist Society meets twice a year at

the temple and receives lectures. This corresponds to the women's *kō* of the Zen temple.

The priests in each temple know, of course, more or less of the theology of their particular sects. Sir Charles Eliot in his *Japanese Buddhism* gives a good account of these, but the followers of the two temples scarcely know the difference. Indeed, some younger people hardly know which temple their family belongs to, as they rarely attend the temple even on the special times for visiting. It is the older people who begin to worry about afterlife and think about Buddha. Many of them will visit a temple at odd times between the big festivals. Some of the old people know many stories and develop theories about the goodness of Amida, but even so they cannot tell the difference between Shaka and Amida and frequently regard Shaka and Buddha as two different deities.

The priests give talks on religion at every *kuyō*, but usually some anecdote from them is all the people remember. The belief in reincarnation, sometimes referred to in a priest's talks, never seems to be grasped by his listeners. Indeed, these *kuyō* are more a meeting of relatives to honor the dead and have a little food and drink together than to learn religion. So, though the priest always gives a talk after having read the sutras, and all listen apparently attentively, they scarcely ever bother to understand what he is talking about any more than they attempt to understand the quite incomprehensible sutras he recites for the souls of their dead.

That one should be thankful to Amida for looking after one in this world and the next, all Shinshū people grasp—beyond this they do not go.

THE POPULAR GODS

The attendance at the Shinto shrine, except on the eve of its festival day in the fall, is restricted to village officials and to stray visits by people at New Year's and for the purpose of making vows or presenting a new baby to the gods. The Buddhist temples are more often frequented, but the chief function of the Buddhist priest is at funerals. More important in the daily life of a peasant are the numerous deities of his house and yard and familiar pathways. More important than the orthodox priest is the praying priest who can cure sickness and drive out evil spirits—spirits more to be feared than the Buddhist hell because more familiar and closer at hand.

The yearly round of festivals is more closely bound up with the phases of the moon and the agricultural cycle than with either formal Buddhism or official Shinto. This is to be expected in an old and stable peasant community with a long tradition of the proper times and ways to gather for social and sacred festivities.

In the household the two deities are Amida in the *butsudan* and the sun-goddess or Inari represented by a *taima* in the *kamidana*.

"BUTSUDAN"

In the *butsudan* is an image of, or scroll picturing, the savior Amida with many golden rays shining forth from him. Here also are the wooden *ihai*, or memorial name tablets of the house ancestors.[12] In addition, other picture

[12] The *ihai* is found in every Japanese household even though not formally Buddhist. Confucianists probably introduced the idea of the tablet to Japan, and Hozumi believes that ancestor worship was a part of Shinto before the Chinese influence. So, although today the *ihai* is a part of the Buddhist alcove, it is not necessarily Buddhist in origin.

scrolls may be seen here. Family photographs may be placed in the *butsudan*. Lately it has become customary to have a large portrait made of the deceased head of the house and his wife and to hang it above the *butsudan*.

The Buddhist altar varies greatly with wealth. A rich man will have a highly ornate black-and-gold lacquer *butsudan* with latticed doors and fine brocade cloths. Poor households have a more modestly lacquered *butsudan* that stands out in elegance from the rest of the house furniture, but which is very humble compared to the *butsudan* of a richer neighbor. Here every morning a man bows and mumbles three times over "Namu Amida Butsu" (which becomes "Namanda, namanda, namanda" in actual prayer). This triple formula, which may be repeated several times, carries all Shinshū believers eventually to the blissful western heaven of Amida. Members of the Zen temple perform a similar daily ritual. This routine ceremony gives a man a feeling of rightness—that everything is in order for the day.[13]

The housewife fills daily two little brass or porcelain cups on stands like candlesticks with freshly cooked rice and puts them as well as a cup of tea in the *butsudan*. Later in the day or evening children or mice eat the rice. There is nothing wrong in this since the essence, not the substance, is for Hotokesama.

"KAMIDANA"

After bowing at the *butsudan*, some people also bow before the *kamidana* (Shinto household shrine), clapping hands instead of ringing a bell. Actually the *kamidana* is usually a little plain wood box high up on a house post by the *tokonoma*, so the prayer is offered by kneeling at the

[13] One farmer remarked that he does not like to sleep away from home as he has no proper place to go in the morning to perform this ritual.

tokonoma. This is not nearly so universal a custom as paying respects at the *butsudan.*

Offerings for the *kamidana* are often placed in the *tokonoma.* Two cups of rice and a cup of tea are the usual daily offerings. In the *kamidana* is kept the *taima* or paper talisman of Daijingu (shrine of the sun-goddess at Ise). The *taima* are distributed annually from the great shrine at Ise through prefectural and village offices. The *kuchō* distribute them in their *buraku,* collect five or ten sen each, and give the money to the village office which in turn sends it to the great national shrine at Ise. With the *taima* is also sold an official Shinto almanac for ten sen, but not everyone buys it, and those who do buy it do not use it.[14] Instead, if a calendar other than the ordinary one on the wall is wanted, a Buddhist one with lucky days and astrological lore is used. In addition to *taima* from Ise, *ofuda*[15] of Mount Ichifusa and Mount Kitadake may be kept in the *kamidana* also. In the evening the first cup of *shōchū* is placed before the *kamidana.*

In the *tokonoma,* presumably Shinto, are picture scrolls of Inari or the Emperor or both. Inari, god of crops, is pictured as an old man holding a bundle of rice. A common Emperor picture scroll shows the reigning (or more often last reigning) Emperor and Empress and above them on the scroll small insets of all previous Emperors back to a glorific sun-goddess, the Imperial ancestress of all the Emperors of Japan and of all their subjects as well.

Often, however, Buddhist scrolls are hung here instead

[14] These *taima* and calendars have been a source of income for the priests of the shrine at Ise for centuries (G. B. Sansom, *Japan: A Short Cultural History* [New York, 1931], p. 371). Kaempfer (*History of Japan* [London, 1727]) also describes this practice.

[15] *Ofuda* are, like *taima,* paper talismans bearing the name of the issuing Shinto shrine. Only those from Ise are called *taima.*

of or in addition to Inari or the Emperors. The commonest is one of many-armed Batokwannon, patron saint of wagoners and horse owners, another is of Miyajidake, god of wealth and brokers, from a temple in Hakata.

Some houses have a Yakushi (god of healing) picture scroll. Owners of Batokwannon or Yakushi scrolls usually hold a small celebration on the respective saint's days. Carpenters and some other artisans have a scroll of their patron saint, the great Shōtoku Taishi. A few rich houses in the village have several such *kakemono* hung up, different ones on different days; the majority of farmers, however, never bother to change the *kakemono*. Except for little ones of Kōbō Daishi or Amida in the *butsudan*, *kakemono* are always hung in the *tokonoma*. An especially common scroll is one of the great and fabulous Kōbō Daishi. Of him it is said in the village that after a trip to China he returned with only three grains of some specially good rice. As he was walking along upon his return, dogs barked at him, and the rice grains fell out of his sleeve. In this manner people discovered about this very good rice. Since then it has become customary to start the planting of rice on the day of the dog. Many people in Suye still observe this custom.

EBISU AND DAIKOKU

Practically every house has a little wooden image of Daikoku and Ebisu in the kitchen (*suijiba*) or *daidokoro*. They are on a shelf in a box high up on a post and usually are blackened with soot, and a farmer may jokingly remark that Ebisusan and Daikokusan like smoke. No prayers are offered to them, but cups of rice are usually given them every morning. The first bit of some special dish is often placed before them and sometimes a first cup of *shōchū*. A bamboo vase with a fresh flower is usually kept nailed to the wall near this shrine. In early spring when bulrushes are profuse a single graceful spear may be seen in the green bamboo vase contrasting sharply with the smoke-blackened Daikoku and surrounding rafters. These are gods of good fortune in general and appear to be of native Japanese origin. Being images, they add a personal touch to a house just as other images do in a *buraku dō*. The very poorest house has a Daikoku (or, if not, an Inari) even if there is no "Daijingusan" or no Hotoke.

Shopkeepers usually have a wooden plaque bearing faces of Daikoku and Ebisu, and in this form the deities are believed to be the shopkeepers' patron saints. The *shōchū* factory in Suye and some of the *tōfu*-makers and small shops have such plaques.

If a household moves, the Buddhist altar is carefully wrapped up and moved too, also the kitchen gods of Daikoku and Ebisu.

There is considerable vagueness about all the deities. One man, for instance, says that the mountain-god called Yama-no-Kamisama is the same as the household-god called Daikokusan. Some say Daikoku and Ebisu, so often seen together, are a married couple; others say they are father and son; still others call them brothers. Their sex is vague and their representation is not always the same. The conventional smiling Daikoku and Ebisu are commonest, but some houses have roughly cut images that look more like some Polynesian product.[16]

SUN

By the front entrance of many farm houses is a bamboo vase with a flower in it. This is for Nichirinsan, the sun.

[16] Buchanan, in his book on Inari, identifies Daikoku with Inari, but no one in Suye does so.

STOVE AND WELL

In the kitchen fresh flowers are kept for the god of stoves (Kama-no-Kamisama), and by the well are flowers for the well-god. Offerings of salt and rice are made to these two gods.

KOJIN

Somewhere in the yard of older households is a stone, or small house containing a stone or mirror. This is the land-god called either Kojin or Jinushi. (Jinushi is also used to mean landowner in the ordinary sense of the word.)

No daily offerings are made to the Jinushi, though flowers may be put before it. Often some of the first grain is put there, then hung later from rafters of the house and used as seed the following spring. Some people hang first grain in the *tokonoma* instead of by the Jinushi.

JIZŌ

Some yards have a stone Jizō in them, usually by the front entrance to the yard. Fresh flowers are given to him, and he receives candles and *shōchū* on Jizō Day. He is regarded as a protector of the house. Occasionally, a household Jizō is some distance from its owner's house. This is probably due to the family's having moved its house but not its Jizō.[17]

CHARMS AND TALISMANS

On the posts by the front entrance to a house are pasted many *ofuda* or paper talismans. These come from various shrines and temples, purchased for a sen or two when some member of the house went shrine-visiting. Sometimes a wandering pilgrim sells *ofuda* for five or ten sen apiece. They are purchased to ward off evil influences and sickness from the house. By the barn there are often spe-

[17] For more about Jizō see Wayside Stones, below.

cial *ofuda* for horses and cows. The sacred power of *ofuda* is sometimes used to cure disease by being laid on the diseased part. *Ofuda* are a source of income for Shinto priests. Some Buddhist temples such as the Zen one in Suye and the big Yakushi *dō* in Uemura also sell these talismans but not the Shinshū temple in Fukada. *Ofuda*, usually from an Inari shrine, are often put on sticks in rice fields to insure a good crop.

A special form of *ofuda* is the *goddon*. The term *goddon* is believed by one *kitōshi* to be derived from Godzu Tennō. These talismans consist of crude horned demons or naked babies stamped from wood blocks onto rough white paper by means of black ink. They are made by *kitōshi* on the first of the second month (lunar), the day of Tarotsuitachi. They are sometimes put in barns or in houses, but most often they are folded up and put on a string around the neck or pinned on the back of one's clothing. They serve as a protection against disease. Sometimes a pair—male and female—are stamped on paper. The Tendai *kitōshi* says they may represent Godzusama and his wife. The orthodox Shinto priest does not make them any more since he "learned they came from India," i.e., are not native Japanese. But the Inari *kitōshi* and Sambō Kōjin *kitōshi* (Tendai) and several other minor priestly persons have the old wood blocks and make them every spring.[18]

In addition to house *ofuda* and *goddon*, there are many personal charms or *omamori* that people carry. These are small bits of cloth or dirt wrapped in white paper and are dispensed by most Shinto shrines and the *kitōshi*. There are *omamori* for easy child delivery and for sickness. The earth of Ichifusa taken with one on long trips, as when

[18] See also article by the author on Godzu Tennō in the *Journal of the American Oriental Society*, Vol. LIX, No. 1 (1939).

going to the barracks, is considered to be an *omamori*. A regular *ofuda*, if used as an active charm, as in curing disease or locating where a person drowned, becomes an *omamori*.

Gohei are white (sometimes colored) paper pompons cut in special ways from plain white paper and fixed in the split end of a bamboo stick. They are a part of all Shinto ritual, official and unofficial. They are often placed by springs and waterways to honor the water-god. Praying priests (*kitōshi*), both Shinto and Buddhist, also use them in their rituals. Only priests make them but at certain times, as in *hoshimatsuri*, they are given to laymen. *Kitōshi* also give them out for various purposes, to cure disease, purify land, etc. With the round metal mirror, *gohei* serve to represent the god in Shinto shrines.

"NANTEN"

By the toilet is planted a *nanten* bush (*Nandina domestica*). The usual explanation of it is that, if a man is overcome while using the toilet, as well he might be, he can grab at this bush and immediately recover. Some people document this statement by citing an actual case that occurred many years ago. A schoolmaster in Menda said *nanten* is regarded as purificatory, though no one in Suye said so. The leaves of *nanten* are sometimes used in serving ceremonial food, as, for instance, *sekihan*.

"HOSHIMATSURI"

Once a year, usually around New Year's, a praying priest is invited in to perform a purifying ceremony for the house and land called *hoshimatsuri* (star ceremony). *Gohei* on a bamboo stick is used in this ceremony and afterward put in the *tokonoma* or by the Jinushi. By means of this ceremony all evils are dispersed from the house, and presumably no sickness or harm will come to the inhabitants. The Shinto priest, all the *kitōshi* and also the Zen priest of Suye perform *hoshimatsuri* but not the Shinshū priest in Fukada.

A man's house is full of people even when he is alone, for most of these gods are regarded as, in a sense, persons. They are referred to with the honorific *san* or *sama* similar to the English "mister" or "sir." When speaking of them, people say *ano sh'to*, meaning "that person." The people of Suye dislike being alone or doing things alone, and so, with the numerous gods of the household, if one must be at home alone or one's children left there, neither need feel lonely.

STONES, IMAGES, AND WAYSIDE OFFERINGS

"DŌ"[19]

At the entrance of the *dō* is always a stone for holding water. It is full only on festival days, at which time visitors wash their hands and mouth before entering to pray.

In the *dō* are various images. The commonest in the Kuma region is Kwannon. Kwannon images are by no means uniform. Some have many arms. A specially famous one in Kurohiji to which people make pilgrimages is such a one and is called the thousand-armed Kwannon; it is also called the easy-delivery Kwannon. Other images look more like Amida (as seen in the Kamakura outdoor statue); others are the standing, slender more conventional Kwannon. Kwannon is regarded in Kuma as a protector of pregnant women.

Yakushi, considered good for curing diseases, is another deity often found in *dō*. There is a famous one in Uemura

---

[19] The *dō* have already been described in connection with their value in *buraku* life (see chap. iv).

to which people from all over Kuma County come on its two holidays in July—the day of the ox in summer *doyō* (the period of great heat) and on the eighth.

Images of Jizō and Amida are both commonly found in *dō*. It is not unusual for two or more different images to be in the same *dō*. This is often the result of amalgamation, each image having once been in a separate *dō*. The images are most often of wood, usually painted, and vary in height from a few inches to five or six feet.

Nearly always a *dō* houses some Buddhistic figure; occasionally, however, a Shinto god is enshrined, usually alongside the Buddhist one. The Shinto god is represented, as a rule, by a round metal mirror and *gohei*, though at the Ebisu shrine in Taragi the god is represented by a wooden figure.

The figure in a *dō* is kept supplied with offerings of fresh flowers or greens, an old beer bottle frequently serving as a vase. Any person living near by may give these flowers.

WAYSIDE STONES

The stone Jizō is one of the commonest roadside images. Occasionally, he is in someone's yard; very often he is at the entrance to a *buraku* or *mura*, acting as a protector of the *buraku*, a guardian of the entrance. Sometimes Jizō is put by a dangerous place: there is one by a place in the river where children swim in summer and where, at one time a few years ago, a child was drowned. In this case the god acts as a protector of the children swimming in this place.

Jizō, being of stone, is deaf. There are many humorous references to this in everyday conversation. He is considered to be a god who can cure deafness. If a man is deaf or growing deaf, he should collect stones with holes in them and present them to some particular Jizō—not all Jizō

will do—and he will then be cured of deafness. One Jizō in
Imamura is especially good for curing earaches. One goes
to him, lights a candle and incense before him, kneels, and
claps hands Shinto fashion or says "Namu Amida"
Buddhist fashion. There is no fixed rule. If successfully
cured, a person may present this Jizō with a banner on
which is written the donor's name and age; or the cured
person may make a brightly colored bib and tie it around
the Jizō's neck.

Most Jizō, however, have no stones or candles given
them except on Jizō Day, the twenty-fourth of the sixth
month by lunar calendar. Then each *buraku* holds a celebration the night before, gives a Jizō in the *buraku* candles,
incense, and *mochi* and holds a small party, all members
drinking merrily together. Jizō is also connected with
wedding ceremonies, as previously noted.

The orthodox Buddhist conception of Jizō (as a protector of children's souls in Hades) is held by a few people.
Most people, however, do not express this belief. He is
said to like children, but he is also just as much a protector
of dangerous places for adult and child alike, a protector of
buraku entrances, a healer of deafness or earache, a holder
of brides. In this last respect there may also be some connection with children, but I have never heard it expressed.
Jizō also figures in the *rokujizō* of funerals (see p. 216).

While most Jizō are carved to represent a characteristic
Jizō type man in sitting posture, some are merely stone
pillars with a stone cap on top.

KŌSHIN

There is another form of wayside stone almost as common as Jizō. It is not cut in the shape of any man but is
merely an upright slab with some inscription. It is variously called Kōshin, Kanoe, or Sarutahiko stone. Professor

Katō considers both these and Jizō to be phallic in nature.[20] The Jizō at weddings may be regarded as connected with sex and fertility, but, in general, neither Jizō nor Sarutahiko stones have any phallic significance in Suye today.

Like Jizō, these stones are considered to be protectors, and their special domain is crossroads. Nearly every *buraku* has a Kōshin which is kept supplied regularly by old people with fresh flowers. One man said that in the old days crossroads were very dangerous. Here a man would lie in wait for his enemy and, when the unsuspecting victim approached, leap out and cut him down with a sword. Hence, Kanoe stones were put at these places.

Sarutahiko was the guide of one of the early gods of Japan and is thus a Shinto god of roadways. Yet, on most of the stones the Buddhist term *kōshin* is written. Kanoe are celebrated every sixty days on a *kumi* system. There are no Kanoe in Kakui.

Kōshin is often confused by people with Kojin-san, the house-property-god. Suijin, the water-god, is also sometimes referred to as Kōshin. Kōshin stones are sometimes at a crossroads where there is also a well. Erskine mentions Kōshin on page 5 of his *Japanese Calendar and Festival Lore*. Here he merely lists the Kōshin days of 1933. He calls them "Metal Positive Monkey Days" and also lists "Wood Positive Rat Days and Earth Negative Snake Days." None of the rat or snake days is observed in Suye, however.[21]

[20] Genchi Katō, "A Study of the Development of Religious Ideas among the Japanese People as Illustrated by Japanese Phallicism," *Transactions of the Asiatic Society of Japan*, Second Series, Vol. I, Suppl. (December, 1924).

[21] The calling of Kōshin days "Metal Positive Monkey Days" may provide some clue to the alternative name Sarutahiko ("monkey man"). *Kanoe* means wood positive. It is possible that from this the villagers came to call these stones Kanoe stones or stones celebrated on Kanoe days. This was learned only after leaving Suye so the connection, if any, I have not been able to determine (see also Aston, *op. cit.*, p. 197).

Besides these two most common types of stone there are a few odd ones, e.g., an Ichidonsan stone, good for toothache. One offers toothpicks at this stone. It is of the same shape as the nonanthropomorphic Jizō.

Natural springs and streams used for water or for washing are usually honored with a *sakaki* branch or a *gohei* on a stick.

The water-god, Suijin-san, resides in wells and streams and is, if anything, beneficial. The river-god, Kawa-no-kamisama, on the other hand, is a rather dangerous deity. He thinks nothing of drowning children, hence the Jizō being placed where children swim. There is a saying that there is never a flood but that the river-god claims a victim.

The water-god is transmissible. Thus, if a new well is dug, some water from another well may be poured in, thus insuring the presence of Suijin-san. A well-digger always offers salt and *shōchū* to a newly dug well and prays that no harm may come to users of the well. When a new bridge is built, *shōchū* is offered to the river-god in order that no harm may come to the users of the bridge. This can be done indirectly by presenting the offering by some well or spring where the bridge-building party is being held.

Similarly, if a new stove is made, ashes are taken from an old one to insure the presence of the stove-god. Whenever charcoal is made in a charcoal oven, *shōchū* and salt are offered to the oven-god (Kama-no-kamisama—same as the stove-god); when new tea is roasted, salt and *shōchū* are again offered to the stove-god.

The sex of these deities is uncertain, and their other attributes are also vague. The image is definitely regarded as a person, is always addressed or referred to with the honorific *san* or *sama*, and, like the household gods, is spoken of as *ano sh'to*. A man sitting in a *dō* or by a roadside Jizō does not feel alone as he would if sitting by a deserted roadside, and a mother feels her children to be more or less safe playing in the *dō* of this or that deity. Further, different Kwannon or different Jizō, etc., are regarded as having different powers and so are in a sense separate individuals but all of the same species. Thus, a Jizōsan is always Jizōsan, but this Jizōsan is by no means the same as that Jizōsan.

By the entrances of some *buraku* are placed special *ofuda* made by the official Shinto priest at special prayer times (*kitōdoki*) in spring, summer, and autumn. They ward off disease and evil influences from the *buraku*.

There is a curious correspondence between the way humans are protected by *kitōdoki* ceremony at these three seasonal changes and the way the horses are bled to protect their health by *chizashi* at about the same time. It is possible that a change of seasons was formerly considered to be fraught with danger to horse and man. Horses (and cows) are by far the most important animals in village life. Formerly they were offered as gifts to Shinto shrines,[22] and so if man is to be protected at this time his horse should also be protected.

HEALING PRIESTS (*kitōshi*)

Kitō means prayer, and, in Kuma at any rate, a *kitōshi* is a man who makes a profession of prayer. Sometimes he is called *majinaishi* (one who makes charms and spells). A *kitōshi* is usually a keeper of some small shrine or temple.

---

[22] At Hachiman celebration in Menda and Aoi in Hitoyoshi people contribute their horses to march in the ceremonial procession of the god's house (*mikoshi*), through the streets of the town. Typically, the owners receive in exchange a gift for their trouble.

In Suye there are three *kitōshi*—two of Inari shrines and one of a degenerated Tendai temple whose object of prayer is a little Indian-looking figure called Sambō Kōjin. In addition to these three recognized *kitōshi*, there are several individuals who claim power to cure by prayer, one being a very poor, very old man, the other a rather well-to-do woman. The woman claims to cure by power of the sun and Amaterasu, and the village Shinto priest considers her a heretic. If she were ever to gain a large following, the government would undoubtedly prosecute her for lèse majesté as it has the founders of other too popular sects of Shinto such as Ōmotokyō.

When a man (or woman) feels sick or suffers from some ache or disease, he goes, or one of his relatives goes for him, to a *kitōshi*. The *kitōshi* inquires into his case, learns his date of birth, and then goes into the little alcove before the god and prays. A praying priest, either Shinto or Buddhist, may wave *gohei* over his client to rid him of evil influences and will usually give him an *ofuda* or *omamori* to take with him and some advice on what to do to recover.

Kitōshi are careful never deliberately to disparage a doctor's power as then the police would interfere. The powers of a *kitōshi* to heal are considered by many to be as great or greater than any doctor's, and besides they are much cheaper. One takes a *jūbako* of rice or some eggs worth about fifteen sen as payment for the prayer, while the doctor in the next village costs a yen a visit; furthermore, the *kitōshi* is a fellow-villager.

If a cow or a horse should fall ill, a *kitōshi* is at once consulted. If a man is planning to build a house or barn, he calls in a *kitōshi* to perform a land-appeasing ceremony. The *kitōshi* comes, puts *gohei* on sticks in the four corners of the area where the building is to be constructed, and a fifth one in the middle. The builder brings twelve river pebbles which are purified by the *kitōshi*, and then the builder puts them in the ground between the sticks. If the lunar year has thirteen months, as it sometimes does, thirteen stones are used instead of twelve. Only river pebbles are pure. The *kitōshi* gives advice on a good day to begin building and tells whether or not the proposed location is a favorable one.

If a man has been bewitched, he visits a *kitōshi*, who by prayer will drive out the possessing spirit. In Kuma this is mostly a dog's spirit, though sometimes that of a cat or a fox. Women desiring children sometimes go to a *kitōshi;* sometimes they visit a Kwannon *dō* or the Kwannon in the Zen temple. When any emergency, such as a drowning occurs, those concerned rush to the *kitōshi* for advice on where to find the body. Sometimes he gives advice on whether a given marriage will be successful.

At New Year's time *kitōshi* are hired to perform purification ceremonies (*hoshimatsuri*) in houses and to ward off evil influences and diseases for the coming year. Another form of *hoshimatsuri* is that performed for a man who is in a dangerous year, such as twenty-nine or forty-one. *Gohei* are used in this ceremony to drive out evil influences. *Kitōshi* perform a ceremony similar to *hoshimatsuri* once a year for certain groups of people in a *buraku* of the same surname.

In Suye by far the most popular and influential *kitōshi* is a blind one in the little Tendai temple (Rengetsuin) in Oade. Very few villagers beside the Shinto and Zen priests realize that the place is of the Tendai sect. Actually it is a combination of Buddhist and Shinto elements. A straw rope and *gohei* (*shimenawa*) hang over the entrance, a typical Shinto feature; in the shrine are brocades and a bronze bell of beautiful tone, which are Buddhist. When praying, the priest at regular intervals strikes the bronze bowl-shaped bell, which can be heard clearly in Kakui and Kawaze as well as in Oade. Its note is frequently heard at varying times every day of the year. The god he uses for prayer is Sambō Kōjin, a kind of *kami* (Shinto deity) though the image is Indian in appearance. The prayers he recites are Buddhist sutras. People from many *mura* other than Suye come to him for healing prayer. He is referred to as Kegyusan, probably from Kengyō—a priest's rank. The Shinto priest refers to him rather contemptuously as *mekura* (blind one).

The temple is one of ten surviving from an original sixteen in Kuma County and is said to be three hundred years old. Formerly these temples had only blind priests, but more recently seeing priests have come in. The keeper of the Oade temple was adopted by the former blind priest as that priest did not have a blind son, but the present heir apparent is the blind priest's son who is not blind.

The festival (*matsuri*) day is the twenty-eighth of each lunar month, the twenty-eighth of the eleventh month being the big *matsuri* day, at which time many followers bring rice and *shōchū* as gifts to the temple.

The next most important *kitōshi* is the keeper of an Inari shrine in Kakui. His adoptive mother received a message from Inari in a dream and so established the shrine. When she died, he neglected it and then, after a while, he became ill, and one night dreamed about a fox. On going outdoors the next morning he found a fox hole behind his house. Regarding these things as signs from Inari, he mended his ways and built a new house for the god. This was about fifteen years ago. In 1936 yet a newer and larger building was made to house the god. The priest performs cures much like the Oade *kitōshi* except that the whole paraphernalia is Shinto. The orthodox Shinto priest of the village approves of him, whereas he disapproves of the Tendai man.

Inari is a god of crops, more especially of rice, and, as such, many farmers have him in their houses. He is also the god of prostitutes and *geisha*, and, as such, he is enshrined in every *geisha* house and brothel. Thus by a curious combination the main Inari shrine of Suye, besides being patronized by farmers and sick people, is regularly visited by *geisha* from the Menda restaurants. They come, dressed in gay *kimono*, the first and fifteenth of every month (new calendar) to pay their respects. After praying, they sit about on the platform smoking and talking before walking the two or three miles back to Menda. They form a sharp contrast to the farm women and doubtless serve as a strong inducement to their husbands to visit Menda restaurants.

The celebration (*matsuri*) of Inari is the first day of the horse in the second month by lunar calendar. At this time many people visit this and other Inari shrines, offer *shōchū*, candles, or rice to the god, in addition to the customary copper, then sit about eating, drinking, and making merry. The food is served by the wife of the Inari keeper.

Any farmer with an Inari in his house makes special offerings to it on this day also. People always refer to Inari as *Oinarisan* (Honorable Inari).

The third *kitōshi* in Suye keeps a Kitadake shrine. Kitadake is a mountain between Suye and Youra near Hirayama. The mountain is referred to by the people as Kitadake-san. There is a shrine there. The *kitōshi*'s shrine is in Kakui and is a branch of the main one on the mountain. The *kitōshi* himself is very old, so his adopted son does most of the work. The son also has a small Inari shrine of his own, and, like the other Inari shrine, it was founded as the result of a dream. Foxes, dreams, and Inari are often associated.[23]

The blind priest is so busy at his business that he follows no other occupation. The main Inari *kitōshi* is a farmer, as well as a *kitōshi*, while his wife makes *tōfu*. They have many children to support. The Kitadake *kitōshi* is very poor, and his son works as a delivery boy in the *shōchū* factory and does his *kitō* in spare time. None of the *kitōshi* is very high socially, low middle being about the highest.

There is no doctor in Suye, and the available doctors from the neighboring towns are expensive. Furthermore, the doctor from the next *mura*[24] is little better than a quack. None of the doctors shows any social conscience, and many a child dies in Suye for this reason. So, while the farmer is quick to pick up what is more useful when he can afford it, such as electric lights instead of oil lamps, rubber shoes instead of straw, he as yet sees no value in such doctors as he can afford. Rich families for the most part do not go to *kitōshi*, going instead to Hitoyoshi doctors, but not many peasants are rich enough to do this.

The practices of the *kitōshi*, especially the Tendai man, date back to the study of *On-yō-dō*, the way of Yin and Yang in the Heian period (tenth century).[25] The praying priests described in the *Tale of Genji* performed functions for the people of the court similar to those which the *kitōshi* fulfils today in Kuma.

[23] The Inari cult is very widespread in Japan (see Rev. D. C. Buchanan, "Inari," *Transactions of the Asiatic Society of Japan*, Second Series, Vol. XII [1935]).

[24] Moved to Menda in 1936.

[25] Sansom, *op. cit.*, p. 226.

BEWITCHMENT, DOG SPIRITS, AND FOXES

In every *buraku* there is at least one woman with an unsavory reputation as an *inugami mochi*, or sorceress by means of the dog spirit, a dog-spirit carrier. A possessor of this spirit is not necessarily evil by nature, but the dog spirit which she has cannot always be controlled and sometimes acts as a free agent to work harm.

A household where there is such a spirit always has a little Jizō or some other god's image housed somewhere on the property. This is "in reality" a monument to the dog spirit. Offerings made to it are to appease it and keep it satisfied. It is believed that originally a dog's head was buried underneath the stone. Possessors of the dog spirit can cause sickness or death to their enemies. People dislike very much to speak of sorcery and are strongly averse to mentioning names; to talk too freely about sorcery might bring it down upon one. The spirit of the dog when released in the victim's house is sometimes heard uttering strange sounds and in that manner can be detected. Unless the spirit makes a noise, the person possessed might not know what is the matter with him and might try different cures for his disease; but, as soon as the presence of *inugami* is ascertained, one must at once go to a *kitōshi*.

Kitōshi, who work for the well-being of man, are nearly always men; witches, who work evil to man, are for the most part women. Women are said to harbor deeper and longer grudges than men. The witchery power stays in a house and is inherited through the female line, so that sometimes a daughter-in-law takes it up after the mother-in-law. Sometimes it is the house rather than a person that carries the spirit and to have a fight with the people living in such a house is dangerous.

The spirits in the house can be of two different types.

One is *bimbōgami* (poor spirit) which brings bad luck to the house it resides in. The other is *fukugami* (lucky spirit). This spirit does many things to help its house prosper. For instance, when people of the house are selling rice, it gets inside while the rice is being measured and puffs it up so that they do not have to give the full measure; on the other hand, when they are buying rice, the spirit tramples it down so that the measure has to be increased. Such a spirit must also be appeased and be made content or it will leave the house. Its favorite food is *sekihan*, and the inhabitants of the house usually keep a bowl of that in its niche.

Reasons for cursing are envy and jealousy. If a man is very rich, some neighbor who is an *inugami mochi* may, while not disliking the rich man, merely covet his neighbor's wealth—and, presto, out goes the dog spirit and the rich man's horse (value 150–200 yen) dies, or his house burns down. Jealousy is more likely than envy to give rise to sickness and death curses and such curses are purposely begun. Witchery is often referred to as *kaze*, wind, because one cannot see it.

The following information concerning *inugami* and other curses is on the authority of the Tendai *kitōshi*.

If the curse is done through the water-god, it may be cured with black metal as the water-god does not like black metal. One must bury some under a stream.

When the cursing is done through a mountain-god, the curser drives nails into some wood or tree. The curse may be lifted by the *kitōshi*'s removing the nails or by his praying for the victim's release. (It is believed by the villagers that this type of cursing is done when the curser wishes to kill his enemy.)

In feudal times Lord Sagara told the people who had *inugami* (*inugami mochi*) to do some form of worship to it in order to keep it satisfied such as erecting a Jizō or a *dō* or by putting some sutra in a stone box, burying it, and putting a stone over it. Some people put up a Jizō so that the dog spirit will not speak (a stone Jizō does not speak).

The dog spirit is in those houses where people are not sincerely religious. This dog spirit can leave the person or house and possess someone, especially an enemy of its "owner." This is different from ordinary cursing inasmuch as the dog spirit leaves a person and possesses the other person quite of its own accord. It can be exorcised by the *kitōshi*'s praying or by his striking the possessed with fire or by feeling on the body with a paper cut in diamond shape[26] to find out where the pain is—and, where the pain is, there is the dog spirit. The priest then prays to get rid of it, through Sambō Kōjin. The person possessed often shivers.

As in other parts of Japan, there is a belief in bewitchment by foxes, but there has not been a specific case in recent years. There are certain spots that are famous as having been haunted by foxes. One interesting belief is that frequently a fox train may be seen going along the railroad tracks. It consists of a row of many lights. This is because, when the railroad was built, several fox homes were destroyed; so today the spirits of these foxes occasionally form such a ghostly train. People are rather afraid of all such manifestations of the fox spirit.

[26] The cakes of Girls' Day are also diamond shaped. This shape may have a sacred sexual significance.

BELIEFS SURROUNDING THE THREE CRISES OF LIFE

BIRTH

Birth beliefs are primarily Shinto but contain many Buddhist elements. As already noted in chapter vi, a pregnant woman considers herself under the protection of Kwannon. The soul of the child is supposed to come from the *kami*, native gods of Japan, more especially the *uji-gami*, patron god of the *mura*, but when and how is not very definite. At the time of the naming ceremony, offerings are made to the *kamidana* and in the *tokonoma* of *shōchū* and cakes. However, this naming ceremony is rather a mixture of Shinto and Buddhist features. The *shōchū* and cakes offered at the *tokonoma* are Shinto. The name is sometimes pasted by the *tokonoma*, too, but the tasseled rosary is Buddhist and the name paper is more often placed by the *butsudan*.

The afterbirth is wrapped up in paper. At sunset the father of the child takes it away and buries it in the yard or near the family graves, after which he steps over the spot to insure the child's obedience. If some animal, as for instance a dog, should run over the spot before the father steps on it, the child will fear that animal. Sometimes the afterbirth is thrown into or buried under the toilet.

The umbilical cord, when it comes off within a week or ten days, is carefully wrapped with a bit of the child's hair and put away in a safe place with the child's name written on it.

The name of a child is sometimes given or changed according to the advice of a *kitōshi*. Thus, one boy's name is Toru, but, as he was born in a bad year, the *kitōshi* advised that he be called the name of some animal. Sheep (*hitsuji*) was chosen, and so the child is called Hitsuji or Hischan in everyday life, though the village office records him as Toru. After five years of age he will be safe and can be called by his given name.

The child's soul is, at first, not very stable, so he is kept at home until the visit to the *ujigami* shrine of the village or the *buraku*. Before this, if he crosses water, the water-god may take his soul. Should it be absolutely necessary to take a child across before the proper time, some salt must be offered to the god. There is some connection between this taboo and the animals' (horses and cows) naming ceremonies. All calves and colts have a naming ceremony (*kamitate*) on the third day after birth. The name is chosen in the same manner as that of babies, written out and pasted by the *butsudan*, but before this is done there is a ceremony called *kawa watasu* (crossing the river). Some water is spilt in the yard, and the cow and the calf are made to cross the pool. Some people explain this as being equivalent to the first crossing of a river by a baby; others, however, think that this symbolizes the bath which a child is given on its naming day.[27]

In Suye there is no indication of any initiation ceremonies, though Mr. Mogami, of Meiji University, tells me that there is some suggestion of them in Konose, a village at the other end of Kuma.

MARRIAGE

At marriage the *butsudan* is opened so that the ancestors may know of the happy event. On some occasions the *san-san-ku-do* marriage ceremony is actually performed

---

[27] Freud, in his *A General Introduction to Psychoanalysis* (New York, 1935), states that water in dreams is frequently connected with childbirth. The ceremonial aspects of a man's life in Suye have many points of significance to a psychologist.

in front of the *butsudan*. The connection of Jizō with marriage has already been mentioned in chapter vi. No priests are involved in the wedding ceremony.[28]

At funerals the Buddhist priest comes into his own. His chief sources of income are funerals and memorial services.

At death the man's soul does not immediately leave the house but hovers about until the funeral. After burial it starts its journey to heaven or hell, depending on its virtues in life and the prayers of its living relatives. The soul of a purely Shinto believer (only the Shinto priest in Suye) does not go to the paradise of Amida but hovers indefinitely about the village shrine.

When one dies, the soul goes either to heaven or to hell. Heaven is in the west, and there dwells Amida. Those who believe in Amida and are good during their lifetime, i.e., charitable, go there. The regular belief is that souls become gathered into Buddha's lap on death and become Buddhas. One's death and becoming a Buddha is called *nehan* (nirvana).

Some younger people (twenty to forty years of age) believe that there is no heaven and hell except in one's self. That is, if one is sincere and does good acts, one has a heaven in one's self.

The belief in *nehan* as a loss of self and desires is not known in the village; belief in reincarnation is also lacking. There are, however, a few popular beliefs, referred to as superstitions: that if one is very scared of snakes, one was once a frog, and that, if one looks very much like some grandparent who has died, one is referred to as that person

---

[28] In cities and towns some people hold the ceremony in a Shinto shrine with a Shinto priest officiating. This, however, is a recent innovation.

reborn. This latter is considered to be not literal but in a manner of speaking.

Most of the ideas of heaven and hell come from the priests' talks and are not very much thought about by the people except when they get old. Certain of the funeral preparations are done in order to facilitate the dead man's progress in heaven, for instance, the *rokudo* Jizō, the board stand with six (or three in most *buraku*) candles. These candles are to be offered to each of the six Jizō who guard six different stages through which a man must pass on his way up. The three *mon* (now represented by one or two sen) are to pay the man who poles the boat across the river on the way to heaven. Most of these things are done as a matter of custom, and many people cannot explain why they are done. This applies to the rice placed before a corpse and later thrown into the grave to be eaten in after-life when all souls gather at Zenkōji, a temple in Nagano. Folded white papers are worn in the hair of female mourners and behind the ears of male mourners during the procession to the grave, where they are thrown in. Another bowl of rice with various funeral foods is placed on a tray in front of the coffin. A piece of paper with a hole in the center is pasted to the rice bowl, for the evil spirits to escape through.

One characteristic attitude is that, according to one's belief in life, so will one's soul be disposed of at death—if Shin sect, one goes to Amida's heaven; if Zen sect, to some other type of heaven; if Shinto, to the village shrine.

Each *buraku* has certain burial customs peculiar to itself. Despite the fact that most people of the village are all of the one Shinshū sect, any variation in burial custom is conventionally ascribed to the dead man's being "of a different sect." There is no feeling that one method of burial is worse or better than another.

Souls as fireballs, or *hidama*, have a much stronger hold on the imagination. A man will speak rather academically about Amida's heaven and life after death but becomes really interested in talking of *hidama*. Many people say they have seen them. There are two kinds:

1. *Hidama* (fireball)
   If one is disrespectful of rice or *mugi*, and, for instance, burns it, it may become a *hidama* with a tail and whiz out of the house. This is an ill omen for the inmates of the house.
2. *Hitodama* (a ball of light about the size of an electric-light bulb—the human soul)
   If a man is about to die, his soul takes this form and is seen by his relatives, regardless of distance. After a person dies, such a *hitodama* hovers about its house. Souls of people whose lives were not good and hence do not go to heaven are likely to become *hitodama*. People often see these fireballs just before someone dies.

THE YEARLY FESTIVAL CALENDAR

The village holidays are, for the most part, reckoned by the lunar calendar. This lunar calendrical system of rural Japan is practically identical with that of rural China. Indeed, the following description of the Chinese calendar, written in 1867, could be applied with equal truth to the observance today in Suye Mura:

The Chinese year contains thirteen or twelve months, according as it has or has not an intercalary month. Consequently the great annual periods, as the winter solstice or vernal equinox, do not fall in successive years on the same day of the same month. Generally, in five successive years there are two intercalary days. The months are spoken of as the first month, the second month, etc., no distinct name for each month being in common use. The month which is intercalary is known as such in common conversation and in legal documents. For example: if the sixth month is intercalaried, there are two six months in that year, viz., the *sixth month*, and the *intercalary sixth month*. [In Suye there are no festivals held during the intercalary month.]

A month has never twenty-eight or thirty-one days, but always either twenty-nine or thirty days. A month is one *moon*, the character for month and moon being identical. The number of days in a month is intended to correspond to the number of days which it takes the moon to make one complete revolution around the earth; and as one such revolution requires between twenty-nine and thirty days, some of the months are reckoned to have twenty-nine and others thirty days. It follows that the number which indicates the age of the moon at any particular time also denotes the day of the month, and that the moon on the same day of successive months from one year to another always presents the same appearance. For example: on the fifteenth of every month the moon is full, on the first there is no moon; the first quarter ends about the evening of the seventh, the third quarter ends about the twenty-second of every month. This plan of regulating the number of days in a month by the number of days which the moon requires to make one circuit around the globe is very convenient and useful to farmers and sailors, enabling them to calculate with precision and remember with readiness the changes of the moon and the changes of tides.[29]

The Chinese have another additional system of seasons and periods called the joints and breaths—twenty-four in all. These have been but partially preserved in Japan. The first day of spring, the days of little heat and great heat, of little cold and great cold, appear to be survivals. The spring and autumn equinoxes celebrated as Higan in Japan are part of the Chinese series of joints and breaths. And, as in China, in rural Japan a time of change of season is dangerous. Whereas the Chinese eat something strengthening on such a day, in Suye a *kitōdoki* ceremony is held and sacred *fuda* put at *buraku* entrances.

The first, eighth, fifteenth, and twenty-fourth are all local *mura* rest days; some *buraku* also observe the twenty-eighth as a rest day.[30] On such days people work only in the morning, while in the afternoon, *kōgin, dōnenkō*, school meetings, etc., are held. If it is some special celebration (*matsuri*) in addition to being a *buraku* rest day,

[29] Justus Doolittle, *Social Life of the Chinese*, II (New York, 1865), 14.

[30] Kaempfer in 1692 noted that the first, fifteenth, and twenty-eighth of every lunar month was a holiday in the regions in and around Nagasaki with which he was acquainted.

then there may be visits to temples or relatives. If a celebration comes one or two days before one of these regular
rest days, then the latter is canceled. The young men's
school holds classes and military drill on these rest days.
While the school and village office observe Sunday as a
holiday and ignore the local rest days, the farmers continue
work on Sunday as on any other work day.

It is notable that the fifteenth of each month, the time
when the moon is full, is almost always the day of some
deity or celebration.[31] Other favorite days for festivals
are the first (dark of the moon), eighth (first quarter), and
twenty-third (third quarter). There are very few holidays that do not fall on one or another of these days. The
day before a celebration is *goya* (eve); the day itself, *matsuri*.[32]

In every house is a calendar with a sheet for each day
giving in big black figures the Gregorian date. Below, in
smaller figures, is the lunar date and remarks as to what
kind of a day it is—the day of *tomobiki*, for instance,
which is unlucky, the day of *daian* which is lucky. On unlucky days one does not move or start a business venture.
Daian is good time to start any new venture.[33] There is
also a zodiac of twelve animals; these are in order: rat, ox,
tiger, hare, dragon, snake, horse, sheep, monkey, cock,
dog, and boar. There is usually a picture of the animal of
the day on the calendar. This zodiac comes from China,
several of the animals, such as tiger and sheep, not being
native to Japan.

[31] It is probable that every full moon once had a celebration. Unfortunately,
I have no data on the fifteenth of the fourth month.

[32] Marcel Granet (*Festivals and Songs of Ancient China* [New York, 1932])
notes that the full moon in China was also important as a time of festival.

[33] Even in Tokyo many candidates for the diet announced their candidacy on
a day of *daian* in the 1936 elections.

The days and years are each named after these animals in order, so that every twelve days and every twelve years they repeat. The combination of the animal of the hour and day, the number of the month and the animal of the year one was born, are of great value to soothsayers and *kitōshi*. One's disposition through life is determined by the day and year of one's birth.

If a woman is born in the year of the horse, it is said she will cause trouble to her husband, so such women have difficulty in getting married.[34] This belief does not prevent women of Suye from marrying, however.

William Erskine in his *Japanese Festival and Calendar Lore* describes many such beliefs. Much of what he says is restricted to priests, and many of the celebrations he lists do not occur in Suye. Most of the lucky and unlucky days, like the zodiac itself, date back to the introduction of Chinese culture into Japan.

All the major festivals such as New Year's, Girls' Day, Boys' Day, and Bon are characterized by visits among relatives, banquets, and gay drinking parties. Lesser festivals are marked by smaller drinking parties. Often a group of close neighbors, after visiting some local shrine or after paying respects and making offerings to the deity of the day, sit together in front of the god and exchange drinks, and sometimes, of a moonlight night, sing and dance.

The yearly festivals were more generally observed in the old days than they are today. Increased work demanded by the money wheat crop and other side work encouraged

[34] A tragic tale based on this belief is "Miss Mori," by Idwal Jones, in the *American Mercury Magazine* for April, 1933.

by the prefectural government have tended to reduce these celebrations. Various economy programs and especially the new economic reconstruction all deplore excess "vain" expenses and encourage people to do work and more work. Also, as already noted, the towns have tended to commercialize certain of the yearly festivals so that villagers go to the towns to enjoy the fair and the crowds, neglecting the local celebrations.

There is another series of holidays, the national festivals. These are marked by village shrine celebrations attended, as a rule, only by village officials. The rest of the villagers continue work as usual on such days. If they live along the prefectural road, they put out the national flag. The calendar indicates the national holidays with crossed flags. People off the road do not bother much about the flag, although the headman is constantly urging everyone to buy and display one. These national holidays are celebrated by the new calendar. While the new calendar and its holidays are easy to adopt in cities where the seasons are less important, it is much more difficult for a farmer to observe holidays which come when he is busy in the fields.

The *mura* is gradually increasing its number of working days. Before Meiji all holidays were by lunar calendar. Now national holidays by new calendar give school children a holiday, but come at inconvenient and untraditional dates for the farmer to stop work. On the other hand, many of the old lunar holidays have been reduced to half-holidays or merely to the making of special foods or cakes by the housewife. Neither school nor village office, as government institutions, observe these local holidays.

The lunar new year comes just at the end of winter (February by new calendar). Leafless plum trees are in bloom, and spring will soon arrive.

The new year by new calendar is a national holiday and is marked by a shrine celebration, but not much else. The third and fifth of January are also national holidays. About a month later, when the lunar new year comes, almost a week's holiday is taken by villagers. At this time relatives call on one another, take gifts, and receive feasts. In the old days one called from house to house, taking a gift to each one; but today, for economy's sake, all relatives gather in one house. One year the family goes to a party of the wife's relatives, next year to a party of the husband's relatives. The relatives take turns in giving a party.

The day before New Year's, *mochi* have been pounded by the family. Three large round *mochi*, called mirror *mochi*, are put before the *butsudan* and three in the *tokonoma*. Other little ones are given to Daikoku, perhaps one to a neighboring Jizō. They will be left until the thirteenth or fourteenth, when fresh *mochi* will be pounded for Small New Year's. The old mirror *mochi* will then be eaten.

New brides of the past year visit their homes at this time, all debts have been paid or settled for the coming year, and the servants receive their annual salary at the end of the year. New servants have been contracted for and old ones dismissed. At this time the servants are given new clothes. A manservant receives material for *kimono*, footgear, a belt, a pair of shorts, and a towel;

[35] The dates given below are all by lunar calendar unless otherwise noted. The villagers refer to months by number rather than by name, and this same rule will be followed hereafter when referring to lunar dates.

while a maidservant receives material for *kimono* (including the lining) and underskirt, footgear, and an *obi* (*kimono* belt). They are also given a little pocket money. This is one of their big holidays, and they usually go home for a day or two.

Everyone visits shrines and temples. New greens are put at graves and *gohei* by waterways. Most people also visit the village Shinto shrine to pay New Year's respects. People of the mountain *buraku* visit Kitadake shrine in Youra.

On New Year's morning the wooden shutters of the house are not opened at the usual early hour; indeed, some are left shut all day. In the morning the family eats special red rice and a special soup prepared with taro the night before. A minimum of actual cooking is done on New Year's Day. The calling on relatives begins in the afternoon. Everyone looks festive, and everyone is sporting new clothes and new *geta*.

School is in session only one hour. It is only in rural regions that this is done as the towns do not observe lunar new year.

New Year's calls and festivities last from three to seven days. On the seventh day *nanakusazōni* (or *zushi*), a soup of seven herbs, is made for supper (see Table 1, column 4). Only a few villagers still observe this custom, some saying that they are too busy, others that it is too much bother. Nanakusa Day is the first of the five big traditional Japanese celebrations referred to as *sekku*. The others are the boys' festival, the girls' festival, *tanabata*, and Chrysanthemum Day. This latter is not observed in Suye.[36]

On the eighth the Yakushi *dō* in Imamura holds a cele-

[36] There is, however, a chrysanthemum exhibit on Meiji Day in November (Gregorian calendar).

bration. Tea and beans are served by a *kumi* of *buraku* women.

On the morning of the fourteenth, *mochi* are again pounded for the celebration of Small New Year's (*koshogatsu*). Three small dumplings on a stick called *kushidago* are put in the *tokonoma*. In the afternoon children make up beaters of rice straw bound with rope and go about beating the ground. They are supposedly beating moles. Such beating is said to get rid of moles from the fields. Only children do it, and the belief is not taken very seriously. In the evening the family gathers about the fire pit to make special dolls called *shunnamejo* and toys of various kinds. A stick of acacia wood (*kokanoki*) three or four inches long and about three-fourths of an inch in diameter is taken. The bark is cut off on one end and a face painted on. Paper is cut into *kimono* and put on. A sharp piece of bamboo is stuck into the bottom—and a doll is made. They are usually made in couples and will be placed on sacks of rice before the *tokonoma* or in the storehouse where rice is kept. The next day they are removed and placed before the Jinushi. Jumping monkeys, millet heads, and other toys are made and also put there. The dolls insure plenty of helpers at rice-transplanting time four months later, the millet heads, a good millet crop.

The father usually does the knife work, while children cut out the dresses and mark them with ink spots to indicate family seals. Mole-beating and *shunnamejo* are local Kuma customs.

Also local is the custom of cutting *mochi* into special shapes on this day. They are cut into small square or oblong pieces to represent grains of rice, or into twisted long pieces for ears of millet or into small round ones for money (*ōban-koban*—ancient coins). All these are put on branches

PRAYER AT A SHRINE IN MENDA ON A *MATSURI* DAY

After this first duty the old ladies will go off and enjoy the fair

SHUNNAMEJO, MILLET HEADS, *MOCHI* ON BRANCHES, JUMPING
MONKEY, AND A TWIRLING MONKEY—ALL ON A BAG OF RICE
BY THE *TOKONOMA* (FIFTEENTH OF THE FIRST MONTH)

of *yanagi* (willow) and *yenoki* (Chinese nettle) because these two trees are used on festive occasions and because in the old days *mochi* and coins used to grow on these trees. The branches of *mochi* are to assure a good crop and good income through the new year. The branches are offered at the *kamidana* and the *butsudan*, which is cleaned out and freshly decorated with flowers. A branch is put in the toilet to ask the toilet-god (Benjo-no-Kamisama) to protect one from bladder trouble, one in the kitchen, one at the stable's entrance, one at the house entrance and often one at the bath, and one at the Jinushi. Outside the house branches are taken to the local *dō*, to any near-by Jizō, and to the well-god. A branch is taken to the family graveyard. After being removed, the *butsudan* branch is put away and saved until the first thunderstorm in spring, when it is burned.

The first of the first month marks the end of the old year, and all old obligations are cleared before that day. From the first to the seventh, festivities and parties occur in abundance, there being a constant round of visits to relatives and eating of *mochi*. The fifteenth marks the close of New Year's festivities, and, with the making of *shunnamejo* and wooden millet heads and *mochi* branches, thoughts are turned to the coming work on rice, transplanting, and resulting wealth.

Some of the significance has been taken out of the celebration on the fifteenth due to the fact of the winter crop of wheat.[37] Incidentally, there are no festivals concerning winter wheat-sowing or harvesting.[38]

[37] Many festivals are marked by the making of wheat cakes (*dango*), however.

[38] It is worth noting that the national festival, Kinensai, occurring February 17 by new calendar, is to pray for good crops. Formerly this occurred in the middle of January.

On the sixteenth is held an Ise *kō*. Ishizaka Buraku celebrates at an Amaterasu shrine on this day, also.

On the twenty-third is held a moon-viewing holiday, at present mostly unobserved. Offerings are made to the moon.

SECOND MONTH

The first and second are holidays. The first is called Tarotsuitachi. On this day the spirits (*taro*) of the mountain and the river change places. To see one of these normally invisible beings is to be affected mentally. No one ever goes swmming in the river on this day for fear of drowning. *Goddon*, as described above under Charms and Talismans, are made at this time by *kitōshi* and worn as charms against disease until the first day of the horse, the festival of Inari.

The first day of the horse in the second month is the big Inari festival. People visit all the Inari shrines of the village, pay honors to the god, present rice and *shōchū* to the shrine, and receive feast food and drink from the priest in return.

On the ninth, Hirayama, the mountain *buraku*, has a special fire-prevention ceremony (*hinokitō*, prayer about fire, i.e., against fire). It seems that once long ago—so long, nobody remembers—a big fire wiped out all the houses in Hirayama, so that ever since they have kept this ceremony. A Shinto priest called Ogata (there are many Shinto priests called Ogata in Kuma) from Tsuiji in Menda does the ceremony. He performs a Shinto ritual (*oharai*) before the *tokonoma* of the house in which the ceremony takes place. It is a different house each year, the priest having come from Tsuiji from old times. It is said that most fires occur on the ninth, nineteenth, and twenty-ninth of the month, and so Hirayama picked the ninth as a good day for the ceremony. It chose the second month because it is a slack period, firewood has all been cut, and other agricultural work is not yet under way. After the ceremony there is a party with the priest seated in the place of honor. Half the *buraku* acts as host, and half as guests each year. Everyone over fifteen years of age brings one *shō* of rice; those under, even if only one day old, give one-fourth of a *shō*. Some people also bring *shōchū*. The party is held only in big houses, since everyone in Hirayama comes. *Omiki* is served, then *shōchū*, and fish and also mushrooms. The women are not served fish, but *kiriboshi*, a kind of *daikon* salad. Each house head is given a *gohei* on a bamboo stick to take home and put in the *tokonoma*. These were made by the priest and will serve to protect the house against fire.

The fifteenth is the day Buddha entered nirvana. This is observed only by old people.

In the spring equinox (March 21 by new calendar, movable by lunar) comes Higan. It is a week's celebration, the middle, equinoctial, day being a national holiday as well. At this time there are lectures at the Shinshū temple in Fukada. Pictures of hell are shown at the Zen temple. The autumn Higan is more important than the spring Higan. Both Higan periods are good periods for social *kō*. At this time women visit Aoshima Shrine in Hitoyoshi to avert female diseases.

THIRD MONTH

On the third is Girls' Day. A family to which a girl has been born in the past year, especially if a first girl, invite relatives in to have a feast. The relatives send ahead of them gifts of dolls. These are all placed in fine array in the *tokonoma*. This is the *sangatsu no osekku*—the third month's festival. It is also called *momo sekku* (peach festival) and *hina matsuri* (Doll Day). Special green diamond-shaped *mochi* made with the herb *futsu*, picked by women during the previous day or two, are prepared. A two days' holiday is observed.

The fifteenth is the eve (*goya*) and the sixteenth the festival day called Otake *matsuri* in honor of Ichifusa, the great and sacred mountain of Kuma. This is one of the big festivals of the year. At this time many people make a pilgrimage to Mount Ichifusa. To make the ascent, people leave the night before or very early in the morning and sleep on the mountainside near the shrine. Formerly many people passed along the road through Suye on the way to Ichifusa, but today they go as far as the foot of the mountain by railroad instead. Some people only go to the branch shrine in Yunomae at the foot of the mountain.

On this day soldiers returned from the barracks during the past year make a pilgrimage to return their *omamori* of sacred earth. Newly married couples make a point of walking to the shrine halfway up Ichifusa on this day.

There is a belief that, if a married couple on the way up pick a piece of cedar called *sawara* and stick it in the mountainside, the marriage will prosper if the branch takes root and grows.

Some people go all the way to the summit. On the night of the fifteenth the path up the mountain is full of young people, and the teahouses along the way do a big business in selling *shōchū* and *sake*.

In the old days this, like other events, was much more generally observed. There are several songs for Ichifusa Day.

SANGATSU JŪROKU NICHI
NO UTA

1. Kyō wa hi mo yoshi doko e
   Shindera mairi
   Harai baba mo dete mi yare
   Mago tsurete
        na yoe.

2. Kasa wa wasurete
   Menda no chaya de

   Sora ga kumore ba
   Omoi dasu
        na yoe.

3. Otake yama kara dokoe
   Yuyama o mireba
   Yuyama onago ga dete
   Maneku
        na yoe.

4. Otake gozankei
   To ucha yūte
   Deta ga
   Otakya nazukete
   Kinagusan
        na yoe.

SONG OF SIXTEENTH OF
THIRD MONTH

1. Where to on this day so fine?
   To visit the Shin temple.
   Come out too, old woman Harai
   With your grandchild.

2. The umbrella forgotten
   At the Menda inn
   If the sky becomes clouded,
   You will remember.[39]

---

[39] You will remember it and, by association, me.

3. From Take mountain where to?
   If Yuyama were seen
   Yuyama women coming out
   Invite you in.

4. One leaves the house
   To worship Otake.
   Otake is only named
   One's heart's enjoyment (is sought)

The umbrella figures in the song because it usually rains on the day of the pilgrimage.

On the way back, on the sixteenth, people visit Cat Temple (Nekodera) in Mizukami.

Green *mochi* are made on Ichifusa Day. It is called *yakimochi* because it is always served roasted (*yaki* meaning roasted).

The Ichifusa rain has a peculiarity of coming down in spells: first hard rain, then a drizzle with a promise of stopping, then another downpour. There are two explanations of why it rains on Ichifusa Day. (1) There was once a priest at the cat temple who was murdered. His mother, angered by this, called her cat to her, and, cutting her arm open, she told the cat to suck her blood and take revenge for the murdered priest. The cat did as it was told and was later found dead at Ichifusa. Since then as a retribution it has always rained on Ichifusa Day. This story also explains why the temple in Mizukami is called Cat Temple. (2) With so many people going to Ichifusa, especially young couples, there is much urinating and secretion of semen. This angers the god of the mountain, so he brings down rain to wash away the dirt.

A variation of the cat story is this: When the first lord of Sagara came into power, he murdered the previous lord. The murdered man's wife (or mother?) took revenge through a cat and brought pestilence upon the land. Finally Sagara had a shrine built for the cat at Mizukami and made it law for all people of Lower Kuma to make a pilgrimage to it every sixteenth of the third month. Thus people came to visit it on that day and also, for some reason, Ichifusa at the same time. This is the story told by the priest at Ichifusa shrine who says that the sixteenth is not the real Ichifusa Day but that it is on the fifteenth of the eleventh month. This latter date is the anniversary of its founding, more than eleven hundred years ago.

At both the shrine and the temple, rice wafers (*sembei*) are sold at this time with pictures of the famous cat.

Ichifusa is usually referred to as Otake-san or Otake-sama, *take* meaning high mountain. Some people seem to think Otake-sama is a separate god, but the word is used mostly as a personalized term for Mount Ichifusa.

The twenty-first of the third month is Kōbō Daishi Day. Many people visit the small *dō* of Kōbō Daishi (Daishisan, Dainiuyurai) in Furu Taragi, which is run on a *kumi* system much as Yakushi and Kwannon *dō* are in Suye. One house in Imamura has a small shrine in the yard to Daishisan. The owners give it *dango* on the twenty-first of the third and sixth months. Other villagers regard this Daishi shrine as in reality a dog-spirit shrine, and the old lady of the house has a bad name as a sorceress by the dog spirit.

FOURTH MONTH

The first is *kitōdoki*, a prayer day. For most people this merely means a half-holiday, though some *buraku* gather and ask the Shinto priest to read a ritual prayer to keep sickness and harm away from the *buraku*.

The fourth is Wind Day (*kazadoki*). Special cakes, called *kazadago*, are made of wheat and rice flour stuffed with bean paste. The holiday is out of respect for the wind-god so that wind will not harm the crops. There is a second Wind Day on the fourth of the seventh month.

The eighth is Buddha's birthday. On this day the Zen temple, the Oade *kitōshi* (Tendai), and the Shaka *dō* in Aso Buraku have celebrations.

At the two temples a special drink, called *amacha* (sweet tea), a kind of licorice tea, is prepared. This is placed in a wooden tub. The tub is on a stand, and over it is a framework elaborately decorated with fresh flowers to form a miniature temple of flowers. In the tub is a small figure of Shaka six or eight inches high. People visiting the temple drink this *amacha*, dipping it out of the tub with tiny bamboo dippers. The liquid, having been poured over the Shaka's body, becomes sacred and can cure all ailments. For a sen or two one can fill a bottle of the *amacha* to take home. All members of the family, especially the babies and old ladies, rub some of the stuff on the forehead, legs, and ears.

At Shaka *dō* in Aso the celebration is run by *kumi*. The *kumi* whose turn it is makes the *amacha*, cleans up the *dō*, and serves tea to visitors.[40] A group of *buraku* women march in procession to the *dō* dressed as wrestlers and perform a wrestlers' dance in the yard. Some young men wrestle and receive contributions of money from people watching (a custom observed at all shrine and other public festivals—people performing in a side show always receive contributions). Because the Shaka *dō* requires some preparation and calls for a *buraku* holiday, in certain

---

[40] All *dō* are taken care of on the *kumi* system—Kwannon in Oade, Kawaze, and Kakui; Yakushi in Imamura; Amida in Nakashima. A few small Shinto shrines are thus looked after, for instance, Tenjin in Kakui. However, a local Inari praying priest or *kitōshi* also takes care of this Tenjin shrine, and, since it was housed in the Zen temple before Meiji, it is not typically a Shinto shrine.

years when the lunar date comes too late in the season
and would interfere with farm work (rice-transplanting or
silkworms), the celebration is moved to the eighth of
April. The temples, however, always celebrate by the
lunar calendar, since all preparation there is done by the
priest's wife, and any free member of the family (usually
the grandmother) can visit the temple and bring the
amacha home.

FIFTH MONTH

On the fifth is the *gogatsu no osekku*, the fifth-month
festival, which is the boys' festival all over Japan. Most
of the people in the village celebrate this by the new calendar because the lunar date is a very busy time. The wheat
harvest, transplanting, and spring silkworms come in
quick succession. The lunar fifth of the fifth month is
bound to come during one of these work periods. All
houses with boys, especially those where a boy had been
born during the past year, put out banners representing a
huge carp[41] or some historical hero. A house where a first son
has been born has the largest festival. Special long wheat
cakes wrapped in bamboo sheaths are made, and large
snails caught in the rice fields are eaten mixed with greens.
Relatives invited to the feast usually bring banners, small
swords, and sometimes dolls representing ancient warriors.

The shape of the cakes made on Girls' Day (diamond
shape) and on Boys' Day (long and round) are probably of
sexual significance, though no villager remarked on any
such meaning. They say that the bamboo sheath is used
and bamboo shoots are eaten at this time to make the
boy grow, like a bamboo shoot, even bigger and greater
than his father.

[41] The carp swims upstream and, when about to die, does not wriggle—signs
of strength, daring, and courage.

On the fifteenth, *hagidago*, special rice balls rolled in bean paste are made to celebrate the end of *nagashi*, the rainy season. This coincides with the end of transplanting, and some people say the celebration is for that.

At the end of transplanting, parties (*sannabori iwai*) are held by exchange labor groups. At this time *dango* are given to Hotoke and Daikoku. There is much drinking. These parties take place simultaneously all over the *mura*, when there is a three-day holiday. Smaller parties are held by each group as they finish their own transplanting. Shortly after this each *buraku* holds a memorial service for the souls of insects killed (*uetsuke kuyō*). The Shinshū priest is invited in; he reads a sutra and gives a talk on Buddhism. Afterward there is a small party.

On the twenty-third is a moon-viewing, not much observed.

SIXTH MONTH

The sixth month has many holidays.

On the eighth Yakushi *dō* in Imamura has its second celebration done on the *kumi* system. On the first day of the ox in *doyō* (the great heat period) it is also celebrated. Yakushi, of the Buddhist pantheon, is a god of healing. He is the only deity who has three *matsuri* instead of one. The little *dō* in Imamura has local celebrations on both the eighth and the day of the ox, tea and beans being served by the *kumi* system. The celebration of the day of ox is the larger one. On this day the men of the *buraku*, using a separate *bancho* from the women, hold a drinking party in the *dō*.

The Yakushi in Uemura, about five miles from Suye, is the most famous one in Kuma. On the eighth of the sixth month older people from many parts of the county visit it. On the first day of the ox in *doyō* all the young people put on their finest and make the pilgrimage. It is a big holiday, and the trip to Yakushi is an excellent opportunity for young men and women to meet.

The contribution to the deity is always one sen. Thus the *kumi* or priest in charge can always estimate the number of visitors by the number of coppers. At big *matsuri* such as Yakushi as many as five thousand people come during the day; at little *buraki dō* celebrations, thirty or forty people.

The thirteenth is Amida *goya* and the fourteenth Amida Day. The fourteenth is also Gion *goya* and the fifteenth Gion Day.

On the fifteenth there is a *segoki kuyō* at the Zen temple, i.e., a memorial service. It is believed by some that it is a service for all the dead of the village. A family *ihai* can be brought to the temple at the time and thus be included in the service. It is a very elaborate service with three visiting priests from neighboring villages assisting the local priest. A bamboo and straw hut is built in the temple where offerings of fresh vegetables are made. There also is some sacred rice mixed with eggplant used in the ceremony. Colored paper banners and lanterns are hung around the temple. At the end of the service the banners are taken home by villagers, who put them later in their *daikon* fields to avert insects. Besides vegetables, offerings of rice and money are brought by villagers who attend in great numbers. The service itself is very similar to a funeral with all the villagers acting as the family.

The seventeenth is Kwannon *goya;* the eighteenth Kwannon Day; the twenty-third, Jizō *goya;* and the twenty-fourth, Jizō Day. There is a proverb on when to visit these deities:

Asa Kwannon ni, hiru Amida	In the morning Kwannon, at noon Amida
Yokkoro Jizō ni, yū Yakushi	In the afternoon Jizō, at night Yakushi

Amida, Jizō, and Kwannon are all celebrated together in Oade Buraku. A *kumi* and *bancho* system is used, three and four houses to a *kumi*. Everyone contributes one *shō* of rice. Then the *kumi* whose turn it is this year makes offerings to the Amida, Jizō, and Kwannon of the *buraku* on the proper days. On some convenient day, before people become too busy with silkworms, the *buraku* holds a party together at the house of one member of the *kumi*. The party is called *rokugatsudō* and replaces separate parties on the actual *matsuri* days. Formerly two and a half *go* of rice was also collected from each house on such occasions to make *sake;* but, since the government has imposed a heavy tax on *sake* manufacture, this no longer can be done. The *buraku* making of *sake* was also done in the old days in Imamura on Yakushi Day.

In the *buraku* of Kawaze and Kakui people gather in the Kwannon *dō* in the evening of *goya*, present candles, cakes, bow to Kwannon, then sit and drink together and enjoy the moonlight. The next day a party is held in the house of a member of the current *kumi*. Just what Amida, Kwannon, and Jizō are good for is not clearly understood. One man thinks that, since farmers celebrate them, they must be good for crops.[42]

Wagoners and horse-brokers hold special parties for Batokwannon, their patron deity at this time, sometimes accompanied by a small *kō*.

[42] See also section on The Popular Gods above.

Gion is celebrated in Taragi and in Hitoyoshi; in the latter especially on *goya*, although three days are celebrated. No one works in the fields on this day as it is said that Gion did so once and became blind in one eye and so told the people not to work in the fields on this day. (A one-eyed person is often jokingly referred to as Gion.) Many people from Suye visit the Taragi *matsuri*. Some households make *dango* in honor of the day. Gion is defined in Japanese dictionaries as a group of eight gods, but in Suye Gion means the one-eyed god referred to. (In Aso County and in Suye, to some extent, the belief is that Gion worked in a cucumber field and lost his eye, and in Kumamoto City followers of Gion shrine eat no cucumbers on this day.)

SEVENTH MONTH

The fourth is Wind Day, similar to the fourth of the fourth month.

The seventh is Tanabata, which is the *sekku* of the seventh month. Many people call it Tanabatasan. On this day some man of the family goes out and cuts a bamboo tree. This is brought home, and children tie on its branches slips of colored paper. On the slips any scribble is put— names, words, anything. The story of Tanabata, a national legend, is described by Hearn in the *Romance of the Milky Way*. (It is the story of the weaving princess who abandoned her work on her honeymoon day and as punishment was separated from her lover. They now reside on different sides of the River of Heaven and meet only once a year on Tanabata Day. The stars Altair and Vega gave origin to the legend, which comes from China.)

In addition to this legend, most of the villagers believe that on Tanabata the souls leave their abiding-place and begin their journey to earth for Bon. Some say that the

Tanabata colored papers are put out in order to attract the attention of the souls.

The thirteenth to the fifteenth is Bon, a big holiday, comparable to New Year's. At this time the ancestral souls are said to come back, to reside in the *butsudan*. They come on the night of the thirteenth and leave on the night of the sixteenth. Any house where a death has occurred during the past year receives visitors. All *buraku* people and all relatives call. They bring gifts of money or lanterns, also rice, *shōchū*, candles and incense sticks, and boxes of cake sold for the occasion at the local cakeshop. Bunches of noodles (*sōmen*), eaten all through the Bon period, are frequently given instead of candles. The guests are given feast food in return, but no fish, as this is in the nature of a funeral memorial. The *sōmen* replaces fish. In some *buraku* all neighbors do not call, but instead each house contributes five sen to the *nushidōri*, and he calls and gives money to the family who is celebrating First Bon (*hatsubon*), i.e., who have had a death in the past year. This simplified Bon calling is a result of the economy movement which is interfering with so many of the established customs.

Graves are cleaned up some days before to prepare for the spirits' return. On the thirteenth water in water containers and flowers in bamboo vases are put at the graves, and incense is burned. Any member of the household may do this, often accompanied by children. If a First Bon, relatives and *buraku* people often offer flowers at the grave of the recently dead. A mixture of rice and chopped eggplant or cucumber is also offered at graves and holy stones by some. (It is interesting to note that the first eggplant of the season is offered to the water-god and is also used at Zen temple on the occasion of *segoki kuyō*.)

Besides doing this, flowers and leaves of *sh'kibi* are pre-

CLEANING FAMILY GRAVES A FEW DAYS BEFORE
BON, SO THAT THE RETURNING SPIRITS WILL
FIND THEM IN GOOD ORDER

A *BURAKU DŌ* ON DAY OF KWANNON CELEBRATION
Visitors are being served tea and beans

sented to Kwannon (Yakushi in Imamura) and Tenjin. Many also put flowers by Jizō, by wells and streams, and by Sarutahiko stones. Jizō not celebrated on Jizō Day are given more flowers than those celebrated. All this is the same as at New Year's.

The house is also cleaned up, the *butsudan* decorated with flowers and lanterns, and offerings of fall fruit and watermelon are made. *Mochi* are also offered. Some people cook rice in a special cooking pot called *shōjin nabe*, from which rice is offered morning and evening to Hotoke-sama. At noon rice is offered from the family meal.

Today, people do not bow to the ghosts as they come in, but they see them off with candles and little pine torches on the sixteenth. Candles are placed all along the path, and torches are placed at the entrance of the path to the house where the ghosts are bidden goodbye. Often a group of neighbors will have a little drinking party together after seeing off the souls.

In Taragi and Hitoyoshi straw boats about five feet long are made and sent down the river loaded with offerings on the sixteenth to accompany the souls on their return. This is not done in Suye.

Bon is a day, like New Year's, for relatives to visit one another; and, as at New Year's, servants receive a two- or three-day holiday and gifts of clothing. Formerly big parties were given, but no longer, due to economy. Bon festivities are further curtailed by the fact that silk cocoons are ready to sell at this season.

A generation ago there were special Bon dances but not now. Only a few verses of a Bon song called the "Dance of the Ginger" still remain, and even these are only remembered by a few old people in the *mura*.

THE DANCE OF THE GINGER[43]

1. Shonga odori nya
   Ashi-byōshi te-byōshi
   Ashi ga soro wa nya
   Ōdoraren.
   > Dokkoi sho shonga e

2. Shonga baba sama
   Meizan suki desu
   Yūmbe kokonotsu kesa nanatsu
   Yūmbe kokonotsu nya
   Shokusho wa senedo
   Kesa no nanatsu ni
   Shokusho sh'ta.
   > Dokkoi sho shonga e

3. Shonga-batake no
   Mannaka goro de
   Sekida kuryu chute damasareta
   Sekida kuryu chute damashimashita ga
   Ima wa sekida no
   Sata mo naka.
   > Dokkoi sho shonga e

1. In the ginger dance
   Beat with the feet, beat with the hands;
   If the feet are not in rhythm,
   One cannot dance.

2. Shonga old lady
   Likes *meizan* cakes
   Last night nine, this morning seven (ate she).
   Last night's nine
   Indigestion did not give.
   This morning's seven indigestion gave.

3. In the middle of the ginger field (we made love)
   He promised to give me the slipper;[44] I've been fooled.
   Now he doesn't even mention the slipper.

---

[43] A Bon song, also used at transplanting and weeding in the old days. Sung, almost chanted, very slowly, each vowel prolonged and syllables repeated; e.g., *odoraren* becomes *oodo, oodooraarenu.* Ginger may have a sexual connotation.

[44] As a sign of betrothal.

A separate observation on the sixteenth is that no bathing or cooking can be done as no water should be boiled because no boilers are heated in hell.

On the twenty-first is another holiday. On this day the souls have reached their destination. Most of the people remove their Tanabata branches on this day, and some farmers put them in the fields as scarecrows.

The twenty-sixth is moon-viewing. This moon, called the three-horned moon, is famous because the dark silhouette of the full moon is seen within the shining crescent. Wheat cakes and flower arrangements of *kaya* grass are offered to the moon. As one must be up at three in the morning to see this moonrise, very few observe it.

EIGHTH MONTH

On the first is *hassaku no sekku*. Many people make *dango*. No one knows just what the day is—some say to celebrate the ripening crops, others that it is one of the five *sekku* (which it is not).

The fifteenth (Jūgoya or Jūgoyasan) is a holiday in honor of the moon. On the night of the fourteenth the young people of the *buraku* gather and bring with them rice straw which they have collected from various houses. One giant *waraji* (work sandal), one giant *ashi naka* (local work sandal), and a giant straw rope are woven. The footgear are tied together and placed by the nearest sacred stone—either Kōshin or Jizō. Just after the rope is finished, it is coiled up like a dragon and some incense is stuck into it. The children crowd around, mumble a parody of a sutra, then dive at the rope, and a tug-of-war is on. The winning side is said to have good crops. As a matter of fact, neither side ever wins; the children just tug and shout for hours. If one side gains too much, some people jump to the other side. (Sometimes done on a *buraku* basis.)[45]

On this night the moon begins to get smaller, and the saying is that it is being swallowed by a dragon. It allows itself to be thus swallowed by a dragon in order to save mankind.[46]

If the moon rises early this night, one must sow wheat early; if it rises late, sow late.

Susuki (kaya) grass and sweet potatoes are offered to the moon. So many sweet potatoes are cooked on this occasion that even a new bride will eat them. The point of this saying is that a new bride is very dainty, and sweet potatoes are said to make a person pass wind.

HARVEST MOON SONG

Jūgoya ban ni
Bobo sen mono wa
Saki no yo de
Oni ga kine tsuku
Are kine tsuku
    Yoi yoi

On the night of the fifteenth
Him who does not copulate,
In the next world
The devils will pound with a pestle
Will pound him with a pestle.[47]

Toward the end of the month, or the beginning of the month in some years, the *kaiko gokuyō* is held. This is a memorial service for the souls of dead silkworms and, at the same time, a celebration to mark the end of a suc-

[45] For a description of the same custom as observed in Kagoshima see H. B. Schwartz, *op. cit.*, pp. 43–45.

[46] The same story was told of the sun during the eclipse of 1936.

[47] The phallic significance of the pestle is well appreciated by the singer.

cessful silk-raising season. While formerly the service used
to be conducted by one of the local praying priests (*ke-bō-
zu*)[48] in each *buraku*, now all members of each of the two
silk-growing associations gather at school where a memorial service is conducted by either the Buddhist or the
Shinto priest. After the service a banquet takes place,
given to the villagers by the heads of the association, and
paid for by the spinning company sponsoring the association. The year 1936 was the first time all members of an
association held such joint ceremonies and parties.

NINTH MONTH

The ninth is Old Village Shrine Day (see below).

Except for an Ise *kō*, there is no festival in Suye itself
on the fifteenth. However, many *mura* shrines in Kuma
celebrate at this time, some early in the month, some later.
People visit the *matsuri* of different *mura* during this season.

On the sixteenth an Ise *kō* meets. The twenty-third is
a moon-viewing night not much observed.

Sometime during this month used to be the festival of
Suwasan at the village shrine, now celebrated on the
twenty-seventh of October by the Gregorian calendar.[49]
This is one of the biggest local holidays, and the only one
in which Suye as a *mura* celebrates. National flags are
out, and no work is done. Many people, besides the usual
official representatives, visit the shrine. *Sekihan*, the festive red rice, is cooked in most of the households. Formerly great feasts used to be held in all the houses, and large
containers of food were kept in the room to serve the
guests. A special soup, *tsubono*, used to be made of taro,

---

[48] See p. 232.

[49] Kaempfer records that the ninth of the ninth month was the *matsuri* day
for Suwa in the Nagasaki region. See also section on Shinto, above.

konnyaku, *gobo*, *tōfu*, and seaweed to be served to the family in the morning and to guests in the afternoon. Now only a few still make the soup, most of the people merely make *mazumeshi*, rice mixed with the foregoing vegetables —a very popular dish on all formal occasions.

In the morning there is a ceremony at the shrine; in the afternoon, a banquet at the Shinto priest's house to which all the dignitaries are invited. This is one of the big banquets of the year, and the only one on a *mura* basis.

The night before the festival day (*goya*) there are sacred dances at the shrine performed by a number of visiting priests. This is the only time that these dances are held in Suye, although similar sacred dances take place on the Hachiman and Gion *goya* in Menda and Taragi, respectively. Many people attend the dances.

Sometime during this month comes the autumn Higan (September 21 by Gregorian calendar—the autumn equinox). At this time there are lectures at the Fukada temple. No special events at the Zen temple in Suye take place. This is the seven-day Higan period in which pilgrims make the rounds of the thirty-three Kwannon *dō* in Kuma County as described under *kumi* (chap. iv). There is a Kwannon for easy delivery in Kurohiji Mura which is considered to be especially effective. On the middle day of Higan many people from surrounding *mura* visit it. It is a similar sort of holiday and trip as on Yakushi Day and the trip to Uemura Yakushi. Everyone dresses up, and young people have a good time. This day is a national holiday, with a ritual at the village shrine.

On the middle and the last day of Higan some people, especially of Hirayama, go to Kitadake shrine on Mount Kitadake on the border of Hirayama Buraku and the next *mura* of Youra. They take *shōchū* to the priest. The priest is at the shrine the whole week. Kitadake is a Shinto shrine while Higan is a Buddhist celebration—but a Buddhist celebration peculiar to Japan.

On the twenty-fifth is Tenjin Day.[50] Officially it has been moved to October 25 by the new calendar and then celebrated in Taragi as well as in Kakui Buraku where the shrine is located. It is done by the *kumi* system. Men contribute fifteen sen each for *shōchū* and gather at the shrine to make an offering. The smaller Inari shrine *kitōshi* prays. Afterward a small party is held. Women of the *mura* still informally observe the old lunar date by visiting the shrine, making an offering of *shōchū*, and then having a party either at the shrine itself or at someone's home.

TENTH MONTH

The ninth, tenth, and eleventh form the Aoi shrine celebration in Hitoyoshi, which is celebrated today by the new calendar. People from all over Kuma visit it.

The fifteenth and sixteenth are Hachiman days, now celebrated with an elaborate ceremony and big holiday in Menda by the new calendar. Many Suye people go, and the celebration goes on for two days.

On the twentieth is an Ebisu celebration in Taragi now held by new calendar. Some Suye young people go. The shrine is unusual for a Shinto building in having an actual wooden image (of Ebisu) in it.

All these town shrine celebrations are attractive to young men of the surrounding *mura* because of the wrestling that takes place. Anyone can participate, and they all join in. At the end of the performance the audience throws in money, which is divided equally among the participants.

---

[50] Tenjin is a deification of Sugawara Michizane, a famous scholar and courtier of the ninth century. Owing to court politics, he was exiled to Kyushu. He is the patron saint of learning and school children plant trees by his shrine.

About the seventh or eighth is Torikoshi. On this day the priest from the Fukada temple comes to some house in a *buraku* and prays for the ancient ancestors of the *buraku*. A small party follows. Some *buraku* (e.g., Kakui) do not observe Torikoshi. Though the ceremony is in a different house each year, there is no *bancho* for Torikoshi.

On the fifteenth is the old Ichifusa Shrine Day. On the evening of the fourteenth *tōfu* is toasted on special bamboo sticks in the fire pit. Thus prepared it is called *dengaku*. It is done in honor of Otakesan (Ichifusa shrine).

The twenty-second to twenty-eighth is Goshōki, or week of celebration of the deathday of the founder of Shinshū sect. The *sengo kuyō* is held at the local Zen temple this month. These two last events are noted above in the section on Buddhism.

On the fifteenth, parties called *shiwasu wasure* are held to bid the old year goodbye.

Toward the end of the month a night watch is kept by the *buraku* firemen. This watch is on the *kumi* system, three or four firemen watching each night. The reason for it is that so much money and rice are available for paying up debts. There is a rush of threshing grain to finish off before the end of the year. On the last day of the year *mochi* is pounded for New Year's.

Until a few years ago the temple rang a bell at midnight one hundred and eight times to disperse one hundred and eight devils, and to mark the end of the year. After this bell was rung no debts could be collected.

The yearly round of ceremonies can be graphically represented in the form of a circle to represent the yearly

TAKING GIFTS OF VEGETABLES AND FIREWOOD TO SHINSHŪ
PRIEST IN FUKADA ON FOUNDER'S DEATH DAY (*GOSHŌKI*)

This is the only motorcycle in the village and is owned by the *shōchū* factory.
The vegetables and firewood are gifts from Kawaze Buraku. The man at the wheel
is Keisuke Aiko, to whom this book is dedicated.

EATING AND DRINKING OF SHRINE OFFERINGS AFTER
COMPLETION OF A SHRINE CEREMONY

Left to right: village office clerk, assistant headman (drinking), a *kuchō*, a village shrine representative (*ujikosōdai*), the priest, priest's son, and village headman. Picture also illustrates winter clothing for men.

revolution of the earth around the sun, and a wavy line to represent the rotation of the moon about the earth (Fig. 4). The idea of the year as a circle is not alien to Japanese thought as the term for a full year is *maru-ichi-nen*, a round year.

From Figure 4 striking rhythms of village life may be noted. First is the fact that the four phases of the moon are marked by holidays. The full-moon series forms the most important set of festivals (Bon, Ichifusa, Small New Year's). The dark-of-the-moon series, with the notable exception of New Year's, forms a less important series (Tarotsuitachi and many other holidays have no particular significance). The first-quarter series are more important than dark of the moon and less important than full moon (Fire, Yakushi, Tanabata, Torikoshi). The three-quarter moon is rather less important than the first quarter (this is the best shown in the contrast between the parallel holidays of the eighth and twenty-first of the seventh month). On Tanabata, when souls leave the other world to begin their journey here, everyone makes cakes and constructs Tanabata trees. On the twenty-first, when the souls have safely returned, there is scarcely any observance of the day at all.

If the year be divided in two at Bon and the beginning of New Year's work, the fifteenth of the first month, then two other lines can be drawn to divide the circle of the year into even sixths. The two corresponding moons of Ichifusa Day (fifteenth of the third month) and when *dengaku* are made (fifteenth of the eleventh month) are concerned with Ichifusa, the sacred mountain of Kuma. The corresponding moons of the fifteenth of the fifth month and the fifteenth of the ninth month are concerned

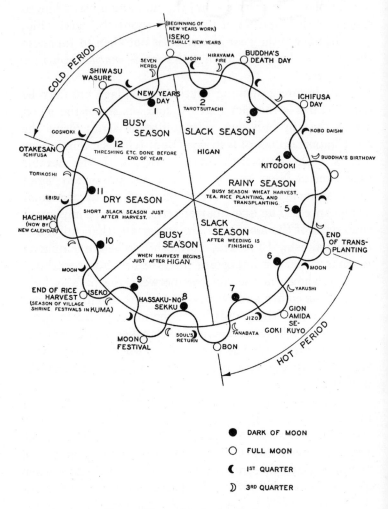

FIG. 4.—Chart of the lunar calendar year

with the end of rice-transplanting and the end of harvesting, respectively.

This lunar cycle is gradually being broken up. Some of
the old holidays are losing meaning. New dates and new
occupations are throwing it off. For instance, the village
shrine celebration now comes by the new calendar before
harvesting is all finished, and the school ignores most of
the lunar dates.

Much of a villager's belief comes from outside his local
group—the school, the village office, etc. So, while the
festival calendar and the agricultural cycle show some positive correlation, not everything in the beliefs of the community can be interpreted by reference to the environment
and means of subsistence of the community.

There are, however, some things of positive social value
which reflect their social value through various ritual
usages. The importance of rice has already been discussed
under foods—its numerous names; Inari, the god of rice;
the fear of wasting or destroying the all-important and
sacred grain. More indirectly the liquors made from rice
(*sake* and *shōchū*) form an important element in all Shinto
rituals—the offering of the wine and the communal drinking of the sacred wine. *Shōchū* mixed with snakeskin, in
Kuma at least, is regarded also as a good cure for venereal
disease.

Bamboo, pine, cedar, and cypress, the most used of all
trees, all have their ritual recognition. Bamboo, green all
the year, is of value to the peasant almost as soon as it appears above ground in the form of bamboo shoots. Full-
grown bamboo is used in basketmaking, bridge-building,
and innumerable other ways. It forms, with the pine, the
ritual decoration at New Year's time. Pine, cedar, and
cypress are the chief woods used in housebuilding and

wherever solid wood is required. All are evergreen. The
cypress and pine are symbols of long life. The wood of the
mulberry bush has special values, a teacup made of it having curative properties.

The importance of wind and rain is recognized in the
community. Too strong a wind may blow ripened rice
down into the wet paddy; lack of rain can be even more
disastrous to this all-important crop. So the wind is honored twice a year. The gods of water are recognized in
many ways—offerings to rivers and wells and dances at
waterfalls in case of drought.

The necessity of aid in farm work is expressed in the
making of dolls at Small New Year's.

Similarly local specialists all have some special patron
deity. The carpenters look to Shōtoku Taishi, a famous
prince of the seventh century, for protection; wagoners
and horse-brokers are looked after by a special many-
armed Batokwannon. For silk-raisers there is a deity of
silkworms; and for shopkeepers, Ebisu and Daikoku as
gods of good fortune.

Months when much work is being done are notable for
the fewness of festivals, i.e., from about the first of the
fourth month to the fifteenth of the fifth month, lunar,
busy with wheat harvest, rice-planting and rice-transplanting, and first crop of silkworms; and eighth and ninth
months, harvest. Periods of rest—sixth and seventh
months, eleventh and twelfth months—have many big
festivals. These rest periods are also notable for many *kō*
parties and visits to relatives on holidays.

The two Higan periods (equinoctial weeks) do not appear in the chart as they are movable dates by lunar count.
Spring Higan comes about the second month—a slack pe-

riod for work. Autumn Higan comes about the eighth
month in the slack period just before harvest.

Those holidays celebrated by the *kumi* system (Yakushi
at Yakushi *dō*, Kwannon at Kwannon *dō*, etc.) involve
the village forms of co-operation and exchange. Those on
which relatives visit one another (New Year's and Bon)
involve an even exchange of banquet for gift. Those where
the *buraku* calls on a family, as at Bon, follow the pattern
of a party for a gift.

As Granet says of ancient China: "The festivals are
great assemblies which mark the tempo of the seasonal
rhythm of social life. They correspond to short periods
during which people come together and social life is in-
tense. These periods alternate with long periods in which
people are scattered and social life is practically at a stand-
still."[51]

All the *buraku* holidays such as Kwannon and Jizō
serve as opportunities for the *buraku* to get together for
parties and a good time. Work is forgotten and good feeling reigns. On the larger holidays of New Year's and Bon
all one's relatives are united by having a party together.

Every celebration, whatever its avowed purpose (e.g.,
Kitōdoki to keep diseases from the *buraku*, Bon to honor
the ancestors, Yakushi Day to celebrate Yakushi), always
in matter of fact follows one of two patterns; either the
buraku gets together for a party or a man's relatives get
together for a party. This is one reason for the seasonal
nature of the holidays, i.e., at periods when there is no
work and at periods just after some intensive labor.

Festivals in the towns are fine opportunities for trades-
men to sell their wares. Stalls are put up along the road

[51] *Op. cit.*, p. 221.

leading to the shrine or temple. Everyone first visits the deity and throws in a penny, then visits the side shows, buys a toy, and joins in the good spirits of the crowd.

The reason for choosing the full moon as a holiday date is not clear. The moon is a much-celebrated planet, there being frequent dates on which it is nominally celebrated and one day (fifteenth of eighth month) when it is very actively celebrated. There is also a myth of the moon allowing itself to be swallowed by a dragon to save mankind. In country life a full moon is always noticeable and impressive. None of these reasons adequately explains why the full moon should be chosen as the important festival day. The whole pattern seems to have come into Japan with the lunar calendar from China.[52]

[52] With so much of Japanese belief coming from China, it is rather surprising to find no eating or offering of pig in rural Japan and no evidence of the important Chinese system of Yin and Yang, or the use of firecrackers to disperse evil spirits.

The reader is also referred to an analysis of the data presented here in the author's article, "Some Social Functions of Religion in Rural Japan," *American Journal of Sociology*, XLVII (September, 1941), 184–89.

CHAPTER VIII

CHANGES OBSERVABLE IN THE SOCIAL ORGANIZATION OF SUYE MURA

IT IS well to keep in mind the conception of society as a network of relations, with individuals as units, in discussing the organization of Suye Mura and the changes it is undergoing. We shall thus avoid the fallacy of thinking of the community as having a substance independent of its constituent members. This community or network of individuals having social relations does, however, possess a persisting structural form which is more constant than the ever changing elements of the structure itself (e.g., changes brought about by birth and death, immigration and emigration). It is the changing relations affecting the structural form which are to be dealt with in this chapter.

Before discussing the changing relationships, internal and external, affecting the society of Suye Mura, it is well to give a brief résumé of that society as it is. External economic and social relations are with the near-by towns. Political relations are through the village office with the prefectural office. The *mura* itself is made up politically of local house clusters called *buraku* united by a common school, village office, and village shrine into a *mura*. Paddy-field rice constitutes the economic base of the society. Besides the farmer there is, and apparently always has been, a small group of shopkeepers who have tended to be all located in one *buraku*. The basic social structures are the household and *buraku*; the fundamental economic systems, based on rice, are the many co-operative and mutual-aid arrangements within the household and between households within the *buraku*. Less striking, but also present, is co-operation between households, members of which are related. Connected with the co-operative systems, indeed at the bottom of most of them, is the principle of reciprocity—some return must be made for any gift or favor or service received. The misfit or nonconformer is either an individualist or a man so poor that he cannot keep up his end in exchanges. An important social sanction consists of withholding co-operation. A characteristic of all phases of village life is the round of seasons, there being a time of the year for all things. The beliefs and festivals of the community reflect the importance in village life of the local house groups called *buraku*, the predominant place of rice in the local economy, and the round of seasons and seasonal occupations.

The basic pattern of life in Suye is evidently an old one. It has survived a long and varied history and probably dates back at least to the time of the introduction of Chinese civilization in the sixth century. One reason for its stability is perhaps that Kuma has always been off the main line of travel, being as it is a dead-end valley surrounded by mountains. The effects of the Meiji revolution and of Western civilization are present, however, and many changes are taking place. These changes affect both relations within the *mura* and relations external to the *mura*. By internal relations are meant those social relations existing within the *mura*, between *buraku* and between households within the *buraku*. External relations are the relations of people in the *mura* with places and systems outside the *mura* such as the towns, the feudal lord, or the central government. The changes themselves are of two types: those directed by the government and those not so directed.

Ordinarily, changes in a social structure are thought of as, to a degree, inevitable and uncontrollable results of changes in the course of time, or changes as the result of contact with another, rather different, social structure. In Japan, however, there is the unusual situation of controlled structural change. The government, carrying on the paternalistic attitude characteristic of the pre-Meiji period, has made a point of carefully controlling the changes and Western influences as they affect rural Japan. The farmers, used to orders from above, continue to this day to accept at face value whatever comes from government sources. Of course, one aspect of a social structural form cannot be changed without affecting other aspects, and so, as we shall see later, many unintended changes have come into Suye Mura in addition to, and sometimes as the indirect result of, the carefully introduced changes directed by the government.

In the old days the *buraku* lines were sharply marked, each *buraku* living more or less independently with its own head (*nushidōri*) and its own shrine. Since Meiji the *mura* unity has increased at the expense of *buraku* isolation. The agricultural association with its branch heads, the *mura*-wide "societies," and especially the school have brought all the *buraku* in the *mura* closer together, giving them many more common interests than before. Within the *buraku* the exchange-labor groups and *kumi* groups are giving way in the face of these government-directed changes; they are also in large degree affected by new economic forces as noted below.

The external relations of inhabitants of the *mura* have changed even more, if anything, than internal relations.

Politically, the external relations have been changed from political allegiance to the lord of Sagara at Hitoyoshi to loyalty for the Emperor of Japan; local loyalties are replaced by national ones. There is still a strong feeling of attachment, however, for Kuma County among all its inhabitants. The old five-man *kumi* responsible to the lord for crimes and debts of any member was abolished with Meiji, but the various kinds of three- or four-household *kumi* are doubtless descended from them. Here is an example of where a political external relation has disappeared leaving only the local house groups. It is parallel in some ways to the no longer official but still locally recognized county. Each is still a functioning group locally while their official functions have been absorbed by the more centralized political units of *mura* and prefecture.

Economic factors are also important in changing the external relations of the *mura*. This is largely due to the coming of the machine to the countryside. Busses, railroads, and improved prefectural roads bring Hitoyoshi and other more distant places much closer to Suye. An increased use of money is a corollary to the increased dependence on machines. The bicycle makes it easy to go to the town of Menda in a few minutes, and the large increase in manufactured articles makes it necessary to go more and more often to Menda. Furthermore, money is necessary to purchase a bicycle to make such trips or to buy a ticket to travel on the railroad. The changes in external relations, owing both to money and to machines, in their turn affect the internal relations of the *mura*. Another reason for the breakdown of *buraku* lines is their increased common dependence on the towns for manufactured goods.

In the old days between feudal lord and the farmer stood the *samurai*. All farmers were of equal status, relationships being with fellow-*buraku* members. After Meiji these class distinctions were abolished and the *mura* became more or less self-governing units responsible to the prefectural office. New social classes, based on money and occupation, have grown up in the *mura* as a whole to replace the older geographical *buraku* units and the governing classes of *samurai* and feudal lord. This reshuffling of social classes has brought in its train new strains and disfunctional situations.

The outstanding element in Japan's response to Western civilization is the controlled form in which the government has allowed it to reach the countryside. The substitution of central governmental control for feudal control has resulted in a great emphasis on nationalism. Whereas, formerly neither the farmer nor the government was ever much worried about such an abstraction as patriotism so long as the farmer produced his rice, today, as a powerful tool of social control, nationalism is stressed in education, in conscription, in public talks in the school auditorium, and in the encouragement of societies such as the Women's Patriotic Society. The Emperor is used as the symbol of the nation and represented as the father of his people in all such propaganda.

Western ideas, as far as the government approves, are dispensed to the people; but, in so far as the government disapproves, the people seldom hear of them.[1] The controlled changes, such as national societies and government schools, have affected the internal relations of *buraku* as already noted, causing them to act together (*a*) in the interests of the *mura* and (*b*) in the interests of the nation. They have affected external relations through such things

---

[1] An excellent article on thought control, entitled "No Left Turn," is to be found in *Fortune Magazine* for September, 1936.

as the government railroad, conscription, and education in widening the range of contact, both personal and ideational, of the local farmer.

As the government-controlled systems such as schools, national societies, and the agricultural association come into the *mura*, the local forms tend to break down. The *nushidōri* and *buraku* co-operative forms are being replaced by the branch heads of the agricultural association. An association system of rice-transplanting is substituted in one *buraku* for the older exchange-labor system. Similarly, the Women's Patriotic Society is intended to take over the functions of the *buraku* mutual-aid systems. The uncontrolled factors of money and machines also play their part in breaking down the old *buraku* co-operative forms. Certain of the new government-directed associations may be regarded as attempts to replace these weakened local economic systems with strong centralized ones.

The older soldier classes have been replaced by the modern conscription system. It is interesting to note that, just as the older social classes were distinguished by special dress, the new *mura*-wide societies are marked by uniforms. The members of the Young Men's Association all wear special uniforms at meetings, as do Reservists and members of the Women's Patriotic Society. This puts all the members on a common footing and under a hierarchy of officers stemming from Tokyo.

The older haphazard means of education have been replaced by a national school system which serves as an ideal tool for introducing Western knowledge and ideas to the country in a perfectly controlled manner. The role of the educated man is important in this respect. The agricultural association system of rice-transplanting was instituted by a retired schoolteacher in his *buraku;* it is the returned college graduate who has introduced many agricultural changes in the *mura*. Both of these men have great prestige in the *mura* as a whole.

Farming production has been stepped up through the government agricultural advisers, by the new methods of using paddy fields to grow wheat in the winter, and by the encouragement of chicken-raising and other secondary farming activities. Formerly the winter was much more of a leisure period given over to festivals and banquets than it is now. Furthermore, the government encourages economy and discourages "vain" expenses at celebrations of such events as births, weddings, and funerals, which fact tends to make all parties very uniform. This policy also accounts to some degree for the curtailment of festivals. The variety of festivals in many cases has simmered down to the housewife making a few special cakes to present to the household gods and then going off to work as usual. As festivals and banquets diminish, corresponding reciprocal exchanges are bound to diminish, and one more factor is added to the breakdown of the *buraku* as a closely integrated social unit. The introduction of threshing machines and an emphasis on using spare time to make side products have further emphasized this trend toward a leveling of the rhythms of social life.

Besides these directed changes occurring in the society there are several changes which are unintended but inevitable results of government control. Such, for instance, is the growth in the *mura* of a special class made up of schoolteachers, having little in common with villagers.

In contrasting the controlled response of Japan to Western civilization with that of China, Dr. Hu Shih points out that in China the Western influences have been haphazard, penetrating diffusely, and without any effective leadership and that the result has been sometimes drastically disintegrating. He fails to remark, however, that similar uncontrolled penetration is occurring in Japan. As they did toward the end of the Tokugawa era, money and the merchant class are spreading and increasing in influence quite independently of the carefully laid plans of the government. It is just this point—the increased use of money and its disintegrating effect on the older social structures—that is so striking in the rural life of Japan today.

The old *mura* system was based on rice and co-operation. Any changes which affect these things affect seriously the whole social structure. As money comes in, co-operation goes out. The breakdown of the co-operation systems of the shopkeeper *buraku* in contrast to the paddy *buraku* is a good illustration of this phenomenon in Suye Mura. Even in some of the paddy *buraku* the richer farmers are resorting to contract labor in transplanting.

With an increased dependence on money comes an increased use of hired labor rather than neighbor's help. The use of hired labor does away with the bother of troublesome exchanges of value. On the other hand, it brings in the new classes of employer and employed which, until recently, were nonexistent in rural life.

The merchants of the towns, through commercializing various festivals, have helped to lessen the importance of the corresponding local *mura* festivals. On the farm, machine-made goods are replacing homemade ones, and mechanical tools are tending to break up some of the smaller *kumi* systems such as the now defunct one for making straw rope. Money and machines have also directly affected the household economy by replacing many home industries with manufactured articles.

The essential nature of the change brought about by the increased use of money is the change from regarding money as a handy tool for buying and selling, i.e., exchange, to regarding money as a desirable thing in itself. The shop-keepers all have this latter attitude and are characterized by stinginess. When a group of people becomes like that, even though they be farmers, they can no longer co-oper-ate trustfully, and the close integration of a *buraku* based on labor exchange and rotating *kumi* breaks down. A man who, perhaps, indicates the direction of future change in this aspect of *buraku* social forms is the pear-orchard proprietor mentioned in chapter iv. He has located him-self on a border between two *buraku* and so belongs to neither. Though he could easily associate himself with one or the other by a gift of wine or a "face-showing" party, he chooses to remain aloof. Thus he never gives any aid or co-operation in housebuilding or funerals, nor does he receive any. If he dies, his family should theoretically have to hire men to bury him—an unthinkable procedure in normal *bu-raku* life. In actual fact some men would probably volun-teer to bury him even though he does not deserve it. It is significant that he is not native to Suye and has no rela-tives in the *mura*.

Another isolated case that may indicate future trends of change is the one family in Suye belonging to a Shinto sect. As already noted, these sects are characterized by healing through faith, harking back to the godly ancestors of the Emperor, and a religious fervor lacking in most of the older Buddhist sects. The one family in Suye belong-ing to such a sect is well to do and, as a rich house, uses more money than the average. Rich men tend to become isolated from the rest of the *buraku* and to lose some of the social values accruing from democratic co-operation and exchange in the things of everyday life. Thus, it is plausible that with this "deprivation" the household has turned to this revivalist sect just as the Orokaiva people of New Guinea have taken up the Taro cult to compensate for certain social "deprivations."[2]

With the advent of the new economic groups with divergent economic interests, the close integration of the *buraku* based on mutual aid is weakened. This weakening of the integration of the *buraku* is another factor in the replacement of *buraku* isolation by common unity in the *mura*. If the change continues very long, however, it is doubtful whether even *mura* unity and the agricultural association will be able to take care of all the disfunctional situations likely to arise.

The central government is aware of the dangers, and part of its agricultural program, including the agricultural association, is no doubt aimed to avoid or counteract changes in the social structure which might prove unsettling to the equilibrium of rural society. Thus, in addition to nationalism and other moral measures, the government is applying economic remedies. In this way it is more likely to be successful than the advisers of the Tokugawa government who prescribed only moral maxims for economic ills. It is interesting that one of the remedies of the government, the encouraging of the agricultural association in co-operative selling of grain and buying of goods and even co-operative manufacture of articles, has created troubles in the business world, and businessmen are protesting against the increasing activities of the national agricultural association in manufacturing and retailing its own goods. The farmer now demands government manufacture of fer-

[2] See F. E. Williams, *Orokaiva Magic* (Oxford, 1928).

tilizer, while the businessman objects to government manufacture of work shoes.

There are other influences breaking down the particular-
ism of the *mura*. One of these is the newspaper. Its influence is not great, but some people read it and gain a
wider outlook. Sometimes they discuss the news with one
another, although there is remarkably little of this as
yet.[3] Most of the changes in social relations have come
about by social contact rather than through the printed
page. Even in the schools it is the influence of their teachers rather than their books which affect the thoughts and
acts of children.

New forms of recreation affect the external relations of
the *mura*. As yet they have not changed greatly in type
except for the occasional movie; for younger people the
movie in the neighboring towns is becoming an increasing
attraction. The festivals have become more of an interest
to the people as county fairs than religious ceremonies
and *buraku* parties are on a smaller scale and less frequent
than formerly.

Other examples of uncontrolled changes in the society
are a few foreign words in the vocabulary and the use of
certain foreign clothes, as, for example, in work. But such
changes scarcely affect the structural forms of the community. The fundamental undirected changes in structural form have come with the increased use of money and
machines and with it a breakdown of local co-operative
systems (*kumi*, *kattari*, etc.) in favor of hired labor.

Most of the changes affecting the internal and external
relations of the *mura* are interdependent. The changes

[3] During the course of this study in Suye the assassinations of February 26,
1936, occurred. Only a few village officials and schoolteachers so much as
discussed the matter, and many people did not even know what had happened.

from a rice economy to a money economy have brought an increased use of machines and a breakdown of co-operative forms. Social classes have changed from feudal lord, *samurai*, and farmer to new ones based on money or occupation which are a result of the new money economy and in turn affect the internal relations of the *buraku* to one another and increase the unity of the *mura*. Even the uncontrolled spread of a money economy and the growth of central authority in Tokyo since the Meiji revolution are related factors of social change. Without a fluid exchange, impossible so long as rice was the predominant means of exchange, much of the real power of government had, perforce, to be left in the hands of local feudal lords. So, just as money and machines, while breaking up certain old co-operative forms and giving rise to new possibly antagonistic capital and labor groups in the *buraku*, give the *mura* greater unity, so the *mura* in turn are becoming less isolated as they are drawn together in a common dependence on national economic forces.

The changes taking place in the social structural form of Suye are, then, of two kinds: those affecting the internal relations of household, *kumi*, and *buraku* and those affecting the external relations of the *mura* and people in it to the environment, i.e., near-by towns, Hitoyoshi, the county as a whole, and the nation. These changes in turn take two forms: those directed by the government and those not so directed. Directed changes are such things as the school, conscription, the agricultural association, and various national societies. The outstanding uncontrolled factors are the change from a rice to a money economy and the related phenomenon of an increased use of machines.

One problem remains unanswered, How far are the changes now observable in Suye Mura the result of Western influence, controlled and uncontrolled, and how far the results of the natural evolution of the native society? We have already seen that money was beginning to make itself felt before Meiji. The introduction of machinery, the abolition of *samurai*, and other changes may have only *accelerated* native tendencies of development rather than *changed* the course of that development. The very fact that so many aspects of Western civilization have been so successfully controlled by the government as they came into the country is evidence in favor of the theory of acceleration rather than of drastic change. Indeed, it is probably impossible for a given type of society to be drastically changed by contact with another, in this case Western civilization, and still survive. Evidence from Polynesia would seem to indicate that this is true. In order to survive, it would seem, there are two courses open: either to reject the new order as much as possible, admitting it only in pieces as China is doing (not always successfully), or to adopt Western culture in controlled form. Japan as a nation has deliberately chosen to introduce the new civilization under careful official control. On the whole, and in spite of such uncontrolled factors as money and machines, Japan has succeeded in this policy, especially in the countryside, as demonstrated in Suye Mura.

APPENDIX I

ECONOMIC BASE

Agricultural statistics for the year 1933, as compiled by the village office, are given herewith:

LAND

Area of village*..................... 1,134 sq. *ri*†
Government forest land............. 3,620 *tan*†
Village government land (forest)..... 645 *tan*
Village government land (other)..... 42 *tan*
Private land:
    Taxed......................... 6,961 *tan*
    Untaxed....................... 6 *tan*

FARMHOUSES

Landowners....................... 32
Landowner and tenant at once....... 112
Tenants.......................... 71
                         ————
   Total......................... 215

OF THIS LAND:

Paddy land....................... 165 *cho*† owned by villagers
                                  85 *cho* owned by outsiders
                                  (66 per cent village owned)

Upland........................... 115 *cho* owned by villagers
                                  15 *cho* owned by outsiders
                                  (89 per cent village owned)

* Includes 2,510 meters east to west; 8,820 meters north to south.
† One sq. *ri*=5.95 sq. miles; 1 *cho*=10 *tan*=2.5 acres.

In 1934 the percentages were 65 per cent village-owned paddy, 87 per cent village-owned upland.

	Acreage (in *tan*)	Crop	Money Value (in Yen)
Rice.....................	2,620	4,732 *koku**	941,783
Mugi (wheat and barley).....	968	1,105 *koku*	12,548
Millet....................	107	240 *koku*	1,200
Sweet potato...............	60	24,000 *kwan*†	1,200
Taro......................	22	10,120 *kwan*	1,012
Daikon....................	22	12,960 *kwan*	648
Tea......................	20	980 *kwan*	1,960
Fruits (persimmons, chestnuts, pears)...................	16	1,474 *kwan*	1,495‡
Soy beans.................	30	30 *koku*	290
Azuki beans	25	20 *koku*	360
Undai (rape seed)...........	21	27 *koku*	351
Soba (buckwheat)...........	10	2 *koku*	18
Others....................	38	7,005 *kwan*	1,439

* One *koku* = 10 *to;* 100 *shō* = 5.1 bushels (U.S. dry measure).

† One *kwan* = 8.2 lb. (avoir.).

‡ One thousand yen of this is the produce of one commercial pear orchard.

SERICULTURE

Number of silkworm-rearing families .. 144

Mulberry fields .... 244 *tan*

Total of all crops................. 5,222 *kwan* = ¥29,040

DOMESTIC ANIMALS

	Cattle	Horses	Pigs	Chickens
Number of keepers.................	65	155	7	130
Number of animals.................	70	205	15	1,214
Number of animals produced........	14	4	10	79,160*

* Eggs.

FORESTRY

Number of people engaged in forestry................. 5

Timber...........................	1,337 *koku*	¥ 412
Charcoal.........................	14,400 *kwan*	1,440
Firewood.........................	105 *kwan* (?)	245
Mushrooms.......................	1,330 *kin**	2,124
Bamboo and others.................................		710
Total..		¥4,932

* One *kin* = 1.3 lb. (avoir.).

Number of people as main occupation................. 3
Number of people as side occupation................51

Carp, trout, ells......................	3,110 *kwan*	¥ 783
Other fish..........................	5,700 *kwan*	570
Total...		¥1,353

Most of the forestry is done by the people of Hirayama, the mountain *buraku*. Most of the charcoal is manufactured by mountain workers hired by a Hitoyoshi capitalist.

There are several shopkeepers and others following non-farming occupations in part or in whole. The village office statistics for 1933 are:

Type of Business	No. of Households	Annual Business
Shōchū......................	I	¥8,000
Stonecutters.................	4	1,331
Straw articles................	223*	1,680
Tōfu.......................	10	1,205
Shopkeepers (including those *tōfu*-makers who also have small shops, tobacco- and salt-sellers, any house running a shop either as a part-time or as a full-time occupation)....................	8	

* Side occupation.

RELIGION AND PRAYING

	No. of Priests	Yearly Income of Priests
Shinto shrine...............	I	¥254
Zen temple..................	I	85
Inari *kitōshi*.................	2	39
Sambō Kōjin *kitōshi*..........	I	46
Other healers by prayer.......	2 (at least)	8

Many farmers have debts. One of the first things a man would do, if by some rare good fortune he came into an unexpected two or three hundred yen, would be to get rid of his debt. One cause of debts is the boom years when silk prices were high. Then farmers bought new land or improved their houses or bought some livestock. Often this would be done with the help of a mortgage or loan. When the price of silk fell sharply, the farmer was left holding the bag. In Japan a man cannot simply declare himself bankrupt and begin again. If a man goes bankrupt, he loses his civil standing and can no longer vote. So, to hold his place in society, a man must perpetually live under the heavy burden of debt.

In 1936 the economic reconstruction began in Suye. The members of each *buraku* were requested to list their debts anonymously in order that the village office might know how Suye stood financially. While some farmers facetiously wrote "enormous" on their slips, most of them faithfully did as told. Debt is a touchy subject, so it is possible that the sums given are inaccurate, probably being an underestimate.

Debts to individuals (includes brokers)...	¥ 40,079
Debts to bank........................	37,145
Debts to village credit association.......	11,443
Other debts (mostly medical)..........	14,404
Total...........................	¥103,071

Average per household, ¥362.7

Rice and money *kō* which have already been won are considered as debts, since one is under financial obligation to pay out money to them at regular intervals.

Money *kō*..................	¥ 41,845
Rice *kō*....................	141,562
Total..................	¥183,407

Total debt:

$$¥103,071 \\ + \quad 183,407 \\ \overline{\qquad\qquad} \\ ¥286,478$$

On the credit side:

Money lent out or deposited as savings:

To individuals...........	¥	3,959
To bank...............		1,205
To post-office savings.....		3,895
Others.................		1,943
Total........................		¥ 22,739

Kō not yet won:

Money *kō*...............	¥ 12,134	
Rice *kō*.................	40,533	52,667
Total credit.................		¥ 75,406

Net debit:
286,478 − 75,406 = 211,072 yen
Average per household, 740.6 yen

Financial matters of the village are taken care of by the village office and the credit association. The village office collects taxes. The credit association takes deposits from any farmer in amounts from ten sen up. It extends loans to members up to a few thousand yen, subject to approval of the head of the association and the village headman.

The credit association (Suye Mura Shinyo Kobai Kumi-ai) was established in 1923.

Capital...............................	¥ 6,780*
Fund.................................	809

Rate of interest for lending, 12 per cent or less
Rate of interest for depositing, 8 per cent or less

Number of people money lent to..........	148
Amount lent..........................	¥23,879
Number of depositors....................	810
Amount...............................	¥ 8,654

* As of 1933.

APPENDIX II

HOUSEHOLD EXPENSES

Household expenses in Suye are only partly financial. Since most things such as *miso*, pickles, and other edibles are made at home, and the basic food, rice, is homegrown, money is needed only for such necessities as salt and sugar. For banquets deep-sea fish must also be purchased. *Tōfu* and other things purchased at the local stores may be paid for with rice instead of with money. Servants' wages are in rice, and so, frequently, are the wages of roofmakers and others. For co-operative labor such as housebuilding or rice-transplanting no money expense is involved. Money is necessary for manufactured tools, for clothing, and to pay for anything purchased from an out-of-the-village peddler, as well as for anything purchased in the towns. All in all, about 50 per cent of an ordinary farmer's living expenses are in money and about 50 per cent in kind. The increasing importance of the near-by towns as shopping-centers has increased the money expense. Nonfarmers pay more in money and less in kind as they have to buy some or all of their rice. Rich men, owing to fish, wine, and education expenses, also pay a higher percentage in money.

Table 10 summarizes the household expenses of a rich farmer (the headman), of several typical farmers in different *buraku*, and of a shopkeeper in Kakui. The high education expense of the headman is due to his having one son away in college, another in the barracks, and a daughter in high school. The figures are from a survey made under the guidance of the agricultural adviser, a member of each branch agricultural association making the survey in his *buraku;* hence figures for some *buraku* will be more accurate than for others. The purpose of the survey was to obtain a picture of the economic situation of the village before inaugurating a program of economic reconstruction (*keizai kosei*) to reduce expenses and increase the production of each household.

TABLE 10

Household Expenses

Buraku	Farmer	Value*	Rice	Mugi†	Millet	Beans	Shōyu	Miso	Vegetables	Pickles	Fish	Sugar, Salt, etc.	Total	Clothing	House Repairs	Charcoal and Firewood	Electric Light	Furniture and Utensils	Total	Health	Education	Entertainment, Shōchū, and Tobacco‡	Amusement	Wedding and Funeral	Rice-polishing, etc.	Temple Donations, etc.	Total	Grand Total	No. People in Household§
								Food								**Clothing, Shelter, etc.**							**Health, Education, Amusement, etc.**							
Kawaze (rich paddy)	Rich man (sonchō)||	Amt. in yen	270**	20**	20	3	21	40	22	45	120	80	641	300	30	43	50	10	433	88	1325††	180	30	50	12	50	1735	2804	8.0
		% in kind	100	100	100	....	100	100	100	100	......	...	68	......	...	95	50	...	9									13	
	Ordinary farmer||	Amt. in yen	361	53	....	13	14	20	3	11	20	23	518	94	200	10	30	2	336	70	35	92	40	60	46	20	363	1217	9.0
		% in kind	100	100		100	100	100	100	100			91															39	
	Average for buraku	Amt. in yen	332	....	....	...	...	...	...	...	...	29	497	...					162								459	1117	6.9
		% in kind	97										83						9									40	
Oade (upland)	Ordinary farmer||	Amt. in yen	160	40	24	8	20	12	11	15	36	8	334	72	25	30	27	5	159	15	15	105	15	20	10	5	185	678	5.0
		% in kind	100	100	100	....	85	83	100	87	26		84	......		100												46	
	Poor farmer||	Amt. in yen	108	12	10	4	3	4	10	7	3	3	164	8	4	10	6	1	29	10	2	12	3	5	2	2	36	229	4.0
		% in kind	73	100	100	....	...	75	100	86			74			100			67									67	
	Average for buraku	Amt. in yen	220	...	...	...	...	...	...	...	...	22.5	387	...					113								230	730	5.7‡‡
		% in kind	80										75						20									45	
Kakui (shopkeeper)	Well-to-do shopkeeper||	Amt. in yen	216	43	...	3	15	8	19	8	35	19	366	110	180	56	47	3	396	500§§	3	124	2	101	6	20	756	1517	10.0
		% in kind	22	100			74	96	100				37			29			4							25		11	
	Average for buraku	Amt. in yen	203	...	...	...	...	...	...	...	...	20.6	342	...					134								237	712	5.5
		% in kind	57										49						8									26	
Hirayama (mountain)	Ordinary farmer||	Amt. in yen	230	20	16	3	10	12	10	4	30	5	340	26	8	16	5||||	...	55	5	10	137	5	...	...	5	162	557	....
		% in kind	100	100	100	100	90	100	100	100			89		38	100			35										
	Average for buraku	Amt. in yen	215	...	...	...	...	...	...	...	...	24.8	334	...					81								127	542	6.1
		% in kind	84										78						22									50	

* Values for rice and other products were set by the agricultural adviser for Suye Mura. The amount of yen actually spent, plus the amount of home-grown or homemade foods translated into yen values, give the total "Value in Yen."

† Collective term for wheat, rye, and barley.

‡ Mostly for shōchū.

§ Including servants. These figures not all available as the survey on which these data are based did not include this information, hence it had to be obtained indirectly.

|| Actual expenses of an actual household.

** Rice is valued at about 30 yen a koku (5.1 bushels). Thus this "rich-man's" household consumed 46 bushels of rice in a year. Wheat is valued at about 15 yen a koku.

†† One son in college; one daughter in high school.

‡‡ For eleven houses. Hence figure difference from that given in Table 5.

§§ Wife of head sick during year and finally died.

|| || Kerosene in Hirayama.

APPENDIX III

SUMMARY OF TALKS AT A MEETING TO ENCOURAGE TAXPAYING, AT SUYE MURA SCHOOL (AUGUST)

The headman's address:

Thank you for so many attending this meeting in spite of the severe heat. Mr. Hayashida, the headman of Okaharu, has come to make a speech for you. He has taken not a little interest in our meeting. Our school master and the village councilors are also kind enough to be present. Recently we have had drought and other natural calamities, on which account conditions of tax payment have become a little worse. The people who are present today are, however, I believe, all honest payers, so I am very happy to see you here today. Taxpaying is one of the greatest duties we, developed people, are to discharge without fail, as members of the state and of a local self-governing community as well. It is, as it were, their blood. Without it, they cannot move. In other villages drought has often been turned into a dishonest excuse of failing to pay taxes. I believe there are no such people among you. As you see, bad payments result in deterioration of school equipment and other public arrangements. It causes a general loss for your village. Thinking of this, please be sure to pay your tax.

The schoolmaster's congratulatory speech:

Several people have now been honored for good tax payment in front of me. I congratulate you upon them from the bottom of my heart. Allow me to speak about the impressions which I have had while seeing this meeting. It goes without saying that tax payment is one of the most important duties you should discharge. Seeing, however, that some fail to pay, it is difficult to carry out. I have often heard people say that agricultural improvement should be started from the spiritual side. This is quite true. The people just now honored are a living illustration of this spiritual recovery. A number of taxpaying groups have also been honored. This shows well how you unite with each other. This good condition is, I think, partly attributable to efforts of the headman, village councilors, etc.

The other day when I visited Konjo Mura in Yatsushiro County

319

with the *seinen gakkō* students, I compared it with your village in various respects. I wondered how this village, which was poor in individual economy, has become such a good one that it is famous all over Japan. I concluded that the unity of the people there was the most essential factor. Suye is richer in individual economy but is poorer in unity of people. Yet it is a very hopeful village, I believe, because it has so much stronger a foundation. If you unite well, you are sure to surpass it.

I have one more thing to speak of. I was once a teacher in the *seinen gakkō* in Kurohiji. People of that village pay taxes very well. This is, however, largely owing to efforts of its headman. People are liable to become too dependent. Thus, without a leader, they become no good. I hope you will keep up your present good condition with your own efforts. In view of the emergency age we are confronted with, I feel greatly assured seeing how you unite well. Compared with the ordinary ways of life where we are apt to turn devils when we claim our own rights, this meeting is a most peaceful and satisfactory scene. I hope you will make further efforts. At the end I again congratulate you wholeheartedly.

Speech of the reporter of the "Hitoyoshi Times":

I deem it a great honor to attend this meeting. Seeing how you are fulfilling one of the most important duties you have to discharge as members of our state, I feel greatly reassured. I hope the people honored just now will continue their good conditions and also that Suye will become one of the best taxpaying villages. I congratulate you by this speech, though it is so poor and short.

Okaharu headman's speech:

Your headman said at the beginning that I have come here especially to make a speech for you. This, however, is not so. The other day he telephoned to me and said, "How about coming to our meeting? It will be very interesting. Just come and see." Thus I came only to see your meeting. Once I have attended it, however, I cannot go home without thanking you. In this sense I will speak to you. I have tried to systematize my thoughts, but failed, because I have had various meetings such as *kuchō* meetings these days. I have written down what came into my head. I cannot tell whether it will be interesting or instructive to you.

Now Konose Mura and Suye Mura are the best taxpaying villages in Kuma County. I considered why it is so. The fact that the people there are rich cannot be ignored. The efforts of the headman and other village authorities must also be taken into account. The most fundamental cause is, however, the unity of the people. Though the average house-

hold tax (*kosūwari*) in my village is ¥16.50, which is very little
compared with yours, over ¥20, the condition of payment is very bad.
Your village has recently been selected for the economical reconstruction work. This work, however, should be preceded by a spiritual reconstruction work. It is true that General Araki said that the enemy
abroad is nothing to be afraid of; it is an internal trouble that makes us
most afraid. Some foreigner said, "It was Rome that ruined Rome."
Why was Toyotomi's army defeated by Tokugawa's at the castle of
Osaka which was one of the strongest castles in Japan? The former had
as good a leader in Sanada Yukimura as the latter had in Tokugawa
Iyeyasu. The real cause of defeat lay in the internal strife, or lack of
unity. Germany also lost the Great War, it is said, because women
failed to keep up their first high spirit. Foreigners say that the Japanese
race is not good at living co-operatively. This is an opinion worthy of
serious attention. Shōtoku-Taishi also emphasized the necessity of spiritual unity at the very beginning of the constitution he established. It
is a famous historical fact that Oda Nobunaga, one of the greatest
warriors in the age of disorder and also the master of Toyotomi Hideyoshi, waged a battle upon people believing in Shinshū who knew
nothing about military technique for eighteen years and yet could not
overcome them. This is another good example of how spiritual accord
is powerful. The Chinese character 人 (man) represents two people sup-
porting each other. This also exemplifies the necessity of unity in social
life. It is deplorable, however, that people have become too selfish these
days. We should have a clearer idea of the constitution of our state. It
goes without saying that a state presupposes three constituents—the
ruler, the ruled, and the territory. The rulers of our country have been
of the same blood. We, subjects, are also descendants of our rulers.
The territory has belonged to the former from the beginning, while Germany, where the Kaiser was sent away from the country, Russia, where
King Nicholas was killed by revolutionists at the last revolution,
France, where Louis XVI was beheaded, and other states have been
ruled by those who took the territory by force, at the cost of blood.
The relation between the ruler and the territory or the ruled is quite
different from that in ours. We call the Empress "Her majesty the
Mother of the State" (*Kokuboheika*). This title shows how we subjects
regard our ruler. Is it not fearful that in this country of ours com-
munism, the thought of the terrible Russian revolutionists who killed
their emperor, has been pervading all classes? This fact is, I believe,
attributable to lack of proper spirit on our part. In view of the emergency age, the most essential thing we are demanded to be provided
with is unity. The Emperor Meiji said in his august edict, "both high
and low uniting. . . . ." The Emperor Taishō and the now reigning

Emperor also have stressed the necessity of unity in their various edicts.

These days people have become too materialistic owing to the business depression. There is an episode about Saigō Takamori. One day Kirino Toshiaki, one of his ardent followers and also one of the greatest leaders of rebels in the Meiji civil war, visited Takamori with a gift box. Wondering what it contained, Takamori's younger brother, Jūdō, opened it in a separate room. He found it contained a number of sweet potatoes. When Kirino came home, Jūdō said to his elder brother in a contemptuous tone, "Look here, that fellow brought us sweet potatoes!" Hearing this, Takamori stood up silent and went into the next room. He brought a short sword and, holding it toward Jūdō, said, "Cut your belly and die." Then he reproached his younger brother, saying, "You yourself are a contemptible fellow. You don't know how to receive a gift. It is not the thing that you receive, but the spirit expressed in it." Jūdō became aware of his mistake and apologized sincerely to his brother.

Unity based on materials is easily broken. A young bride who selects her groom, judging him by the money he has, or the clothes he will buy for her, is sure to be disappointed. However, I never say that we can do without material. It is important, but it should go hand in hand with spirit. I hope you will improve your life on both sides.

I am sorry for my tedious and disconnected speech. I am afraid it was not interesting to you.

The headman:

I thank you for your attentive listening to the speeches. What the Okaharu headman said just now is quite to the point. Unity is everything in our life.

Now we will break up. As to the *kuchō*, please gather downstairs. Others may disperse individually. Thank you.

APPENDIX IV

SUMMARY OF A LECTURE BY THE FUKADA SHINSHŪ PRIEST ON THE OCCASION OF THE SEVENTH SEVEN-DAY MEMORIAL SERVICE FOR DROWNED BOY IN ASO BURAKU, AUGUST 13, 1936

[First the priest read aloud a passage from a sutra, then gave the speech.]

Please allow me to speak for a while on this occasion. I have heard that the child of this family was drowned. I know very well that it is very difficult to comfort one's self when one meets with such a calamity. The death was, however, predestined in the previous life. A passage of a sutra says that there are many ways of death—death by the sword, death by fire, etc.—for people are predestined differently in their previous lives. Seeing that we are human beings with feeling, it is natural that we are thrown into sorrow on such occasions. Many people have asked me to tell how to save themselves from the depth of painful sorrow. The most important thing to do on this occasion is how to make the death significant. When I was in Kagoshima, I met a couple who lost their dear child. For the first one week they ate next to nothing on account of sorrow. But then they felt their appetite recovering and came to eat and drink as usual. Think of this case well! It is worthy of being thought out. At first they were so much discouraged as to eat nothing. They cried: "Our dear, dear child was taken away." Then what happened? They came to eat and drink as usual soon afterward. Is this not a sign of their wanting in true sincerity? If they had been truly attached to their child, they should have died with him, or at least tried hard to know to the full what happened to him in the next world. Seeing that they did not do so, their confessed love was false. They were selfish after all. Their child's death was thus made quite meaningless. If instead they had been surprised at the event, led to be conscious of predestination in the previous life, and had found Amida, not only the child but they themselves would have been very happy. It is very fortunate that, meeting with adversity, we are allowed to know of the previous life and finally to receive enlightenment. Some people believe

323

in order to be rich, or to recover from illness. None is more foolish than they. Wealth is not lasting. Kōbō Daishi sang in his alphabetic song that flowers, though in bloom, are destined to fall; nothing is lasting in our life: "Iro wa nioedo chirinuru wo waga yo tarezo tsune naranu."[1] This is quite true. I often meet my friends in Hitoyoshi. They say: "You are now pretty old, aren't you?" Hearing this, I am a little surprised to see that I am no longer young, as I have been unconsciously considering myself to be. All of you think: "I am still young, I can still live long." This shows how much confidence we place in ourselves, how proud we are. We also say: "This is the money *I* obtained. These are *my* own things." Being selfish, we live as if everything belonged to us. This is, however, a great mistake. We live, thanks to our surroundings or to Buddha. Even the fact that you happen to ride with somebody else in a bus is predestined by Buddha in the previous life. We cannot think of ourselves without thinking of Buddha's favor. Conscious of this fact, we should be thankful for everything, far from doing injuries to others. Here is a parable of Shaka who was good at teaching by means of parables.

A man had four wives. He loved one of them dearly, so much so that people said he was loving too much. He loved the second one a little better than ordinary husbands do. The third one he loved as much as ordinary husbands do. As to the last one, he did not care a fig for her, treating her as if she had been a servant. Somehow he became seriously ill. As his death moment was coming near, he began to feel very lonely. He called up the first wife and asked her to die with him. He met, however, with a flat refusal. Then calling up the second one, he demanded the same thing. She declined too, saying that it was impossible for her seeing that even his best wife would not die with him. He was obliged to put the same demand to the third one, because he felt so lonely. She answered that she would follow him, but only as far as his grave, not dying with him. As there was no choice, he called up the last one he had been loving least of all. She, however, said, to his surprise: 'I am ready to follow you to the next world. I am yours.'

The meaning of the parable is this. The first wife is our body, the second, reputation, wealth, social position, etc. The third, relatives who follow a coffin to the grave, and the fourth our soul. We neglect our spiritual life, leading a selfish life. The final thing to depend upon is, however, our soul. At death we must leave our body, wealth, wives, and children in this world. It is only the soul that goes with us to the next world. Conscious of this fact, we cannot but be surprised and be afraid.

[1] "Iro ha, etc.," is a verse written by Kōbō Daishi to include all of the Hiragana syllabic alphabet which he is said to have invented.

It is, however, too late to know of this at the deathbed. Those who know that they enter the land of purity as soon as they die are the happiest people in the world. Now, let us come back to Kōbō Daishi's song: "Ui no okuyama kyo koe-te asaki yume miji eimo sezu," which means to obtain enlightenment, getting firm belief after overcoming worldly thoughts. It is only when we give up all confidence in ourselves and truly seek after something to depend upon that we hear the voice of Nyōrai [Amida]. Nyōrai never forsakes those who ask for help sincerely. Nyōrai lives within ourselves. Only his existence is suppressed by our worldly thoughts—or money, or reputation, or a grudge, Once, however, we meet with difficulties and are conscious how poor our power is, how all things around us are inconstant, how we are altogether made of sins, we are thrown into the sorrow of entire solitude. It is this moment that we are allowed to hear Nyōrai's voice. Then a life with Nyōrai as the center will begin. It will be quite different from the former life with ego as the center. Our view of life will be totally changed. However, mind, you have not obtained the true belief while you think that it is you that came by that belief. There have lived a number of great priests of the Shinshū sect. They have, however, never thought themselves great. The true belief is that in which you put everything in the hands of Nyōrai. "I know everything of you. Trust everything in me." With that belief, we will be prompted to sacrifice ourselves for the benefit of the world in order to be thankful for Nyōrai. Thus a death will be made significant. You will be peaceful in mind, knowing that your child is already in the happy land of purity. You will lead a life full of strength, full of smiles and of light. Then you are in paradise. It does not belong to the next world, but exists in this life.

I am very sorry to have talked so long, with so many digressions and probably in an inconsistent way.

[Then the priest read a passage of a sutra, at the end of which all present recited *Namu Amida Butsu.* A small party followed.]

APPENDIX V

SHINTO *NORITO* AND PRIEST'S SPEECH
SEPTEMBER 27, 1936

THE FIRST *norito*

The first *norito* is the purification *norito:* I pray to you gods living all over the heavens, to cleanse the headman of the *mura*, the people and the school children of sins they may have committed before.

THE SECOND *norito*

I, the priest for the Suha shrine in Suye Mura, say to you, gods enshrined in the shrine here: Please protect the Emperor and keep him ever prosperous. Take care so that the children of the Suye Primary and Higher Primary school can work so hard as to satisfy the Emperor's august mind, and protect them from harms.

THE PRIEST'S SPEECH

At the last meeting of Shinto priests in Kumamoto Prefecture, we decided to co-operate with the school children in holding the ceremony. This decision is, I think, suitable to the present situation of our country. These days the clarification of the national policy has been much talked about. Originally our country was made by gods. Its origin is, however, difficult for you to understand. You will learn about it when you go to middle school. In spite of this nationality, our country has been much polluted by the Western civilization, for instance, Mr. Minobe's case. In this sense this gathering is most significant. I have just heard you sing the song of shrine-visiting, which almost moved me to tears. This is the very thing that you should do as good Japanese children. Your schoolmaster presented a *tamagushi* just now. I'll explain its meaning. *Tama* means one's spirit, and *kushi* a spirit. By offering a *tamagushi* we mean that we offer our whole spirit to the gods thoroughly. A spirit is, as you see, used to push a thing through, that is, to present our soul as far as it reaches the gods to the very inch. Though I want to talk about the relation of the gods and the protégés (*ujiko*), you have been kept standing pretty long now, so I will do so the next time.

BIBLIOGRAPHY

BOOKS

ANESAKI, MASAHARU. *History of Japanese Religion*. London: Kegan Paul, Trench, Trubner & Co., Ltd., 1930.

ASTON, W. C. *Shinto: The Way of the Gods*. London: Longmans, Green & Co., 1905.

BRINKLEY, F., NANJŌ, F., and IWASAKI, Y. *An Unabridged Japanese-English Dictionary*. Tokyo: Sanseido, 1896.

ELIOT, SIR CHARLES. *Japanese Buddhism*. London: Edwin Arnold, 1935.

ERSKINE, WILLIAM H. *Japanese Festival and Calendar Lore*. Tokyo: Kyo Bun Kwan, 1933.

FEI, HSIAO-TUNG. *Peasant Life in China*. London: Routledge, 1939.

Fortune Magazine, September, 1936. Chicago: Time, Inc.

FREUD, SIGMUND. *A General Introduction to Psychoanalysis*. New York: Liveright, 1935.

FUKUZAWA, YUKICHI. *The Autobiography of Fukuzawa Yukichi*. Translated by EIICHI KIYOOKA. Tokyo: Hokuseido, 1934.

GRANET, MARCEL. *Festivals and Songs of Ancient China*. New York: E. P. Dutton & Co., 1932.

GRAY, JOHN HENRY. *China: A History of the Laws, Manners, and Customs of the People*. 2 vols. London: Macmillan & Co., Ltd., 1878.

HEARN, LAFCADIO. *Romance of the Milky Way*. Boston: Houghton Mifflin, 1905.

HOZUMI, NOBUSHIGE. *Ancestor Worship and Japanese Law*. Rev. ed. Tokyo: Maruzen, 1912.

HU, SHIH. *The Chinese Renaissance*. Chicago: University of Chicago Press, 1934.

Japan-Manchoukuo Year Book. Tokyo: Japan-Manchoukuo Year Book Co., 1938.

JONES, THOMAS ELSA. "Mountain Folk of Japan: A Study in Method." Unpublished Ph.D. dissertation, Columbia University, 1926.

KAEMPFER, ENGELBERT. *History of Japan*. 2 vols. London: Published for the translator, 1727. A three-volume edition was published in London in 1926; page references in the text are to this edition.

KULP, DANIEL HARRISON. *Country Life in South China.* New York: Bureau of Publications, Teachers College, Columbia University, 1925.

MITFORD, A. B. [LORD REDESDALE]. *Tales of Old Japan.* London: Macmillan & Co., Ltd., 1871.

MURASAKI, SHIKIBU. *The Tale of Genji.* Translated from the Japanese by ARTHUR WALEY. London: Allen & Unwin, 1935.

NASU, SHIROSHI (Director of Research). *The Village of Shonai.* Tokyo: Department of Agriculture, Tokyo Imperial University, 1935. (In Japanese.)

NITOBE, INAZO (ed.). *Western Influences in Modern Japan.* Chicago: University of Chicago Press, 1931.

REDFIELD, ROBERT. *Chan Kom: A Maya Village.* Washington: Carnegie Institution, 1934.

REIN, J. J. *Japan.* 2 vols. New York: A. C. Armstrong & Son, 1888–89.

SANSOM, G. B. *Japan: A Short Cultural History.* New York: Century Co., 1931.

SCHWARTZ, HENRY B. *In Togo's Country.* Cincinnati: Jennings & Graham, 1908.

SUZUKI, EITARO. *A Plan for a Rural Sociological Survey in Japan.* ("Research Bulletin of the Gifu Imperial College of Agriculture," No. 19.) Gifu, Japan, 1931.

WATANABE, YŌICHIRŌ (Director of Research). *Investigation of Farm Villages, Especially How Farmers Use Their Labor.* (Report No. 1 on field work in Yoshihara Mura, Kyoto Prefecture.) Kyoto: Department of Agriculture, Kyoto Imperial University, 1932. (In Japanese.)

———. *Farm Village Investigation.* (Report No. 1 on field work in Kangamiyama Mura, Shiga Prefecture.) Kyoto: Department of Agriculture, Kyoto Imperial University, 1933. (In Japanese.)

WILLIAMS, F. E. *Orokaiva Magic.* Oxford: Oxford University Press, 1928.

YOSOBURO, TAKEKOSHI. *Economic Aspects of the History of the Civilization of Japan.* 3 vols. New York: Macmillan Co., 1930.

ARTICLES

ASAKAWA, K. "Notes on Village Government in Japan after 1600," *Journal of the American Oriental Society,* XXX, Part III (1910), 259–300; *ibid.,* XXXI, Part II (1911), 151–216.

BUCHANAN, D. C. "Inari," *Transactions of the Asiatic Society of Japan,* Vol. XII (2d ser.; 1935).

SCOTT, ROBERTSON. *The Foundation of Japan.* London: John Murray, 1922.

EMBREE, JOHN F. "Notes on the Indian God Gavagrīva (Godzu Tennō) in Contemporary Japan," *Journal of the American Oriental Society*, LIX (1939), 67–70.

FLORENZ, KARL. "Ancient Japanese Rituals, Part IV," *Transactions of the Asiatic Society of Japan*, XXVII, Part I (1900), 1–112.

HALL, ROBERT BURNETT. "Some Rural Settlement Forms in Japan," *Geographical Review*, XXI, No. 1 (1931), 93–123.

JONES, IDWAL. "Miss Mori" (a story); *American Mercury Magazine*, XXVIII (1933), 466–74.

KATŌ, GENCHI. "Japanese Phallicism," *Transactions of the Asiatic Society of Japan*, Vol. I (suppl.) (2d ser.; 1924).

KOIZUMI, KOICHI. "On the Custom Called Yuhi, as a Type of Labour System in Agricultural Villages," *Report of Imperial Agricultural Association*, Vol. XXV, Nos. 8–10 (1935). (In Japanese.)

RADCLIFFE-BROWN, A. R. "On the Concept of Function in Social Science," *American Anthropologist*, XXXVII (1935), 384–402.

SATOW, E. M. "Ancient Japanese Rituals" (Parts I–III), *Transactions of the Asiatic Society of Japan*, VII (1879), 95–126; *ibid.*, IX (1881), 183–211.

SIMMONS, D. B., and WIGMORE, J. H. "Notes on Land Tenure and Local Institutions in Old Japan," *Transactions of the Asiatic Society of Japan*, XIX (1891), 37–270.

TAKIKAWA, MASAJIRO. "Law, Japanese," *Encyclopedia of the Social Sciences*, IX, 254–57. New York: Macmillan Co., 1933.

INDEX

INDEX

Adolescence, 193–95

Adoption: ceremony, 84; disadoption, 81, 84–85; general description, 81–85; inter-*buraku* and *mura*, 70, 71, 75; *junyōshi*, 83; by marriage, 213; persons adopted, 82–84; position of adopted person, 84–85; reasons for, 81–82; and social classes, 161; son desired, 97

Adultery, 172

Afterbirth, 259

Afterlife, 261–63, 323–25; *see also* Heaven, Hell, Souls

Age: dangerous ages, 252; and freedom, 172; importance of, 87; and kinship terms, 87–88; same-age tie, 87–88; see also *Dōnen*

Agricultural Association: discourages dances, 104; effects of, 301, 304, 308; formation of, 27, 32; general description, 63–65; periodical, 64, 76–77; transplanting system, 137

Agriculture: adviser, 63; choice of crops made free, 8; crop rotation, 36–37; deity of, 254; and festival calendar, 267, 270–71, 278, 293, 294–95, 296, 297; in feudal days, 6; lectures on, 9; national guidance of, 17; new program, 305; produce of Higo and Kuma, 36–43; produce by seasons, 42–43; production of Suye, 314; *see also* Agricultural Association, *Mugi*, Rice, Seasons, Sericulture, Tools, Vegetables

Alcoholic liquor. *See* Beer, *Sake*, *Shōchū*

Almanac, 239; *see also* Calendar

Amakusa, 70

Amaterasu-ō-mikami: *buraku* celebration, 272; priestess, 251; royal ancestress, 223; scroll, 117; *taima*, 237, 239; *see also* Ise

America: depression in, 77; emigrants to, 70

Amida: *buraku* celebration of, 121, 281, 282; in *butsudan*, 237–38; in *dō*, 246, 278 n.; and heaven, 238, 262, 263; lecture on, 323–25; scroll, 240; and Shinshū, 230, 236, 238; and souls, 261; *see also* Shinshū

Amidism, 230, 236; *see also* Shinshū

Amusement. *See* Recreation

Ancestors: and adoption, 81; of *buraku*, 292; and *butsudan*, 89; tablets, 218, 237, 281; *see also* Bon, Souls

Aoi Shrine, 250 n.; celebration, 291

Aoshima Shrine, 273

Araki, General, 321

Archery, 164

Area, of Suye, 19

Army: annual inspection, 66, 166, 167; conscription, 8, 9, 63, 70, 72, 76, 195–203, 304; consolation bags for, 167; diet, 38; and Emperor, 197; in feudal days, 1, 2, 158; in government, 10; military drill, 66, 265; military influence in school, 189; military value of livestock, 44; military value of *shōchū*, 44; Reservists Association, 166–67; soldier's departure, 109, 197–200; soldier's return, 109, 201; soldiers' talismans, 274; song about soldiers, 187; *see also* Manchukuo

Arrow: archery, 164; ritual use, 126

Ashigaru, 2, 158

Aso Buraku, 24, 32; Shaka *dō*, 232, 278; Shintō shrine, 226

333

[PRINTED
IN U·S·A·]

VERMONT COLLEGE
MONTPELIER, VT.

Date Due

Dec 19			
JE 23 '92			

Demco 293-5